The Quest for Purity
Dynamics of Puritan Movements

Religion and Society 26

GENERAL EDITORS
Leo Laeyendecker, *University of Leiden*
Jacques Waardenburg, *University of Lausanne*

MOUTON DE GRUYTER · BERLIN · NEW YORK · AMSTERDAM 1988

The Quest for Purity

Dynamics of Puritan Movements

Edited by

Walter E. A. van Beek

MOUTON DE GRUYTER · BERLIN · NEW YORK · AMSTERDAM 1988

Mouton de Gruyter (formerly Mouton, The Hague)
is a Division of Walter de Gruyter & Co., Berlin.

The vignet on the cover of this book represents the
symbol of the *Agathos Daimon,* the snake of the
Good Spirit, known from Greek astrological and
magical texts. As its Town God, the *Agathos Daimon* was believed to protect Alexandria, which was
famous world-wide for its library with precious
manuscripts and books.

Library of Congress Cataloging- in -Publication Data

The Quest for purity.
(Religion and society ; 26)
Includes index.
1. Puritan movements--Comparative studies.
I. Beek, W. E. A. van.   II. Series: Religion and society
(Mouton de Gruyter) ; 26.
BL237.5.Q47   1988   291.9   88-1358
ISBN 0-89925-376-8 (alk. paper)

CIP-Kurztitelaufnahme der Deutschen Bibliothek

The quest for purity : dynamics of puritan movements /
ed. by Walter E. A. van Beek. - Berlin ; New York ;
Amsterdam : Mouton de Gruyter, 1988
(Religion and society ; 26)
ISBN 3-11-011382-1
NE: Beek, Walter E. A. van [Hrsg.]; GT

Preface

The present volume is the result of a long interaction between cultural anthropologists and historians of religion. Working closely together in one large research program called "Essence and Functions of Ideological Systems", they have tried to bridge the gap between the disciplines. As one of the nodal points on which interests converged, the processes of puritanization emerged from the discussions. After ample preparations, two-day workshop was held at Utrecht University. The proceedings of this workshop laid the foundation for this book.

The workshop was organized together with the Rev. Dr. P. Staples, Dr. L. van Vucht Tijssen and Prof. Dr. J.D.J. Waardenburg. The discussions within this committee have shaped the whole endeavour to a great degree. For the selection of and commentaries on the contributions for this volume I am greatly indebted to the valuable insights of Prof. Dr. A. de Ruyter and especially to Prof. Dr. H.U.E. Thoden van Velzen with whom I wrote the introductory essay: he has been instrumental in shaping the editorial quest for publication purity.

For the financing of the workshop, as well as for all other facilities needed for the production of this text, we are grateful to the Faculty of Social Sciences of the University of Utrecht. For the translation of the Broeyer contribution (Geneva) and for the English correction of all articles we are deeply grateful for the services of Rev. Dr. P. Staples, for which we also thank the Faculty of Theology. Typing has been done with great care and diligence by Paula Duivenvoorde, Petra Nesselaar and Kootje van Spanje. Maps were drawn by F. Stelling. For computer assistance we thank Jos Jaspers.

Contents

PURITY, A GREEDY IDEOLOGY
H.U.E."Bonno" Thoden van Velzen and Walter E.A. van Beek

Purity; a greedy ideology
H.U.E."Bonno" Thoden van Velzen &
Walter E.A. van Beek

Introduction: the Puritans and 'puritans'

In the 16th century, in England and Scotland, militant groups of Protestants demanded from the Church of England far-reaching reforms in doctrine and worship, and greater strictness in religious discipline. During the 17th century, these Puritans succeeded in occupying positions of power and influence, both in the home country and in New England, whence they had migrated in substantial numbers. Nothwithstanding their rise in the hierarchy of social prestige, the number of conflicts with other denominations or sections of the population increased greatly. Their political prominence and spiritual radicalism, and the well-known Salem witchcraft trials of 1692-1693, won them a place in the limelight of academic attention. Less well-known and less written about are the 'Puritans'(1) of other ages and in other parts of the world. 'Puritans' because they too are driven by a quest for purity; by an inexorable desire to cleanse the world and themselves of evil. Most of these 'Puritans' find their source of inspiration in a divine revelation, or are urged to action by their impatience with the corrupt practices of a smug priesthood. Others, no less interesting, are motivated by a political creed. In this book we include as 'puritan' all movements, whether directed primarily at the individual or at the body social, that are moulded by that one supreme aim, **the quest for purity**.

In March 1985, during a two-day colloquium at Utrecht University (the Netherlands), twenty specialists from various disciplines, discussed puritan movements in different parts of the world and from different ages. From the papers presented at this conference, eleven were finally selected for inclusion in the present volume. In all of these cases 'the quest for purity' was a dominant phenomenon. The cases are:

The City of Geneva at the time of Calvin;
The New England Puritans;
The Second Reformation among Dutch orthodox protestants;
The Dutch Evangelicals;
The Wahhābi movement in 19th century Arabia;
The Fulani Jihād in 19th century West Africa;
The Shi^cite revolution in Iran;
The Taiping rebellion in China (19th century);
The Gaan Gadu cult of the Suriname Maroons (1890);
The Mazimu movements in contemporary Tanzania;
Two reform movements in Communist countries (U.S.S.R. and Kampuchea), present-day.

From the beginning two areas of debate structured the discussion. First, once we succeeded in identifying a number of movements that all share this 'quest for purity', questions arose about other characteristics that these puritan groups might share (2). Would puritans, for example, exhibit strong social control with explicit norms about socialization and resocialization? Do all such movements have an eschatological dimension? To what extent are the puritans hierarchically organized? Are they all motivated by an 'internal' justification to rule their fellows? It turned out that the puritan movements discussed varied greatly with respect to several of these characteristics. Among the movements represented here, some do not seem to have any eschatological dimensions (the Second Reformation), while hierarchical leadership patterns are absent from many others (Mazimu e.g.). Rather than looking for some fixed elements of the puritan pattern or model, we gradually came to accept these questions as tools for inquiry.

However, what merited discussion in all cases was, in William James' words 'The Mark of the Beast,' the specter of evil that held sway over the imagination of puritans. In the first section we will depict the various forms of evil as seen by New England Puritans, Muslim Crusaders of the desert, Maroons of the South American rain forest or burghers of sixteenth century Geneva. The ways open to the righteous to cleanse themselves of evil will be discussed; the nature of their beliefs as well as their ambitions of purity. Finally, in the first section of this introduction, attention will be devoted to the forms of social organization of puritans.

'The Quest for Purity,' whether voluntarily accepted or enforced, demands total commitment. It affects all spheres of life, leaving no field of action untouched. Lacking easily fulfilled goals, 'the quest' continues to pursue adepts. After removing one corrupt institution, or removing one particular source of defilement, other evils seldom fail to manifest themselves swiftly. There is something almost inhuman about this 'quest' that is never fulfilled; that keeps on devouring human energy, always asking for more. Borrowing Coser's (1980) concept of 'Greedy Institutions', we will label puritan creeds 'Greedy Ideologies'. Here our second line of inquiry begins: to explore 'puritanism' as a creed that will inevitably clash with other ideologies and with their supporting groups. Demanding full commitment, and always an increasing share of resources, puritanism cannot but bring its adepts into collision with other groups who espouse different beliefs. Hence our emphasis on puritanism as a process that will inevitably find its path towards self-destruction. Once the boundaries to expansion are apparent, and the dangers of self-destruction have become manifest, the search for a solution reveals the fundamental puritan dilemma. Should one compromise by diluting the faith, or perhaps create a sacred enclave, by withdrawing into the wilderness as some 19th century puritans did? Or should one attempt to break through these boundaries with the sword? Various 'solutions' will be discussed in the second section of this chapter.

The final question is what factors might be conducive to the rise of puritan movements. In our last section we shall adress this issue, and offer a modest explanation of the puritan phenomenon.

Characteristics of puritan movements

The Struggle Against Evil

Puritans view the world as a battlefield, where the forces of Good - always in short supply - battle against omnipresent Sin, Corruption and Evil. Among the ideologies of puritan movements, all of which offer an explicit definition of sin, several different approaches to Evil can be discerned. The main distinction is that between personal and collective evil, between evil residing chiefly in the individual, or evil located in the body social. The Christian movements offer examples of the first category. England's 17th century Puritans, the Cathari of Southern France and the adherents of the Second Reformation in Holland, all have a distinct conception of 'personal evil.' Sin stems from the individual who has not truly conquered himself or herself; it has to be discovered through introspection, a critical evaluation of the state of one's heart. Another example is Communism in its revolutionary stages: bourgeois, revisionist ideas may spring spontaneously from the minds of people inducing them to err from the true, revolutionary path. Communist revolutionaries of China's Cultural Revolution hold that, when thinking errs, sinful 'capitalist' and 'revisionist' actions follow automatically. The Communist medicine is private reexamination and public confession (Hinton 1972:250). New England Puritans would concur.

Such an ideology of purity tolerates no debate on the creed, and it brooks no opposition. Any opponent of the basic principles defiles himself, and thereby places himself beyond the pale, forfeiting his claims to be heard. As the Chinese Communists asserted: 'Reactionaries have no right to speak.' (Hinton 1972:75). Wrong thinking is not only sinful, it is also the road to a subhuman status. Ultimately, one becomes the embodiment of evil, the witch, 'the evil from within', transforming the wayward individual into a subhuman or even anti-human species.

This process may or may not be checked by the individual, nor is the sinning individual the only one to blame; the extent to which evil is self-willed varies among ideologies. In the movements discussed in this book, witchcraft is not deemed hereditary. Among adepts of the Gaan Gadu cult, for example, and certainly among the Mazimu, deviant thoughts, sinful fantasies and impulses stem from the individual's heart. Feelings of inferiority, deprivation or despondency may have acted as catalysts. People have to be on their guard almost continually lest they slip and are enticed to commit witchcraft.

Somewhat more complex are those cases which explicitly refer to an outside agent of evil, but where one can nevertheless conclude that external danger plays a secondary role. The New England Puritans are a case in point. They can only be understood from a long historical perspective, as the churches had to struggle continuously against witchcraft, but in doing so heavily influenced the witch beliefs they were adressing (Demos 1982:386 ff). But even in the famous Salem case, the devil did nor come uninvited (Boyer and Nissenbaum 1974). On closer inspection, in the Communist purges - or the MacCarthyan anti-communist one (Lifton 1967:457), external and internal instigators of evil join forces. In all of these cases a notion of inherent and self-willed evil interacts with an external, involuntary one, be it Satan, communist infiltration or 'capitalist roaders.'

The second notion, that of evil as a collective phenomenon, entails different characteristics. Here evil, though still discernible as sins willed by individuals, is not primarily defined as a problem of the individual heart. Movements focusing on this concept of evil do not hold the erring individual but the surrounding world as the principal enemy. Evil hides itself primarily in social institutions that corrupt the individual by enticing him, or even pressuring him, to go in the wrong direction. The Evangelicals, for example, deplore and condemn wrong customs and institutions: 'abortion', 'free marriage', 'streaking', 'euthanasia', and 'lèse-majesté', to name only a few (Post, this volume).

Most Islamic movements search for evil in a similar direction. The Wahhãbites, the Fulani **mujahedeen**, and the Shi^{C}ite revolutionaries, all denounce sinful modern institutions and long for a return to a golden uncorrupted past. Such movements define evil institutionally, threatening the believers as a collectivity and from 'the outside.' Hence the call for legislative measures or other forms of collective action. The Islamic examples demonstrate reliance on clearly legalistic solutions to contain evil. Calvin's Geneva was little different. Although sin was defined individually, it was revealed through the overt acts of people and should therefore be corrected with punitive actions by the civil authorities. Sometimes a public confession was demanded, but even that was seen as a punishment rather as an instrument to alter a person's mind (Broeyer, this volume). In these movements, the control of leaders over the thoughts and fantasies of individual members is much weaker than in the first category, but the sway of the machinery of public redress was more far reaching.

Evil Diagnosed

Whatever is considered the source of evil, the definition of the actions and thoughts that amount to evil is something different. The clearest cases of transgression usually involve those acts which appear to reveal that the individual pursues his own aims without regard for communal goals. Selfish, egoistic acts in particular arouse suspicion. Puritan ideologies, greedy as they are, employ a definition of selfishness that touches most spheres of life; that quintessential private passion, the pursuit of sexual pleasure, is seldom left alone. Hence the marked preoccupation of puritan movements with sexual behaviour. To mention a few examples': rigorous sexual ethics are the hallmark of the Wahh⁻abi and Shi^{C}ite movements, and of New England's Puritan and Tanzania's Mazimu.(3) Though the Communists do not regulate sexuality as strictly as these other movements, the unbridled pursuit of sexual pleasures is frowned upon. Sexual behaviour is the most private of all social interactions; as such it is considered a threat by all movements which seek to control the lives of their followers. As Coser (1980:130) argues so convincingly, no greedy institution can succeed in its totalitarian goals without establishing a control over sexuality and over relations within the family. Inevitably, whether in the guidelines for introspective correction given to Puritans, or in the sin catalogues of the Evangelicals, rampant sexuality is most strongly denounced.

Though the values of harmonious family life easily rank among the most sacred tenets of puritan movements (New England Puritans, Fulani, Wahhābi, Evangelicals), strong and intimate family ties are looked at askance. In this respect too, puritan movements show their tyrannical and greedy face: harmonious family bonds should be furthered but they should never become so strong that they put the institutional framework of the movement in jeopardy. Ideological loyalties, in the last resort, should prevail over kinship bonds. The Communists are most explicit on this issue: on each individual rests the responsibility to denounce kinsmen for any ideological deviance.

The loyalty for the Movement should takes precedence over all: other ties and commitments should yield. 'God is a Jealous God' (Exodus 20:3) or, in Lenin's famous words 'The Party is Mother and Father.' The Mazimu were careful not to accuse their kinsmen of witchcraft in public; however, they were often encouraged by their leaders to sever the bonds of kinship and associate with other Mazimu only. Taiping adherents should (and did turn against their father and mother, even beheading them (Zürcher, this volume). In most puritan movements the follower is an isolated entity: the terrestrial side of a single-stranded, exclusive, exacting and vertical relationship.

The conversion experience itself is often a dramatization of the exclusiveness of the new bonds that tie the adept to the Movement; it often represents a shattering rejection of any other link than those that connect the converted with God, the Party or with Scripture (Pettit 1966). A Puritan convert was inclined 'to fancy himself as nothing so much as a man locked up in iron armour' (Greven 1980:72). Self-hate, self-denial, and self-contempt often appear to be the result of this type of conversion: 'mortification of the flesh' is its most common expression.

Greedy ideologies of purity tend to deny their adherents an easy relationship with their own physical existence. New England Puritans conceived of their bodies as a constant source of temptation and distress; the Taiping leadership even denied their rank and file any right of sexuality. Among some puritans, God, the Party or the Movement holds exclusive rights to their members' physical bodies. In other similar movements, puritan ideologies tend to proscribe the sensual pleasure like alcohol or meat, or, in other cases again, periodic fasts are stressed (Walzer 1982:134). Generally, comfort is sin; a state of permanent unrest should shield adepts from temptation. These taboos serve several purposes: the manifest one is health; the latent one is reinforcement of group boundaries. Lowering commensality with outsiders breeds in-group orientation.

In puritan movements, acts that place the social order in jeopardy, and certainly those that further disorder, are cardinal sins. A good, 'purified' society is an orderly one; chaos and order are the weapons of the enemy, clarity and order the signposts of purity. The social order which is sought, one that includes both organizational order and internal harmony, is often considered the primeval way of organizing things, the Order of Old. The Movement strives to reestablish an ancient pattern or organization and community living, and is wholly committed to its smooth functioning. Any act that threatens to disrupt harmony is severely punished. What actions are seen as disruptive differs greatly from one group to another, depending on their perception of risks and dangers. The Puritans tried to curb emigration from the original colonies (Carroll 1969) as underpopulation seemed to threaten their viability. In Calvin's Geneva an infraction of Church rules was punished by the civil administration as a direct threat to the social order (Broeyer, this volume); in Iran any critique of the position of the clergy is considered a menace to the edifice of state (Kreyenbroek, this volume). The Fulani and Taiping, expansionist and military oriented as they were, exacted stiff punishments in case of disobedience. Disobedience is the exemplary social sin of puritan movements.

The ideology of purity is also at war with free will and free agency of its adepts. This shows most clearly during their meetings. One striking feature of both the 'national' festivals and the weekly or regular meetings held by puritan movements is their excessive length. Neither does time count during sermons given by the pastors serving the Second Reformation, nor during the political meetings of Communists. Followers are expected to offer freely of their time, and never is it spent so well as when participating in the audience of their leaders. Sermons, political lessons and speeches may take any length of time during congregations. Puritans accord a high priority to thought control. Long meetings, with interminable speeches or sermons, with their innumerable repetitions and admonitions, just serve that purpose (Riesman 1977). As Lifton showed in his pioneering study on the psychology of totalitarianism, the command and absolute control over the time of subjects brings home more than anything else the absoluteness of power that is delegated from the Supreme Being or the Cause to its servitors. The very monotony and repetitiveness of messages reinforce obedience patterns that are basic to the definition of self of the followers: 'I obey, therefore I am.' (Lifton 1967: 423).

Puritan Ambitions

The puritan movements differ in their levels of aspiration, in their ambitions for spatial control. Mazimu adepts and Second Reformation followers content themselves with being islands of righteousness in a sea of iniquity; New England Puritans sought to establish a pure 'City on a Hill'; the Moslim movements aimed at a just state, not altogether different from the senitorial goals of Communists.

Island Communities. The first option is hardly different from that of many other Protestant sects. The Protestant Reformation doctrine easily accomodates with a position of absolute minority, as they do not only stand apart from 'the world' but also from those other Protestant groups (Graafland 1963; Van der Meiden 1981: 67). Most movements have to accomodate to marginality, in some phase of their existence.

For some movements, the ideal of a community of the pure is too far away from practical political possibilities to be aspired to at all. The Mazimu, for example, maintain a precarious and uneasy balance with the Tanzanian and Zambian civil authorities. Their marginality stems from political realism, rather than from any lack of ambition. Mazimu are puritans who have accepted that they will have to survive in a defiled world: they exhibit an 'Island devotionalism' in which people try to remain 'pure of mind and deeds' in small pockets of the faithful. Although aware that they live among the impure, as true spiritual 'dung beetles,' they strive for staying clean in a foul environment. With such a limited ambition, the call to conversion is not sounded out loud. Practically absent in the Second Reformation, with the Mazimu the missionary zeal is tempered. Purity is a way of life, and exemplary compartment the only a method of conversion.

For puritans who have resigned themselves to living in enclaves, there is little to gain from interaction with the enemy, nothing to learn, nothing useful to expect. The village community often, but not always, is the ideal. Glorification of village life, of community oriented-ness, and of a golden past are frequently encountered. For most puritan ideologies, the pristine condition existed only in the past, and the past therefore should be resuscitated. The Second Reformation offers such examples. But Tanzania's Mazimu form cells within communities, and regard the village community as a threat rather than as the ideal form of the human group. And among Maroons, in the days when restrictive rules were announced by a new deity, the organs of community power-ancestor priests, spirit mediums - were removed or checked by the new wave of puritans that came to power.

A City on the Hill. Most movements, however, do strive for communities of the pure that can be totally controlled. The clearest and most explicit examples are Calvin's Geneva and the communities of the New England Puritans. Theirs is the vision of a perfect Jerusalem, an ideal that had a lasting influence on later American puritan movements. (4) As Broeyer (this volume) indicates, Calvin's Geneva in several respects attained some of these goals of perfection.

The 'City on the Hill' was a well-organized city, with a Church, temple, or other sacred building in the centre; it was governed according to the rules of purity by a well-educated elite. It aimed at becoming 'a light for the whole world'. It was also a city of equals, in which the various occupations and professions formed a seamless social fabric; a city in which ecclesiastical authority was identical with the civil one, and where God's Word, the Bible, the Quran and Shari'a or the Revelations of the Founder were the basis of civil administration and adjudication of law. Such a concept is the negation of the Augustinian separation of the **Civitas dei** and the **Civitas terrena**: no separation between Church and State is aimed at, in fact that very separation is believed to have caused the rot to set in.

Converting the World. A Kingdom of the Purified is the most ambitious undertaking for Puritan movements. All the Islamic movements cherish this ambition, as do the Taiping and the Communists movements. Their mission is to convert or conquer the world in the name of Allah God or dialectical materialism. A true member has to prove himself by persistent recruiting of new converts. More than in the Puritan examples with modest aims, the organization - a fixed hierarchy of positions and responsabilities - is of central importance here. Links with secular power holders are treasured: the lien of the House of Sa'ud with the Wahhābi being a pertinent example (Cudsi & Dessouli 1981). The puritan organizations of the Communist type are the most thorough, trying to combine an intensive form of social control with a highly centralized state.

Puritans with such ambitions heavily rely on a strictly hierarchical organization which not only controls inner life, but also directs the expansion of doctrine. The army figures as the most pertinent example for such groups. The puritan movements of the communist variety demonstrate these qualities most clearly (van Ree, this volume). Life in the villages is modelled after an army barracks: relations between the villagers reflects the hierarchical pattern of officers and their subalterns; the measure and way of punishment follows a military code.

In the Muslim examples, in the city of Geneva and in the communities of the New England Puritans, the army is also taken as a model, but less strictly so. The pure society or 'pure city' is often depicted as an army of the 'just' waging war on a host of the unrighteous. Though this moral battle easily shades over into a military one, the militarization of movements with moderate ambition movements is mainly a rethorical one. In the three Muslim cases, however, with their larger ambitions, battle is waged as a necessary consequence of the moral one. Whereas the English Puritans were in the centre of England's civil war (Finlayson 1983), their New England counterparts viewed their battles against the Indians as a war against Satan (Carrol, 1969). In the Muslim cases the ideology emphatically stressed the issue of a holy war, starting from a position of a perceived opposition. This war had to be legitimated by branding the adversaries as subhuman, as infidels opposing the establishment of **Dar-al-Islam**. Militarism was depicted as a necessary evil: the young warriors were warned not to mistake the excitement of battle, the fascination with horses and the glory of victory, for a lifestyle of God pleasing purity (Fulani jihād). Even in puritan movement with maximum ambitions, like the Taiping, military aggression is seen as inevitable, but as yet another seduction that may capture the believer's imagination and tempt him to stray from the straight and narrow path.

Striking Down the Idols

As puritan movements are reactions against perceived evil in the society at large, purification of expressive forms is almost always deemed important. Most puritan movements are iconoclastic, striving to do away with all kinds of liturgical and ritual embellishments (Mazimu, Taiping), Catholic ritual (English Puritans); the destruction of idols (Fulani and Gaan Gadu), desacrating graves of erstwhile saints (Wahhābi). Former rituals are denounced as idolatry, an accusation often levelled by puritans of the Second Reformation against Roman Catholic practices (van der Meiden 1981).

This iconoclastic tendency towards ritual does not mean puritans can live without ritual whatsoever. The Mazimu collectively interpret dreams; the Gaan Gadu movement installed a new oracle; the Fulani organize prayer sessions; while the Taiping meetings developed an elaborate court ritual. However, as a general rule, these rites tend to be less colourful, and less elaborate than the preceding ones, with a tendency to suppress overt symbolism. As the individual must find his salvation by transforming himself, the function of symbolism is greatly reduced. One Mazimu healer apologized to one of the present authors for using a drum: the time would soon come, she asserted, when prayers were all that would be needed for the believer.

The symbols that continue to exist are identity markers for the movement as a whole, symbols that underline the ideological unity of the whole group. Communist and Protestant puritan groups, the Evangelicals and the followers of Khomeini, all have their days of remembrance to celebrate. Thus, the Fulani have a special prayer meeting, commemorating the day they had engaged in their first battle, which marked their start as a coherent and successful movement.

This poverty of symbolism when coupled with iconoclasm, ties in with the puritans' hostility towards art. While purifying their society, they also purify culture, banning all kinds of artistic expressions from a community's culture, straitjacketing a human group's emotional expression. English Puritans have been known to indulge in a 'tyrannical and disastrous suppression of the theatre' (Trevelyan 1974:512). Art and the quest for purity do not harmonize well. Puritan ideologies do not favour artistic expressions for two reasons. The great majority of art represents a highly individualistic endeavour, difficult to control by the spiritual authorities and, what is more, through its creativity, constituting a menace to the claims of the movement over the emotional life of individuals. The second reason could be a very simple one: there seems to be no real need for it. No artistic excellence can, in puritan eyes, ever lead a soul unto salvation. The mind of the believer should not be distracted by outward appearances, by images which of necessity are always but a weak reflection of greater truths, or perhaps even misleading; hence the urge to do away with representations of God, Allah or The Cause. Where the old ways were once replete with such arts forms, and therefore with the seductions of earthly distractions, art should never again be allowed to occupy such a great role in the life of the community.

One form of art may prove the exception to this rule. For puritan movements, as is the case with totalitarian regimes, the art of singing is tolerated or even encouraged. Singing is the most collective of all artistic expression and the one most easily controlled. The role of singing in gaining control over thought and emotions should not be underestimated. Movements that concentrate on the emotional side of religious experience, like the (definitely non-puritan) spirit churches, rely heavily on singing to bring forward a controlled extasy. Usually this far exceeds needs, wishes, and goals of puritan movements as emotions are given a limited and well-delineated role to play in their meetings. Still, their striving for control over emotions is just what makes these ideologies greedy, so singing is important. When puritan systems lose some of their stringency in the quest for purity, when the movement becomes an institution, a gradual renaissance of the arts may be noticed.

Between the first and the last things

All Christian and Muslim instances of the puritan movements as well as the Taiping see themselves as the followers of a tradition, not the trendsetters of a new one. Their quest for purity presupposes pure doctrine, a firm foundation of infallibly secure beliefs. In fact the main ideological thrust of a new puritan movement is exactly this, to purify doctrine. Most movements try to restore the pristine clarity, simplicity and appeal of the Founder. Shunning new, intellectualistic, modernist or revisionist interpretations, they turn back on the original texts, a theological movement often called Fundamentalism (Barr 1977). Inerrancy of the central source, hostility towards sophisticated interpretations and an assurance that those who do not share their point of view are not true 'believers', such notions and attitudes are hallmarks of Fundamentalism (Barr 1977:1, 1984:5 ff). Thus, the quest for doctrinal purity is a quest for **repristinization,** turning the tables of time, reentering the communities of old. These puritan movements explicitly refer to the old society where the tradition has been founded, as the ideal one. This does not apply to all puritan movements of our set, e.g. the Communist movements, or Mazimu Gaan Gadu. As a model it seems to be limited to the movements of Protestant and Muslim origin (though not to the Second Reformation, e.g.), (but - as we have seen-these form an important section among the movements). In these cases repristinization is a central focus; recreating the conditions of the original emergency of the ideology can become almost obsessive, as in the Fulani case (van Beek, this volume) where even the old order of battle was imitated. Creating the Community of the Prophet and re-creating Israel's Exodus (Shipps 1984) can be used as a rethoric in order to have the followers stick together in times of adversity (Walzer 1982); but it can also become an overt imitation of the old communities. Geneva, the Fulani and the New England Puritans are pertinent examples. The most complex case would be the Taiping, where the notion of a pristine situation called for an intricate interpretation.

This harkening back to the ways of the past can be extended further in those movements where the ideologies point back to an even more distant pure past. Both Christianity and Islam have a two-phased 'Garden Syndrome': their doctrines depicts a double loss of innocence. The first was with the coming of death and sin into the world of individual human beings. After that man tried to shape an acceptable society on his own and failed. Revelation stepped in and created a perfect community of converted around the founder of the religion, a community to be gradually corrupted later by man's innate proclivities towards evil. This 'double Garden' motive is a central element in these puritan movements, so the battle against evil has to be followed up and reinforced by the repristinization of society (turning back to the founder) as well as fighting against evil (striving to the original purity).

The puritan's vision of the future, their eschatology, testifies to two related aspects: their tendency to halt the progres of time and their fascination with death. They deny specifics of history (in Whitehead's terms) 'the eternal greatness incarnate in the passage of temporal fact'. The actual historical situation is, in a sense, an aberration: no longer of pristine purity, not yet redeemed by the ultimate purity. Puritan movements do not in themselves develop eschatologies nor elaborate on existing ones. They do, however, develop the belief and heighten the commitment to existing eschatologies. For the people of Geneva, the New England Puritans and the Evangelicals, the expectation of the Second Coming is much more relevant and important as an everyday aspect of their religious life, than it was or is for their contemporary Protestant fellows. Still, the actual content of their predictions is not at variance. Thus, eschatological issues, that may have been latent in the tradition, are habitually picked up by the puritan movement and reactivated, just as they pick up many issues in a lax religious practice (Davidson 1977).

More important, still, for puritans is individual eschatology: the private future in the expected hereafter. Not all ideologies leading up to puritan movements have an explicit notion of an afterlife; of course the communists most definitely do not. Again, the Muslim and Christian movements offer the clearest examples, but also the Taiping have some vision of a glorious life-after-death and a definite set of rules how to reach that ultimate destination, the continual quest for purity being the most important means to that end. A puritan's life is not his own but committed to the greater cause. In some instances, like the regime of Pol Pot, the cause is callously indifferent to individual lives and suffering, but that is an extreme case. Most puritan movements do value individual human life, as it is the prime mover of purity; i.e. they value individual lives in sofar as these are vessels of purity: the individual is the battle ground between the forces of good and evil. Death then not only puts an end to that battle, but can be the culmination of a noble endeavour, when and if the forces of good score a victory. Though in this life a lasting purity is never to be achieved- as purity is not a state but a never ending quest - one's faltering and probing steps on the road towards purity faster hope for a continuing state of total purity after death.

Death as a focus of individual life finds expression in the collective institutions of puritanism too. The New England Puritans lived with death (Stannard 1977) in many ways. Funeral services were the high-points of social life, graveyards formed with the churches the center of religious existence. The art of sepulchral decoration in America never survived the decline of Puritanism. Among the Fulani the readiness to die was an important value in life, and, as in argued (van Beek, this volume) a decisive factor on the battlefield. This, of course, is the most glorious way of dying, in a direct confrontation with the forces of evil (which, in the Fulani case, happened to consist of devout Muslims). Iran's thousands of eager youngsters flock to the battlefield with Irak to fight 'the renegate monster', who considers himself a good Muslim too. The Taiping adherents, in the wake of their Nanking realm, astonished friend and foe with their stubborn resolution to die fighting for a lost cause. Of course, as Lifton argues, the loss of identity when the individual valuation of oneself becomes dependent on the unattainable standards of purity, is a way a death in itself (Lifton 1967). In short, though puritans may live a difficult life, they die a glorious death.

Puritanism, a programme for failure

A successful puritan movement is a **contradictio in terminis.** For the great majority of people, to live a life of perfect purity is an impossibility. The demands made on the average individual are too high, and clashes with fellow human beings are bound to occur. A movement that takes the quest for purity seriously is doomed. Why? Three sets of reasons present themselves: the contradictions within the ideology itself; problems between its quest for purity and the demands of practical reality; and finally the unintended consequences of the temporary success of the movement.

The unattainable ideal

For all human beings, purity can only be a goal to strive for; attainment of this state is impossible. In fact, most puritan movements explicitly view purity as a process, a quest, not a state; the direction taken by the individual is what counts. For those movements, this unattainable ideal has advantages as well as drawbacks. The first considerable advantage is one of mental control. The sheer crushing challenge to become ever purer, and the concomittant failure of individuals to live up to the ideology's high demands, places adepts in a vulnerable moral position. No one succeeds to stay clean, so all are guilty of impurity in some way. Hence a puritan movement's reliance on a guilty conscience, reinforced by obligatory confessionals and constant exhortations. Calvin considered the unattainability of purity- in his words piety - as an important asset for the Church and the City (Broeyer, this volume). Individual members are constantly kept 'on their toes exhorted to be vigilant and alert at all times against the encroachment of evil, whether coming from within or without. Unrest usually results from this like, for example, the 'salvation panic' mentioned for the English Puritans:

'A struggle between faith and doubt ensues, with the candidate careful to indicate that his assurance has never been complete and that his sanctification has much been hampered by his own sinful heart.' (Morgan 1963:91)

Searching for revealing dreams (Mazimu); for the slightest transgressions of morality (Iran) or for bourgeois contra-revolutionary thoughts is a daily and strenuous occupation, even more than humanely tolerable (Korea, Kampuchea).

'For a Communist the question of correcting mistakes is a question of whether or not one can carry on the revolution. For this lesson we paid a heavy price. We only learned it through mistakes. A good revolutionary must revolutionize his own mind first before he can lead the masses.' (Hinton 1972:251). And: 'If you don't transform yourself you can't lead the masses to fight the enemy.' (ibid., p. 250)

In brief, the quest for purity keeps believers in a permanent state of dissatisfaction. This reflects on themselves and on their fellow believers. Puritanism is a greedy ideology, always asking for more; commitment is never wholly satisfactory (Erikson 1979).

All Puritans Are Equal

A second strain of puritan unrest stems from the dilemma of equality. Most puritan ideologies start from an explicit notion of equality of all men before God, Allah or the Revolution. Each believer's first responsibility is towards himself or herself. Neither age, nor sex or social class are held to make a significant difference. But in real life social differentiation cannot be suppressed sufficiently. Particularly when puritans develop organizations with status hierarchies, some puritans become more equal than others. The same ideology that advocates equality, at the same time supports inequality, of leaders and followers, of commoners and clerics, of the elect and the non-elect. Most puritan movements gradually come to accept a stratified society, something which they did not seek in the first place.

The relative position of men and women is a moot point as well. In most puritan movements women are routinely assigned a subordinate, traditional role, stressing the time-honoured duties of procreation, and socio-emotional leadership rather than its more instrumental form. No puritan movement of our set is led by women, and in most of these women are practically absent from the ranks of leadership. It is only during the most turbulent times that Communist puritan groups allow women a position of prominence. But when the days of external threat are over, the party knows only token female comrades. Tanzania's Mazimu leave leadership positions with women only in exceptional cases. In most Mazimu groups women are offered supporting roles, such as those of spirit mediums, the 'foot soldiers' of the cult. Even among the Taiping, bent on promoting the status of women, the leadership was exclusively male (Zürcher, this volume).

The Trap of Organization.

This brings us to another type of contradiction, not within the ideology, but between ideology and practice. Although most puritan-ideologies assume that the proces of purification in individuals would or should suffice to generate a pure society, in many cases forms of organization quickly grow among Puritans. The New England Puritans were quite outspoken about this connection: they quickly jumped from individual to national purity and (such despite the fact that their church order was often congregational and recognized the autonomy of the local church):

'The Government of God is the only government which will hold society, against depravity and temptation without; and it must do by the force of its own laws, written upon the heart. This is that unity of Spirit and that bond of peace which alone can perpetuate national purity and tranquility.' [The Spirit of the Pilgrims, 1831 (cited in Miller 1966: 36)].

Beliefs such as these fostered the need for corresponding social organizations. Many puritan movements have developed strong organizations e.g.: puritan Communism, the Evangelicals, Calvin's Geneva, the Taiping, Iran, all show this characteristic. Why would people who have convinced themselves that nothing matters so much as the cleansing of the heart, advance hierarchies that cannot but cherish mundane concerns as well?

A first reason might be the hierarchy of priorities that is so established among puritans. If one cannot think of a more worthy aim then the quest for purity, and no rival goals dilute this priority, than any measure that will further the Cause can only be welcome. Secondly, depending on the ambition and measure of success of the movement, large-scale territories have to be governed and kept subjugated. Thirdly, puritans always feel they will have to defend themselves against the encroachments of a sinful 'world', hence the need for defensive organizations. A final factor furthering organization is the necessity to curtail dissent. The sacred texts can be interpreted in various ways; interpreters themselves have to be watched for any deviations. In the larger puritan movements an organization has to monitor the work of interpretation and implementation that is going on in the society concerned.

Once such an organization exists, the contradiction becomes apparent between its necessarily narrow range of goals and the all encompassing drive of individuals to cleanse themselves and the world of evil. Additionally, control over the overt behaviour of people is quite different from the exigencies of self-examination and self-correction. This might be a chief reason for the often noted dual leadership of such movements: the founder of a movement is usually not the main organizer. The instigator and leader of the Fulani jihād did not wish to move into the newly built capital (van Beek, this volume). The founder of the Taiping movement was gradually isolated from his followers by his staff. 'Organization defeats genius'; while corrupting the founder's original goals, the ideal of purity becomes a victim as well. Leaders turn into bureaucrats; evil is defined as 'everything outside the organization', and sin is detected in transgressions of norms and rules of the organization. Through this 'Betrayal by the Officials'(5) the movement is transformed into an institution, either a denomination (English Puritans, Evangelicals), or a monolithic party (Communists) or an empire (Wahhābi, Fulani, Taiping).

The deeper an organization manages to penetrate individual life, the less the leeway left to followers for cleansing themselves of evil. Individual expressions of purification, which fall outside the range and realm delimited by the organization, are being frowned upon. The poorly organized Mazimu accept a wealth of individual symbols in their interpretation of dreams, while Evangelicals, on the other hand, have to resort to a strictly circumscribed system of symbols and vocabulary in order to express their feelings. Similarly, the original notion of what constituted the ideal man is no longer congruent with the demands of the organization: be it a denomination or an empire. The basic values of Islam - and consequently of the Wahhābi and Fulani cases - are linked to a nomadic existence. But, once a more complex society develops, the ideal man becomes an outlaw and a 'pure' person a mystic.

Leaders and Followers

Most of the puritan movements presented here have been led by strong personalities. Examples readily come to mind: Calvin in Geneva; Ousman dan Fodio for the Fulani; Khomeini in Iran; Lenin in the early Soviet State and Pol Pot in Kampuchea; all of them strong and well-established leaders, inspiring both confidence and commitment among their followers. Although some of these would usually be defined as charismatic leaders, a cult of personality seems to go against the grain of puritan ideology. A leader is required to give guidance during the quest for purity. He should bow to the high demands of puritanism; be the ideal follower rather than an eccentric leader. A leader's unusual performance will ultimately cause distrust among believers trained to view the world as a place of sin. A leader's prerogatives will arouse the hostility of puritans striving for egalitarian worlds (Tai Lui 1973).

The creation of dynasties appears to contradict this. The Korean case will be interesting in this respect (van Ree, this volume). The clearest example, however, is offered by the Fulani. In the Sokoto empire Ousman dan Fodio had been followed by his son, who in his turn was second in a long line of dan Fodio descendants to occupy the emirate's throne. Wahhābites showed the same dynastical process. Both Islamic tradition and the exigencies of a nation state favour the emergence of dynasties; dynastic succession is well founded in ideology and a dynasty was considered a model polity in 19th century Islam countries. As such the repristinization favoured the re-emergence of a Caliphate dynasty. However, as is shown for the Fulani (van Beek, this volume), the exigencies of the empire changed the movement from a puritan one into a social system whose ideology had been subordinated to the demands of politics. Success defeats the quest for purity.

From this point of view, one can understand how several puritan movements can function without a dominant form of leadership. In some cases a collective form of leadership is present: for example with the Gaan Gadu and the Mazimu. The priests of the Gaan Gadu oracle acknowledged a high priest, but many decisions were taken collectively. The same holds true for the dream interpreters of the Mazimu. Among all movements, the Second Reformation seems to be the most acephalous one: though their ministers hold important positions, the tendency of the movement is clearly 'inward oriented', rendering marked leadership patterns both superfluous and impossible.

On the whole, the tendency of puritan movements seems to be towards positional charismatic leadership (or in Weber's terms, the routinized charisma), in which the leader has to fit into a predefined role that limits his personal expression and trims his style of leadership(6).

The best example is that of the Dutch Evangelicals who have a well-defined set of leaders. However, the authority of these leaders is respected primarily because the organization they give guidance to grants them such a position (see Post, this volume). Succession to office is contingent upon fixed bureaucratic procedures, thus enabling the organization to replace or appoint leaders smoothly.

The notion of positional charisma offers a compromise for the inherent conflict between strong leadership and egalitarian tendencies. In the quest for purity all are equal, and puritan ideologies often state so explicitly. If some people achieve a higher spiritual refined status, closer to the ideal of purity, then this is considered their personal achievement. The ideology implies or directly suggests a fundamental equality of all followers, which is often expressed in greetings (brother, sister, comrade), and in equality of dress and living conditions. These egalitarian forces will ultimately clash with the need for a strong and lasting organizational structure. This conflict is reflected in Cromwell, the Puritan, of whom Brailford (1961:393) writes: 'He felt a fraternity with his fellow-believers, which levelled social distinctions and made the poorest of the Saints his equal.' At the same time, Cromwell was at pains to drive home the lesson that the various groups of Puritans 'must learn the fact of unity and cooperation' (ibid.). The last requirement implies organization and hence leadership.

Most puritan movements tolerate a category of intermediary functionaries who as a class may hold considerable powers. In the Islamic tradition these are the **mallams** (scholars) or clergy (Iran). Among the Christians of the Second Reformation, the Evangelicals or the Puritans a category of ministers perform such functions. These intermediaries interpret tradition, and demonstrate the relevance of texts dealing with earlier times for present-day situations. This often commits them to a literal and fundamentalistic interpretation of the Scripture that leaves little room for individual or idiosyncratic variation and elaboration. One way the levelling process works is through the scrutiny of doctrinal novelties, followed, if necessary, by the dressing down of intermediaries by the rank and file. Harmony and consensus are key values for puritans; it is dangerous for their leaders to disregard voices of protest from their followers. Many Christian puritan movements have committees of lay members who scrutinize the performance of their leaders. All puritans watch worldly hierarchies suspiciously, quite alert for signs of increasing social inequality.

Gambits and end games for puritans

The inevitable trajectory of institutional development transforms or corrupts a puritan movement. Once the organization has struck roots in puritan communities, the process of bureaucratic or organizational ossification sets in. This, as we discussed earlier, represents a direct threat to the ideals of purity, and to the basic processes of self-examination and correction. To escape such a fate, the only 'viable' alternative is to let the puritan ideals wither away. States usually do not wither away, but ideals and norms may vanish much more rapidly. The Gaan Gadu cult of the Suriname Maroons present us with such a case. Within a span of five years, the purges and the witchcraft eradication campaign had spent their force, and the new puritanical norms were almost forgotten (Thoden van Velzen, this volume).

Such developments, detrimental to the puritan cause, can be postponed by a number of processes. The first is that of marginalization. When a movement contents itself with a modest role in social life, the quest for individual purity may continue for a much longer time than in those movements which cherish high ambitions. The Second Reformation is the best example of such 'Island Devotion' and, more generally, movements of a pietistic character usually manage to find a safe niche in the general socio-religious environment. As the price for a sustained quest for purity, such movements often curtail their ambitions. Tanzania's Mazimu movement provides us with another example. Small cells of Mazimu members succeed to continue with their cleansing and soul probing by keeping a low profile. Thus, they avoided confrontations with the Christian communities in the area, and evaded government and party scrutiny.

Moving out: the hijra-exodus pattern

A more drastic option is that of isolation. Muslim chronology starts with the year of Mohammed's **hijra**, his temporary exile. Perhaps the move was not voluntary but enforced, but it proved to be expedient. In exile, far from 'the idolators,' one could rally one's own strength, and prepare for a return. Such a pattern of involuntary isolation, serving as a preparation for later expansion, will be called here the **hijra** pattern. The **exodus**, of course, is the more or less deliberate migration from an oppressive social situation to a new and free 'promised land'. While the **hijra** implies a 'reculer pour mieux sauter', an exodus attempts to establish a new society in a new land. Whether **hijra** or **exodus**, many movements instigated by puritan cult leaders seek to build - permanently or temporarily - a pure city or kingdom, out of reach from the forces of evil, in the serenity of blissful isolation. Not all puritans seek isolation: the smaller and less ambitious ones content themselves with their place in a society's margin. But for the bigger and more ambitious movements the trend is clear: away from a befouling environment.

The Wahhābi, Taiping, Puritans and Fulani represent the clearest examples of liberation by migration. Many of the English Puritans settled in North America, far away from an 'idolatrous King' and a 'Wayward Parliament'. The Indians, though far from hostile towards them during the early days of settlement, were soon defined as 'Satan's children'. Though the Puritans did not use the term **exodus**, the notion of 'pilgrimage', which they did use, purveyed the same sense. The Afrikaners present a similar case. Though the motives for their Great Trek were not only religious, the ideas of a 'Covenant people,' a calling and a pure way of life did play a significant role. They moved north, occupying empty lands or emptying the lands of its original inhabitants(7). In the *Retief Manifesto* they wrote (de Klerk 1975:23-24):

'We are now quitting the fruitful land of our birth, in which we have suffered enormous losses and continual vexation, and are entering a wild and dangerous territory; but we go with a firm reliance on an all-seeing, just, and merciful Being, Whom it will be our endeavour to fear and humbly to obey.'

An empty country, or one peopled by creatures who, in puritan eyes, do not deserve the status of humans, facilitates the exodus(8). However, it is not a prerequisite. The Taiping, after they had started in the exodus, made Nanking its stronghold and capital, by no means empty territory before its arrival. The movements, the Wahhābi and Fulani, made their **hijra** to lands where Muslims lived and ruled; they never operated in an institutional vacuum. But for these Muslims the presence of a host society did not detract from the **hijra** as a road to purity.

The Fulani case offers the clearest example. The dissenting puritan Muslims, in revolt against the Hausa states (also ruled by Muslims), had to go west to escape extermination. There they built a new power base, and confronted their enemy in the first and decisive battle (van Beek, this volume). Closely following Mohammed's example, they began their chronology with his exile. Later they moved again against the Hausa states, conquering their internally divided enemies, one after another.

The Shiᶜite case is much more complicated. In the Iranian revolution there is no clear **hijra** in the classical pattern. True, many Iranians who were later to become prominent as leaders of the revolution, among them Khomeini, lived in exile during the last years of the Shah. But the revolution was made in Iran, not elsewhere. On the other hand, Shi^{c}a as a religion can be called a religion in exile, continually mourning the helplessness of man and his inability to overcome the forces of evil (Kreyenbroek, this volume). The martyrdom of Imam Hosein, exalted in innumerable passion plays, was a central symbol for a people driven from their lands of origin, robbed of their religious inheritance. Thus, the Khomeini/Shari'ati revolution may be seen as the conclusion of a long **hijra**, with the erstwhile exiles finally occupying the centers of power.

The **hijra** pattern as a factual emigration is absent in Wahhābi history. The cause was proclaimed in Nejd, and when it spread from there Nejd remained its centre. But even here the sunnitic orthodoxy of Wahhābi requires a **hijra**. Even if no collective migration is undertaken, the individual should follow this sacred path. A Muslim living outside of Islamic territory should emigrate to the lands of the faithful. While leaving the cities of the idolatrous behind him, and trekking to the citadels of pure faith, one performed one's **hijra**. Even a change of life styles might be called **hijra**. The founder of the Saoudi Kingdom Abd al-Aziz used the concept of **hijra** in order to have professed and respected Muslims, the Bedouins, abandon their traditional nomadic life style in favour of agricultural communities (Waardenburg, this volume).

Permanent Agitation

For an ideology stressing the quest for purity no rival doctrines exist. All that is worthwhile, desirable or valuable is embodied in the state of purity that people strive for. Neither compromise nor discussion is possible with puritans. One cannot take a stand away from the road to purity and still be considered a partner. Some of the checks and balances that result from 'contained disagreement', from the acceptance of differences of opinion or even of dissent, all such tolerance that lubricates the social machinery, is lacking in puritan movements. The world is divided between good and evil with no ground in between, and a person who tries to create a neutral territory where parties can negotiate their differences stands condemned. Hence the prevalence of the notion of witchcraft among puritans: people who are the embodiment of evil, voluntarily or involuntarily. The Salem witch case presents us with a notorious and one of the best described instances: when a group of girls could, inspired by Puritan ideology, reveal where evil was located in society, then that Puritan ideology had no means to check those accusations by exposing them to critical scrutiny.

Puritans have a hard time to prove that someone in their midst is an unreliable source of information on evil.

'How intoxicating to feel like God the Father, and to hand out definitive testimonials of bad character and habits.' (Camus)

All puritan movements have a proclivity for witch hunting. The Salem case was far from atypical, as Staples (this volume) argues. Salem had been the nexus of puritan endeavours for many years before the witch craze occurred (Boyer and Nissenbaum 1975), and the tragic events cannot be explained away as a simple 'incident'. Weisman (1984:191-203) has compared a list of pre-Salem legal actions against people suspected of witchcraft in Massachusetts Bay. The list contains 34 known cases. According to Weisman (1984:182), a great number of cases fell victim to a 'deliberate policy of silence on the part of civil and ecclesiastical authorities.' Likewise the revolutionary Communists, the Mazimu, the Gaan Gadu shrine holders, and in some way the Fulani as well, all show this tendency towards the personification of evil, and of an on-going need to purge such nefarious elements from their ranks.

For those dedicated to the goals of purity, its negative and positive effects are evident. Permanent agitation is detrimental to the quest for purity because it prevents the stabilization of a community of the pure; also it often precludes proselytization of the doctrine. On the individual level too, the haunting fear of a witchcraft hunt does not confront one with one's own impurities, but directs attention away to the outward expressions. In this way, the quest for purity defeats its own purpose. On the other hand, witch eradication campaigns and purges create insecurity, and thereby counter the process of bureaucratic ossification. Agitation keeps a society in turmoil; self-righteousness is kept in check; rigidity of social and moral positions temporarily avoided.

In the Salem case, the witch hunt stopped when some important authorities and their wives were implicated. As long as a puritan movement does not occupy the commanding heights the forces of moderation can still make themselves felt. The civil authorities in Salem carried enough weight to disprove the supernatural claims of the girls. When a witch craze is instigated from the societal top, like the Communist purges, or with the help of powerful persons in the government (Mc Carthy's purges), the process is much more difficult to stop. Either other powerful elements in a society's leadership manage to put a stop to the witch hunt (Mc Carthy), or the threat of external invasion and then the armed struggle finally brings the mass killings to an end (Pol Pot regime).

Anyway, also without witch crazes, permanent agitation can be detrimental for the movement. Even if it keeps the individual 'on his toes', it can lead to continuous fissioning of the group. This is a perennial problem in the Second Reformation (van der Meiden, this volume), but also in Communist movements the tendency to separate the new 'True Believers' or 'Right Way' from the degenerating old one is evident.

Explanations for puritans

We have sketched the morphological and dynamic analogies among puritan movements, and charted their trajectories through time. The question of explanation remains: why do puritan movements occur at a certain time and place, and what are the socio-economic and cultural contexts that give rise to such reactions? Like the numerous explanations presented in the literature on religious movements, a hard and fast explanation is not to be expected; we aim at conjectures with some plausibility.

First and foremost, puritan movements are religious movements, and the explanation of their occurence runs parallel with that of religious movements in general. The standard explanation is perhaps Balandier's (1955) 'a retaking of the initiative,' or 'deprivation thesis'. A period of social upheaval, and drastic economic and political change causes economic misery, loss of identity and of legitimate means to express frustration. When living conditions degenerate, and people no longer believe that they can improve their lot, they rally around prophets with their promises of supernatural assistance and redemption.

Such a theory has obvious drawbacks. Some religious movements can, with greater plausibility, be linked with affluence, and particularly with the social dislocations brought about by sudden prosperity (Thoden van Velzen & van Wetering 1983). A second weakness of all these theories is that they are couched in terms of such a general nature: this makes them hard to refute. Practically all known societies are in intensive contact with others, and often with more powerful ones. Such culture contact is seldom advantageous. We would like to follow Durkheim (1950:97) when he suggests that the factors responsible for the genesis of religious movement, and for their success, might vary considerably. Although the majority of puritan movements (Finlayson 1983) arise in times of violent changes and general social uprooting, this certainly does not represent more than a necessary condition. This has been expressed most clearly in the case of the New England Puritans.

'Puritanism cannot, then, be described simply as the ideological reflex of social disorder and personal anxiety; it is one possible response to the experiences of disorder and anxiety, or rather, it is one possible way of perceiving and responding to a set of experiences that other men than the saints might have viewed in other terms.' (Walzer 1965:309)

The same holds true for most other movements described in this volume. The Gaan Gadu cult, the Wahhābi, and the Fulani all share these aspects. They arose in times of change, not in situations of violent crises, though they sometimes provoked such a crises themselves (e.g. the Taiping). Secondly, the destitute did not figure prominently among their membership. The English Puritans were dominated by disgruntled noblemen, by the new intelligentsia of clerics and newly educated gentlemen, like merchants and lawyers (Walzer 1982: 308). The 'deprivation thesis' is clearly insufficient to enhance our understanding of the genesis of the English Puritans. For most other movements the same holds true (cf. Lewy 1974: 316).

As for the 'personnel' of the movements, the main body of adherents comes from a position of relative affluence, a middle class. The English Puritans, as we have just argued, came from a newly created middle class; the Geneva puritans were reasonably well-to-do citizens, often occupants of new positions in the professions. The Second Reformation relies heavily on settled farmers and shopkeepers, while the Cathari had a long tradition of wealth and found support in the artesan class as well as among the landed gentry. The Wahhābi occupied key positions in trade networks, a denomination of merchants and gate keepers for a long-distance travelling. Nineteenth-century Fulani were wealthy pastorals; the Iranian revolution relied heavily on clergymen and shopkeepers, while the Taiping could count on massive support among the Hakka, a relatively wealthy caste within Chinese society. The same connection is apparent in the Gaan Gadu movement where well-to-do boat owners formed the backbone of the movement. At first glance, the Mazimu 'religious cells' appear to form an exception: in most areas they recruited their adepts and patients from among the poorer section of the rural population. But among the affluent cash crop growing farmers of the Umalila plateau Mazimu cells were led by wealthy farmers.

Generally speaking, puritan movements seem to be characterized by a relatively affluent following, in which the middle classes, and merchants in particular, are overrepresented. Puritan movements seem to attract slightly privileged but vulnerable sections of the new middle classes. Ill at ease with their new positions of wealth and influence such individuals become the vanguard of puritan revolt. They appear on the scene as people anxious to protect their newly won share of the 'good life,' fully aware of the many power assets in the hands of an older elite, often perceived as hostile. Their quest for purity implies a levelling action against the classes just above them. Claiming that all can become pure who aspire to it, they replace the ascribed inequalities of rank by the achieved status of virtue (cf LeRoy Ladurie 1979:277).

With this focus on achievement, they embody the attitudes of the new merchant class: individually striving for upwards mobility, but collectively very much tied to the existing order, strong in their individual self-sufficency, but vulnerable in their actual achievements. The quest for wealth through trade strongly resembles the quest for purity: both cannot offer the prospect of a resting place or final destination. Stable, guaranteed positions of wealth or of purity do not exist. Just as one can only stay rich by keeping on one's trading toes, so purity is never won but needs continuous exertion. Puritan creeds are religions of the insecure.

A second characteristic of this rise of puritan movements - and their success - is the 'thin' structure of the institutional environment in which they operate and flourish. On closer inspection, nearly all puritan movements are granted or have won the 'social space' which is needed to develop a kind of counter-society. The puritans who followed the dictates of the **hijra**-exodus pattern actually create the social space they need. In other societies puritans distance themselves from others to find room for their demanding religious experiments. Puritan movements do not spring from a highly organised, tightly woven society, but from the margins of such societies where the institutional framework is less pervasive: England's new gentry; the Fulani who leaned against the Hausa states; the Hakka who could reap but little rewards from the marked hierarchical structure of Chinese society; the Ndjuka boatmen who earned a profitable living far beyond the control of their kinsmen.

A third factor that should be mentioned is the ideological one. In most societies the quest for purity draws from existing ideological wells. Without a dominant ideology in which the notion of purity occupies a significant position, the rise of a puritan movement is improbable. Christianity, especially in its Protestant version, and Islam, both Sunni and Shi^{c}a, accord a fairly high place to the quest for purity. Examples outside these two major traditions are hard to find. It is likely therefore that the presence of the ideological reservoir of both religions was a necessary condition for the rise of puritan movements. However, in view of the near ubiquity of Christianity and the Islam, this line of reasoning has little explanatory power.

Puritan leaders usually insist that they do not strive to create a new society. Nonetheless, they are often instrumental in generating considerable changes, and setting society on a new course. An egalitarian society of pastorals is changed into an empire; a reign of terror replaces a mildly autocratic regime; or the way is paved for a capitalist upheaval: these are only some of the changes that appear in our case studies. This brings us close to Weber's position about the association of Puritans with the rise of capitalism. Even to do full justice to the debate generated by Weber's ideas would require a separate book. But let us reiterate Weber's insistence on the unintended consequences of the Puritan creed, effects that eventually were to undo the movement itself. In other words: Religion brought forth Prosperity, but the Daughter ultimately devoured the Mother! (Puritan proverb from New England see van der Meiden, this volume). We have earlier discussed how the need to build a movement may undermine the puritan position. Other forms of action tend to have the same deleterious consequences. Puritan movements may, for example, create empires, but will lose their zeal for purity as they gain their purposes. The drive to cleanse society of corruption may easily lead to witch crazes and to death and destruction for thousands or, as in one case, for millions. The capitalist state some movements helped to spawn may offer unexpected riches for its citizens, but the quest for purity peters out. They may content themselves with settling in a society's margins, as one denomination among many others.

The outcome always seems to differ from what puritans had in mind at the beginning. Inevitably the time comes when the days of the elect or the visible Saints are over. In this world the last word is never granted to the pure. The 'impure,' those who can live with compromises, who accomodate to worldly interests, will (usually) win in the end. High ambitions are thwarted and the world becomes complacent again, with goals that are modest, but attainable. When virtue makes so few demands that it seems to have come within reach of the common herd, when purity is redefined as mild ascetism, those still longing for greater purity find themselves alone, sighing perhaps with the old revolutionary when he looked again at the complacent society he had helped to build:

'What a misfit I've become,...I feel like a foreigner in my land.' [Sergei Esenin, cited in Walzer (1982:320)]

When confronted with the many social transformations they generated, puritans have only one consolation: 'they may not have the last word, but they did have the first'.

Notes

1. We shall refer to the English and New England Puritans as **Puritans**. All other movements will be referred to as **puritans**, having lost a capital 'P' for clarity's sake.
2. Our colleague of Utrecht University, the Islam scholar Jacques Waardenburg, opened the field for a comparative study of puritan movements with a seminal paper which discussed some of the main features of such movements. Basing himself chiefly on Muslim movements he mentioned the following characteristics (Waardenburg 1982):
   - internal justification to rule others;
   - a sense of calling, either to abstain from the world or to convert the world;
   - clear demarcation of group boundaries;
   - latent or manifest eschatological dimension;
   - strong patterns of social control, with explicit norms about socialization and resocialization;
   - strong organization around a powerful leader;
   - tendency towards economic autonomy in as many aspects and fields as possible;
   - internal social aid.
3. The 'Good Men' or **perfecti**, the Cathari elite, probably held the most extreme views on sexuality: 'Sexual acts which produced new bodies to inhabit the temporal realm had no divine sanction; thus legal matrimony was no better than prostitution'. (Wakefield 1974: 33)
4. In the early history of the Latter Day Saints this tendency has been dominant; their 'gathering places' in Kirtland - Ohio and - especially. Nauvoo, Illinois were to be 'Cities on the Hill' (Shipps 1984). Their later goal is closer to the last category.
5. The reference is to Julien Benda's well known *La Trahison des Clercs* (1928).
6. A clear example of positional charisma is offered by the Latter Day Saints. The top positions in their organization - which is very structured - are routinely assigned charismatic characteristics, such as prophecy, revelation and seership (Gottlieb & Wiley, 1984).
7. Within a migrated puritan movement, the exodus pattern may be repeated, when internal differences threaten the unity of the settlers. A heroic saga of such of such a double trek is recorded in South Africa, where about 1875 groups of 'ultra-fundamentalists' decided

that for them Transvaal held no future, and they set out on 'one of the most hazardous and strange journeys in the history of Western man' (de Klerk 1975:62), through South West Africa, present day Namibia, to Angola.

8. Another interesting example is - again - provided by the Latter Day Saints. In 1845, thousands of Mormons were expelled from Illinois and trekked two thousand miles to the west, to a new place to build their Kingdom, far away from the sources of persecution (Shipps 1984).

References

Barr, J.
1977   *Fundamentalism*, London: SCM Press.
1984   *Escaping from fundamentalism*, London: SCM Press.
Boyer, P.S. & S. Nissenbaum
1975   *Salem possessed: the social origins of witchcraft*, Cambridge Mass.: Harvard University Press.
Brailford, H.N.
1961   *The levellers and the English revolution*, Stanford: Stanford University Press.
Carroll, J.
1977   *Puritanism and the wilderness: the intellectual significance*, New York: Columbia University Press.
Coser, L.A.
1980   *Gulzige instituties: patronen van absolute toewijding*, Deventer: Van Logchum Slaterus.
Cudsi, A.S. & A.E. Hilal Dessouki (eds.)
1981   *Islam and power*, London: Croon Helm.
Davidson, J.W.
1977   *The logic of millennial thought in eighteenth century New England*, New Haven: Yale University Press.
Demos, J.P.
1982   *Entertaining Satan; witchcraft and the culture of early New England*, Oxford: University Press.
Erikson, K.T.
1979   *Wayward puritans; a study in the sociology of deviance*, New York: Wiley. (1966)
Finlayson, M.G.
1983   *Historians, Puritanism and the English revolution; the religious factor in English politics before and after the Interregnum*, Toronto: University of Toronto Press.

Gottlieb, R. & P. Wiley
1984   *America's Saints; the Rise of Mormon Power*, Toronto: Gen. Publication.
Graafland, C.
1961   *De zekerheid van het geloof. Een onderzoek naar de geloofs-beschouwing van enige vertegenwoordigers van reformatie en nadere reformatie*, Wageningen: Veenman & Zn.
Greven, P.
1977   *The protestant temperament; patterns of child rearing, religious experience and the self in early America*, New York:
Hill, C.   *Puritanism and revolution; studies in interpretation of the English revolution of the 17th century*, London: Secker & Warburg. (1958)
Hinton, W.
1972   *Hundred day war. The cultural revolution at Tsinghua University*, New York: Monthly Review Press.
Klerk, W.A. de
1975   *Puritans in Africa: a story of Afrikanerdom*, London: Collings.
Lewy, G.
1974   *Religion and revolution*, Oxford: Oxford University Press.
Lifton, R.J.
1967   *Thought reform and the psychology of totalism*, Hammond-worth: Pelican Publications (1961).
Meiden, A. van der
1981   *Welgelukzalig is het volk: een bijgewerkt portret van de zwarte kousenkerken*, Deventer: Van Logchum Slaterus.
Miller, P.
1939   *The New England mind: the seventeenth century*, New York: Macmillan.
1953   *The New England mind: from colony to province*, Cambridge Mass.: Harvard University Press.
1966   *Life of the mind in America, from the revolution to the civil warm*, London: Routledge & Kegan Paul.
Morgan, E.S.
1963   *Visible Saints: the history of a puritan idea*, New York: Cornell University Press.
Pettit, N.
1966   *The heart prepared: grace and conversion in puritan spiritual life*, New Haven: Yale University Press.
Riesman, P.
1977   *Freedom in Fulani social life*, London: Routledge & Kegan
LeRoy Ladurie, E.
1979   *Carnival in Romans*, Paris, Gallimard.

Shipps, J.
  1984   *Mormonism. The story of a new religions tradition*, Michigan: Ann Arbor.
Stannard, D.E.
  1977   *Puritan way of death: a study in religion, culture and societal change*, Oxford: Oxford University Press.
Tai Lui,
  1973   *Discord in Zion: the puritan divines and the puritan revolution, 1640-1660*, The Hague: Nijhoff.
Thoden van Velzen, H.U.E.
  1977   Bush negro regional cults: a materialist explanation, in: R.P. Werbner (ed.). *Regional cults*, pp. 93-118. Academic Press.
Thoden van Velzen, H.U.E.& W. van Wetering
  1983   'Affluence, deprivation and the flowering of Bush Negro religious movements', *Bijdragen tot de Taal-, Land- en Volkenkunde* 139 (1): 99-139.
Trevelyan, G.M.
  1974   *History of England*, London: Longman. (1926).
Waardenburg, J.D.J.
  1982   'The puritan pattern in Islamic revival movements', in: *Revue Suisse de Sociologie*, 3: 387-702.
Wakefield, W.L.
  1974   *Heresy, crusade and inquisition in Southern France, 1100-1250*, Berkeley: University of California Press.
Walzer, M.
  1982   *The revolution of the saints*, Cambridge, Mass.: Harvard University Press. (1965).
Weisman, R.
  1984   *Witchcraft, magic and religion in seventeenth century, Massachusetts*, University of Massachusetts Press.

A pure city: Calvins Geneva
Frits G. M. Broeyer

A pure city: Calvins Geneva
Frits G. M. Broeyer

The term "puritan"

In his Preface to the English translation of the New Testament of 1557, the Englishman William Whittingham described Geneva as 'the model and mirror of true religion and true piety' (Berry 1969:7). Whittingham was quite familiar with the situation in Geneva, because he had spent some time there, after the persecutions during the reign of Mary Tudor had forced him to leave his native land. One year earlier, another exile, the Scotsman John Knox had expressed his views in no less laudatory terms: 'In other places, I confess Christ to be truly preached; but manners and religion to be so sincerely reformed I have not yet seen in other places' (MacNeill 1962:178). Geneva owed that reputation for piety almost exclusively to John Calvin, whose talents as a religious leader set his stamp upon the city. It was an impression that it long retained. When the poet John Milton visited Geneva in 1639 after his Grand Tour in Italy, the lifestyle of whose inhabitants filled him with great consternation, he was very enthusiastic about the religious and moral climate which he encountered on the shores of Lac Léman (Parker 1968: 180ff).

Milton was understandably well-aware of the similarity between the ideal of piety which was pursued by the Calvinists in Geneva and that of the English Puritans. From the very beginning, the Anglo-Saxon Puritans regarded Geneva as a veritable City of God: a perfect paradigm which could be copied at will elsewhere. Historically, however, it is quite anachronistic to call Calvin's Geneva a 'puritan' city at all. Nevertheless, because the theology of the Puritans is Calvinistic, as well as because its most important elements are also derived from Calvin himself, it is by no means inappropriate to regard Geneva as the capital city of Puritanism. Despite its rather obvious anachronism, the adjective 'puritan' is used in many scholarly publications in order to describe the piety of Geneva in the time of Calvin (e.g. Monter 1967:225).

The actual word 'Puritanism' appears to have been used for the first time in the 1560's, namely as a pejorative word to denote those English people who were dissatisfied with the developments which took place after the accession of Queen Elizabeth in 1558 when the national church was again separated from the jurisdiction of Rome (Trinterud 1971: 3-10). Those who were dissatisfied with the Elizabethan Church believed that the Reformation should be more consistently pursued than the English government was prepared to tolerate. Puritan agitation against the English 'Establishment' was rigorously opposed during the reign of Queen Elizabeth. Many of the Puritans were imprisoned for their beliefs. Yet they did not constitute a coherent party or front. Their opposition can be graded along a spectrum which runs from moderate to radical. Some of them did not even oppose the Establishment at all; although they could certainly be called Puritans. They did indeed have certain grievances against the Church of England, but they tried to realize their ideals as much as possible within the existing framework of the Establishment (Collinson 1967).

The term Puritan changed its meaning in the period after 1625. This was because the Church of England began to attack the typically Calvinistic doctrine of Double Predestination (i.e. either to salvation or to reprobation) and to recatholicize the official liturgy. The term Puritan still retained its pejorative overtones, but it now included people as well who were or who could have been quite happy in the Established Church of Queen Elizabeth and James I. They began to accept the label 'Puritan' as if it had become a badge-of-honour. Even those who emigrated to America, where they were able to organise their local congregations as they themselves saw fit, and no longer had to oppose either a Church polity or a Church order which was imposed from above, cherished the name of Puritan.

Despite all the nuances Puritanism did have a clear Calvinistic background. Several of the Puritan leaders of the first generation, the aforesaid Whittingham and others, had spent their exile in Geneva during the Roman Catholic interlude, when Mary Tudor reigned (Garrett 1966). The most important source of their ideas was undoubtedly the Bible. Indeed, the Anglo-Saxon Puritans had long preferred the 'Geneva Bible' of 1560 which had been translated by the Geneva exiles, the footnotes of which were regarded by its users as highly authoritative and also bore the typical stamp of Calvinism (Berry 1969). It is obvious enough that Geneva and other bastions of continental Calvinism lay behind their protest against the liturgical uses prescribed by the book of Common Prayer and the episcopal hierarchy of the Church of England.

Some historians emphasized the continuity between Puritan piety and the religious movements in the Middle Ages which stressed purity (Ritschl 1880; Morgan 1965). But Puritanism took roots in Geneva. This applies for its specific form of ascetic piety too.

Puritan piety does include a number of elements which, on closer inspection, are derived from Calvinistic theological ideas. So the genetic relationship between Geneva and Puritanism is doubtlessly one of cause and effect. The quest for purity characterizes the Anglo-Saxon Puritans. But, even before the Puritans, in Geneva so much attention was given to the quest for purity that it is now necessary to describe it in some detail in order to establish precisely its nature and function when compared with the same quest of the Puritans.

The political background of the reformation in Geneva

The motivations underlying the practice of piety in Geneva and the practice of Puritan piety differ from each other considerably. Here, the specific features of Genevan piety emerge clearly when compared with those of later Puritanism.

As far as the Puritans - strictly speaking, the actual, historical Puritans - are concerned, what is indeed striking is that they personally decided to practise this kind of piety. Their personal choice of this very form of life can easily be confirmed by an appeal to the historical sources such as the spiritual diaries in which they continually recalled their past conduct and monitored their feelings and their deeds in a life-long process of self-criticism (Morgan 1965:5; cp. Monter 1967: 102). The situation, however, was very different in Geneva where, for several years, an institution known as the **Consistoire** actually monitored public and private morality. Piety in Geneva seems to be a form of life which was imposed 'from above'. The inhabitants of Geneva were prepared to accept this as their own because they were afraid of retribution. The sources suggest unmistakably that Geneva was less dominated by a voluntarily-accepted piety than by the handing out of punishments to those who had transgressed the rules which were then in force. Calvin's Geneva evokes pictures of people like Pierre Ameaux, the manufacturer of playing cards, who was forced to parade through the streets in a penitential garment. And of people like the wife of Ami Perrin, that unflinching lady Françoise Favre, who was pilloried in public for dancing (Parker 1975:98-100). Policies enforced from above played a prominent part in Geneva.

Perhaps it could not have been otherwise. When Calvin arrived there, the town had only recently opted for the reformation, a choice which was clearly politically motivated. In the Middle Ages, there were two predominant powers which had a considerably say in municipal affairs: namely the Duke of Savoy and the Bishop of Geneva. They defined the extent to which the city had the rights to regulate its own affairs. In many respects, Geneva was dependent upon both of these external powers: especially in the field of jurisprudence. But in the middle of the fifteenth century, the Duke of Savoy had obtained a considerable influence in the episcopal elections. The church, therefore, supported Savoy. But the citizens of Geneva were anti-Savoyard, and, because of the stance of the church, from then on also anti-clerical.

A new route for political independence was opened up when Bern became increasingly an external factor of great political importance. A pro-Bern party established itself in Geneva which looked towards Bern for political support. Because of this Swiss connection they became known as the 'Eidguenots'. It had to struggle for a rather long time before it was eventually possible in 1535 to achieve independence with the support of its Bernese ally. It was a difficult struggle which cost the life of one of the leaders of the 'Eidguenots', Philibert Berthelier, who was executed in 1519. The crucially important role played by Bern in the struggle to achieve independence also entailed important religious consequences. Bern had already joined the Reformation in 1528, an example which was followed be Geneva in 1535, the year in which it achieved its independence, and 1536 (Monter 1967: 29-63).

It was especially the South German merchants who first introduced the principles of the Reformation into Geneva at an early date. The city stood at the intersection of several traderoutes. Although there was a severe economical crisis between 1515 and 1535, Geneva was still able to maintain its commercial position by continuing to attract trade, hence the contacts with South Germany (Ammann 1954). And hence its easy access to new ideas.

After 1535, the main goal of Genevan politics was the preservation of its independence. But, also from an economic point of view, one of the great problems was the minuteness of the territory ruled by the city. Potential enemies could be knocking on the city gates in next to no time. So the city of Geneva was compelled not only to pursue a highly delicate political course, but also to devote a considerable part of its financial resources to military defense. Apart from the intentions of the house of Savoy to repossess the city, there were the aspirations of Bern to consider, as well as those of France. In the time of Calvin the conflicting religious loyalties of his supporters and his opponents also had political ramifications. The crucial question was where the city should turn for help from external powers (Monter 1967: 19-22).

A second important political and religious factor in the time of Calvin was Geneva's demographical development. In comparison with another town on the Rhone, Lyon, or with such typical South German cities as Augsburg and Neurenberg, Geneva was relatively small. At the beginning of the 1550's it only had approximately 13,000 inhabitants (Perrenoud 1979:37). Because of adverse economic circumstances, there was an exodus from Geneva at the beginning of the sixteenth century. This explains why it was so easy during the 1530's to demolish the suburbs in order to maximize the defensive capabilities of the town (Bergier 1972:6).

In the decades which followed independence, the population of the town grew, and increased even dramatically after 1550 (Perrenoud 1979: 37). Geneva became a city of refuge for Protestants, especially those from France, although there were others too who came from Italy and elsewhere. Some of the refugees left again later, but others became permanent residents. Both the skills and the capital which they brought with them, also contributed to the long period of economic growth and prosperity in Geneva from 1560 onwards (Bergier 1972:17-24). The arrival of the foreigners, however, provoked much prejudice amongst the autochtonous population, - in most cases quite unjustly-aimed at the French (cp. Roget III 1875:208). Calvin himself was a foreigner too, an argument which was eagerly used against him by his critics. Nevertheless, the oft-defended assumption that the religious atmosphere of Geneva was largely determined by outsiders is quite unfounded. Only those who had actually been born in the town were allowed to sit in the two most important decision-making bodies, namely the Little Council and the Council of Two Hundred. When foreigners eventually were admitted in great numbers to the bourgeoisie and became eligible for seats from 1555 onwards, the most important historical developments had already taken place. Even in such an influential ecclesiastical body as the Consistoire, which set its seal on the religion of the town, the 'locals' were in the majority. Over against the foreign preachers, of which there were between five to ten, there were always twelve elders who were chosen from the ranks of the local population (Pfisterer 1957: 13-15; Parker 1975:126).

The introduction of purity: 1536-1541

Calvin's ministry in Geneva embraces two distinct periods. He worked from 1536 to 1538 and from 1541 to 1564 there. During the first period, Calvin laboured in vain to transform the religious character of the city in accordance with his own ideals. Because the links between the local population and the Roman Catholic Church had only just been broken, the Protestant zeal of the bourgeoisie seemed to be seriously deficient. Many of the inhabitants of Geneva had not accepted yet that the principles of the urban reformation must also have personal consequences for themselves; they remained crypto-Catholics. For this as well as other reasons, Calvin wanted all the inhabitants to make a public profession by receiving a confessional document which he had drawn up himself. This was resisted. In 1538, moreover, new elections to the city council brought into power a majority which was striving for closer political links with Bern, a policy which also entailed the maximum alignment of their religious policies. Calvin was deeply shocked, because he believed that a government should not interfere with the internal affairs of the church. His relationship with the city authorities became so tense that he was sent into exile, together with Guillaume Farel, the man who had originally prevailed upon Calvin to Geneva (Parker 1975:64-66).

It is deceptive to attribute all the historical developments which took place in Geneva between 1536 and 1564 entirely to the influence of Calvin, as is frequently the case. For during his first Geneva period, the role which was played by Farel was at least as important as that of Calvin. Even later, it is not true that everything 'Calvinistic' can be derived from Calvin. Other ministers, such as Abel Poupin, were also influential. Nevertheless, it was certainly Calvin whose role was predominant (cp. Kingdon 1984).

In November 1536, two months after Calvin's arrival, both Farel and Calvin had already proposed a plan to the Genevan government which included a church order. In January 1537, a memorandum, the 'Articles on the Organization of the Church and its Worship' was submitted to the city authorities in order to clarify their plan (Calvini O.S.

I:369-377). What is quite remarkable in this document, and also typical of the practice of piety in Geneva, is the fact that the Lord's Supper constitutes the basis of the **desiderata** which had been formulated. On the basis of the celebration of the Lord's Supper, certain demands must be made of society. For, whenever communicants partake of the Lord's Supper unworthily, or violate in some other way the moral and religious codes, then God's honour is also violated. In order to prevent the profanation of the sacrament, it must be possible to apply sanctions. Above all, it ought to be possible to exclude tresspassers from the Lord's Supper by means of excommunication. In the memorandum it is implied that God has indeed vested the power of excommunication in his church. God desires that all those who lead the kind of life which is unworthy of a Christian and persistently ignore warnings to walk in the ways of the Lord ought to be expelled from the fellowship of the congregation. Such an excommunication. Should remain in force until those who had been expelled had shown signs of repentance. If the Church was unable to exercise its spiritual power, it had the right to invoke the help of the government (cp. Plomp 1969:144-155).

These 'Articles' were indeed accepted: so both Calvin and Farel got their own way in this particular matter. But the 'Articles' were not actually applied in accordance with their original intentions. The banishment of the two men put an end to attempts to remedy this situation. But, even during Calvin's first sojourn in Geneva, it was not the case that the moral rules were completely neglected. Farel and Calvin simply expected far too much. Furthermore, after their departure, the urban authorities still continued to exercise oversight over public morality (Roget I 1870:121-125; 144-146).

After his enforced exile, Farel went to Neuchatel, where he continued his ministry for many years. Calvin retired to Strassburg, from whence he soon restored contact with Geneva. His opponents, meanwhile, made themselves unpopular by conceding too much to Bern during negotiations to settle a territorial dispute. Consequently, two of the four Syndics were elected from the ranks of Calvin's supporters during the elections of February 1540. Moreover, pressure from Bern to ratify the terms of the treaty, which were unfavorable to Geneva, only served to exacerbate during the months which followed the anger which was aimed at the 'Artichauds' (Calvin's opponents were so nicknamed by a play on the word articulants, because of their support for the articles of the treaty with Bern). In June 1540, the 'Artichauds' finally overplayed their hand when one of their leaders became involved in a riot during which blood was shed. From that moment onwards, their influence began to diminish. Meanwhile, Calvin himself had successfully performed a vitally important task on behalf of the city of Geneva. In 1539, Cardinal Jacopo Sadoleto had written directly to the people of Geneva in an attempt to win them back to the Roman Catholic Church. So the city authorities appealed to Calvin with the well-grounded expectation that he would rebut the arguments of Sadoleto. On 21 September 1540, in the end, the Council decided to ask Calvin to return to Geneva (Monter 1967:67-70; Parker 1975:77-79).

Imposing purity and piety: 1541-1564

It still needed eleven months of negotiations before Calvin eventually agreed in September 1541 to return and resume his official ministry in Geneva. Calvin was well aware that he wanted more scope than the municipal authorities would be prepared to grant him. His own ideal was that of a Christian church modelled upon the primitive churches which were founded by the Apostles after the death of Jesus (Calvini 0.11:281; cp. Kingdon 1962:59). His conception of an originally pure church, which must now be repristinated, presupposed that what God wanted was a congregation which took firm action against those who violated or transgressed the divine commandments, a task which the government ought to support. With an appeal to Isaiah 29: 23, Calvin argued that the government was the patron of the church and was therefore obliged to punish all those who stubbornly persisted in their disobedience towards the church. The church should have the authority to anticipate the further decisions of the courts of justice by excommunicating offenders, thereby excluding them from the Lord's Supper. During his first Genevan period, Calvin had not been able to push through his ideas about ecclesiastical discipline. When he was recalled, therefore, it must have been clear enough to him, despite the more favourable circumstances, that he would still be unable to realize his aims without encountering opposition (Plomp 1969:62-136).

Excommunication was also used as a sanction in other centres of the reformation. Usually it was the state which applied this particular sanction. After Calvin's return to Geneva in 1541, it was long uncertain whether the right of excommunication belonged to the state or to the church. For example, the Little Council demanded exclusive rights for itself. Only in 1555 was it finally decided that the Consistoire had the legal right to pass the sentence of excommunication. Compared with the situation elsewhere, the church had obtained in Geneva a unique position over against the state (Roget II 1873:47,69; IV 1879:186-194; Monter 1967:138ff; Kingdon 1962:59).

Such ecclesiastical privileges were self-evident for Calvin. Exactly as a document on church discipline was discussed shortly after his arrival in Geneva in 1536, it happened again with another in 1541 when he was recalled from exile. During the negotiations before his return in 1541 Calvin had ample opportunity to make his wishes known. The necessity of establishing a church court to exercise ecclesiastical discipline had already been noted at that particular time. Before the reformation, the bishops had their own ecclesiastical court called the Consistoire for dealing with matrimonial cases. The name of this court was transferred to the new court which was to deal with ecclesiastical discipline. Calvin acted quick on this issue. Two days after his return he had already persuaded the authorities to set up a committee to draft the new church order. The draft text was ready within two weeks. This text, the famous 'Ordonnances Ecclésiastiques' which set out the new ecclesiastical polity, could now be submitted to the municipal authorities. It was approved by all the official bodies in two months (Roget II 1873; Calvini O.S. II:328-364).

The 'Ordonnances Ecclésiastiques' include regulations for the church offices, religious education and many other matters. But the most characteristic section is that which deals with the exercise of ecclesiastical discipline. Procedures were formally established for supervising and monitoring the conduct of all the members of the local congregation in Geneva. In accordance with the traditional views which obtained at that time, church membership and citizenship actually coincided. The municipal councils elected the elders who sat next to the ministers in the Consistoire (Plomp 1969:166-171; Parker 1975:82-84).

The Consistoire, a means for city purity

On 6 December 1541, the first meeting of the Consistoire took place (Roget II 1873:21). The minutes of the meetings convey a remarkable picture of Geneva in the time of Calvin (Roget II-VII 1873-1883 and Calvini 0.21:287-818). All kinds of infringements of the ecclesiastical rules have been minuted right down to the smallest details. Posterity has remembered in particular the attempts of the Consistoire to prosecute the most notable citizens of Geneva. The policy of proceeding against the upper-classes can be evaluated positively, because there was no respect of persons. But the reasons for prosecuting offenders, and finally punishing them, often seem to be exaggerated. With the virtue of historical hindsight, the style of life which was expected from the citizens of Geneva does indeed look puritanical. This seemingly puritan style of life was greatly encouraged by the strong social control of the Consistoire.

The Consistoire was not a court of law as is all too often assumed. Its intentions were entirely pastoral. Calvin believed that it was the appropriate instrument to put an end to backsliding and to bring back again those who had fallen from the way. So the usual **modus operandi** of the Consistoire was to issue an admonition or warning. Generally, this was effective, so that further measures were unnecessary. In many cases, furthermore, offenders were given to understand that they must go to church and listen to sermons, which was another means of ensuring discipline. In some cases, however, such admonitions were not effective at all. That was the moment at which exclusion from the fellowship of the Lord's Supper could be applied as a sanction. If the offenders still refused to repent of their former transgressions, the government was expected to intervene by enforcing punitive measures. Many cases were referred by the Consistory to the Council. Conversely, there are also cases which the Council referred to the Consistoire. Both Church and State strove together to create a form of society in which the standards expected were very high indeed.

As was earlier the case in the 'Articles on the Organization of the Church and its Worship' from Calvin's first Genevan period, the Lord's Supper was the focal point of church discipline in the 'Ecclesiastical Ordinances'. The Consistoire was expected to ensure that the Lord's Table was not profaned by communicants whose conduct proved that they did not walk in the ways of the Lord. Only those who had repented of their former sins were allowed to partake of the Lord's Supper (Plomp 1969:232-243).

What kind of cases did the Consistoire deal with? (cp. Plomp 1969: 218-231). In many cases, it was suspected that the accused was a crypto-Catholic. Measures were taken against those who assisted at Mass or allowed their children to be baptized by Roman Catholic priests, or such like. In 1546 the choice of Christian names was determined by law in order to prevent Protestants from calling their progeny for example Claude, which could imply devotion to St. Claude, who was indeed venerated several miles from the city of Geneva. In the years 1551 and 1552 this particular prescription brought about a conflict with some of the city notables when Balthasar Sept announced his intention to continue the family tradition by naming his son Balthasar too. He was forbidden to do this (Roget II 1873:247f; III 1875:208, cf. 224).

The Consistoire also dealt with large numbers of matrimonial cases, which is what one might expect given the historical fact the famous

'Ehegericht' in Zürich had greatly influenced the Consistoire. The latter was frequently compelled to consider the validity of matrimonial obligations which were often taken frivolously (Köhler 1939, 1942). Adultery was invariably dealt with as a very serious offence.

And then there were the quarrels which had to be resolved too. In this case, the intentions of the Consistoire and its policy are clear enough. It is obvious that nobody should partake of the Lord's Supper in a state of unrepentence. So it was the policy of the Consistoire that all quarrels and disputes must be settled before those who had been engaged in them could be allowed to come to the Lord's Table. To which list the following kind of offences should also be added: blasphemy, lying, inebriation, dancing, playing with cards, dicing, visiting fortune-tellers, insulting the preachers, not going to church, irregular behaviour during the church services. In those cases too offenders were invariably punished.

Not everything to which the Consistoire objected actually demonstrates Calvin's stamp, nor did Calvin and his fellow ministers succeed completely in creating a society which was morally superior, both to pre-reformation society and to the situation elsewhere. Some cases do indeed support this view. Dancing and gambling for example had already been forbidden before the reformation in Geneva, although the rules were not applied consistently until after Calvin's arrival. Calvin and his colleagues did indeed strive to organize society in accordance with strict norms. In 1546 they even attempted to abolish the taverns, to which many of the dangers threatening the spiritual welfare of the people were attributed. They were replaced by a new kind of institution called 'abbeyes'. What the clergy regarded as the benign social function of the tavern could be allowed to continue in these religious public houses. The atmosphere of this new institution was meant to be Christian. So everybody had to say grace before meals (Roget II 1873:233ff; Parker 1975:100). The experiment turned out to be a complete failure. It had to be abandoned within a few months. In 1546, there was a partial ban on the performance of plays in the theatre, after a discussion in which Calvin himself did not appear to be an avowed opponent (Roget II 1873:235-243; Parker 1975:100ff; Pfisterer 1957:68-73).

Church and State in the quest for purity

The introduction of strict discipline caused Calvin himself much racking of the brain. The discussions were sometimes so heated that Calvin even warned that he would cease preaching and stop attending the meetings of the Consistoire unless his advice were actually heeded. A typical case is that of the candlemaker who had to be prosecuted in 1547 for insulting the clergy in public. This manufacturer, Guillaume Dubois, refused to acknowledge his guilt and accused Calvin of hypocrisy (Roget II 1873:262ff). The machinations of the Consistoire on more than one occasion also provoked complaints, which were lodged with the government. And yet, both Calvin and his fellow-ministers were allowed to continue with their attempt to eradicate what they regarded as sinful behaviour. A civil servant ensured that those who were summoned to appear before the Consistoire actually did so. In many cases which were referred to the city authorities - because the Consistoire did not have the right to exact the necessary penalty- the penalties were actually enforced. The strongest sanction in such cases, which regarded the church more than the state, was banishment. The sentence of death which was pronounced over Michael Servet because he had denied the doctrine of the Trinity - is an exception to the rule, thus making the negative publicity which his burning at the stake has subsequently received partly undeserved. Moreover, this particular case was never brought before the Consistoire, because the secular court was regarded competent to try a case of heresy.

As far as the death-penalty is concerned, one should also consider here all those - including both men and women - who were condemned to death for witchcraft by the secular court in 1545 and then executed. In Geneva the word which was used for a witch, denoted both a 'heretic' and a 'witch', 'herege' and not 'sorcier' or 'sorcière' (Monter 1976: 22). Nevertheless, the case-law was still identical to the penal code of the Emperor Charles V, the 'Carolina', which dated from 1532. It dealt with damage which had been caused either by witchcraft or, rather, by black magic. In the case of Geneva, the wave of executions of those who were supposed to be witches was precipitated by a dangerous outbreak of the plague. Even before the Reformation, however, there had already been a persecution in Geneva for the selfsame reason. Such an outburst of witch-finding could well be an indication that other factors were also involved: the government of Geneva could have been trying to shove up its shaky position by capitalizing upon feelings of anxiety and hatred. But the correlation between witch-finding and the plague renders such an explanation less plausible. The desire to eradicate the epidemic in the former Roman Catholic and later Protestant Geneva, alike, is more than a sufficient explanation. Calvin actually believed in witches. He did not object to the persecution of witches as such, but only to unnecessary torture. During witch-trials, the accusation that the accused had entered into a covenant with the devil played a vital role. Popular belief in witches and the conviction of the elite that people could be induced by the devil to do evil deeds sealed the fate of dozens of victims (Roget II 1873:60ff, 70-78, 154-167; Pfisterer 1957:46-49, 143-147; Monter 1967:72, 90; Monter 1976:11, 22-24, 35 ff, 66; cf. Thomas 1970:66-68). Not only in 1545, but in other years too there were condemnations for witch-craft, although on a smaller scale.

From 1546 onwards, the opposition to Calvin was led by his erstwhile supporter Ami Perrin, who was married to a daughter of the notable Favre family, the fore-mentioned Françoise. The Favre family caused Calvin much trouble. As the result of a political miscalculation on his part in diplomatic relations with France, Perrin was forced into temporary exile in the 1540's. In May 1555 he was involved in a street brawl which was regarded as an act of insurrection. He was compelled to flee from Geneva. After Perrin disappeared from the scene, and with him the leader of the opposition, Calvin had at last the chance to implement his policies with the support of the Genevan government as he thought fit (Monter 1967:74ff, 77-88; Parker 1975:98-101, 124-126; Kingdon 1984:52, 61-64). Although not entirely unchallenged, Calvin's position, even before 1555, was already powerful enough to enable him to get the government to accede to many measures he wanted. In 1543 the Council of Geneva promulgated a by-law prohibiting the bathing of unmarried men and women together. In 1544, the Council accepted Calvin's request that the singing of bawdy songs should also be forbidden. In 1550 Calvin's supporters succeeded in banning the production and the sale of playingcards. Calvin believed that it was quite natural to invoke this kind of support of the government in his attempts to purify society (Plomp 1967:242).
 One highly interesting piece of evidence is the letter which Calvin wrote to the Duke of Somerset on 22 October 1548 (Calvin Opera 13: 54-77, 77-90). The English King, Edward VI, who succeeded to the throne of Henri VIII in 1547, was still a minor, so that Somerset as Lord Protector was the most important leader in England. Calvin expounded to Somerset the ideas which he ought to bear in mind when furthering the cause of the Protestant Reformation in England. A crucial point in Calvin's proposals was that sinfulness should be punished. 'The great and terrible corruption of morality, which I can see everywhere, compels me' - so wrote Calvin - 'to request you to ensure that people are subjected to a good and honorable discipline.' For the glory of God was at stake, even in those matters which people were inclined to treat as trivial offences. Specific offences such as theft, grievous bodily harm and blackmail were indeed treated

severely, because society was affected directly. But marital infidelity, sexual offenses, inebriety and blasphemy were not regarded as very serious infringements. Nevertheless, God did indeed condemn them as very serious transgressions. In order to avert the wrath of God, therefore, strict discipline must be enforced, and a corporate attempt should be made to ensure that people practised piety. 'For' - continued Calvin - 'as teaching is, as it were, the soul of the Church in order to quicken her, so discipline and the punishment of vice are the muscles which hold the body upright and make it strong.' So it was necessary to protect the Lord's Supper lest it be polluted by the presence of those who had committed such misdeeds. For Calvin, Protector Somerset had been placed by God in a position of supreme authority in order to keep the population of England on the right path. In his plan presented to Somerset Calvin is articulating the ideals which the Anglo-Saxon Puritans would try to realize later in their own way.

Internalization of the ideals of piety and purity

In Geneva, Calvin tried to realize his ideals: with ever increasing success. The official recognition of the Genevan government in 1555 that the Consistoire had the exclusive right to excommunicate was also a public recognition of Calvin's ethical and religious goals. This public recognition of the right of the Church set the seal upon the attempts of Calvin, his fellow preachers and his supporters to establish an urban society based upon biblical norms. It is inconceivable that such a goal could ever have been reached without the ministry of preaching. In the first place, Calvin himself used to preach several times a week. Deliberate absence from the official church services was one of the things which could not possibly be tolerated. But it occurred sporadically. Church-attendance was socially self-evident in the time of Calvin, whose sermons were thus heard by the citizens of Geneva week after week. He was indeed a formidable preacher, not only in the sense that he possessed oratorical power, but also in that his sermons were imposing because of their theological substance. A short-hand writer was appointed in 1549, whose special task it was to write down Calvin's sermons. History has confirmed the contemporary belief that Calvin's sermons were so precious that they ought to be recorded for posterity. Even today, those sermons still compel respect and admiration for Calvin's intellectual and religious capacities. So it comes as no surprise to find that his sermons induced many people to accept his insights, given the fact that preaching was the most important means of mass-propaganda. They are a major factor for Geneva's gradual acceptance of Calvin's ideals of a society, which gave to God alone the glory, both in word and deed (Monter 1967:100; Parker 1975:89-96; Peter 1984). A second highly-effective means of propaganda was religious education. At about fifteen years of age, children could be admitted to the Table of the Lord. Before achieving communicant status, however, a long period of religious education was obligatory. From their tenth year, children were expected to submit themselves to a process of catechization. Calvin was greatly interested in religious education, and produced a catechism. In the 'Ordonnances Ecclésiastiques', he included an article on compulsory catechization. At a sensitive age the children were confronted by Calvin's religious ideology in no uncertain terms. Indications have been preserved which reveal the kind of knavish tricks that were played on the preachers by the children, but they seem to have merely incidental.

Calvin, drawn by a student.
Adapted from **Compendium Roberti Gagni super Francorum gestis**

Calvinistic religious education eventually produced a generation of citizens convinced that society should be as Calvin himself prescribed it (Roget II 1873:1; Monter 1967:102-107; Hedtke 1969:82-94).

Finally, the regulations which required the systematic visitations of people in their homes also contributed to the advent of a society in which religious values were indeed taken seriously. It is frequently alleged, that there even existed a well organized system to catch people out in their religious and moral transgressions. This does not fit the facts. The task of the spies was to ensure that the precarious political situation and, thus, the safety of the state, were not placed in jeopardy by internal treachery. Nevertheless, the annual visitation of people in their homes, which was introduced in 1550, was very effective in its own way. Pastoral visiting did indeed constitute a very tight social control. This visitation became mandatory when a clause to that effect was introduced into the new edition of the 'Ordinances Ecclésiastiques' in 1561. Information from the neighbours was also highly welcomed by the Consistoire. Such a deposition of damaging information was not, however, regarded as an intrusion into someone else's privacy, rather, as a contribution to community-building. In Calvin's later years, the number of cases dealt with by the Consistoire increased dramatically. This increase was simply the result of the more effective social control. A community had already been formed in Geneva which actively desired to be recognizable as a community which honored God in all of its activities (Pfisterer 1957:86-90, 94-100; Kingdon 1962:72; Plomp 1969:194, 199 ff, 216-219).

In 1558, the government promulgated by-laws against luxurious living. Yet, Calvin continued to strive to create a pious community without resorting to excesses (Pfisterer 1957:1-85). This does originate another distinction between Calvin and the later Puritans, who produced much more detailed codes of conduct.

In Genevan society, working for one's daily bread was highly regarded. Calvin, in fact, was an opponent of mendacity. In a sermon on 2 Thess. 3. 10, he attacked the practice of begging because mankind was created to be active. Where as in the Middle Ages begging had an aura of sanctity, but Calvin deprived poverty of its earlier glamour. Those who could work were expected to work, because God had bestowed upon people their natural talents. They ought to be used. Work became a vocation and the profits of one's labour became a divine blessing. Partly due to the skills of many of the new inhabitants of Geneva, who had sought their refuge there for religious reasons, bringing their capital and their relations with them, the e-conomic malaise of the first half of the sixteenth century came to an end. Industry and commerce sprung up in Calvin's lifetime. Such signs of progress could be regarded in Calvinistic Geneva as an indication of the grace of God. Even during the course of one's daily labours, the community of Calvin in Geneva sought to ensure that God obtained the glory which was His by right (Bergier 1972:19; McKee 1984:100, 118-120, 123 ff).

Legitimation of the quest for piety and purity

It is quite remarkable that Calvin also stressed, in his correspondence with Lord Somerset, how a life-style can be imposed by external means. Likewise, the Puritans attended later to the possibility of external discipline, by which the power of sin could be contained. But, in the historical form of Puritanism, there is still more emphasis upon self-discipline. In England and New England sinners were repelled from the Lord's Supper. But many refrained even from communicating, because they did not have an experience of conversion and felt unworthy to participate in the Lord's Supper on the grounds that their sins might pollute it.

Puritan piety was largely inspired by speculations on the subject of Predestination, which was one of the central tenets of Puritanism (Haller 1965:83; Wallace 1982). They based their teachings on Calvin. Yet, despite popular prejudices on this point, this doctrine was never quite so central in Calvin's own works. He used it to set wounded consciences at ease. Predestination meant that believers did not ulti- mately have to torment themselves about their sins, because God had already decided before the creation of the world which part of mankind He would elect to salvation and which He would reprobate (Wendel 1950:199-216; MacNeill 1962:210-212). In practice, however, many people were indeed tormented by this doctrine: do I belong to the elect or to the reprobates, and how do I know that I belong to God's elect? Calvin had pondered upon those questions. In the 'Institutes', Book III, 24, 4, he dealt with the problem of the right and the wrong way to attain certainty about one's own election (Calvini O.S, IV:414ff). But the Anglo-Saxon Puritans continued this debate **ad infinitum.**

Elect or reprobate? To solve this existential problem the Puritan followers of Calvin appealed to logic. Logic was then a very popular discipline. It was one of the basic subjects in the university curri- culum. On the basis of the relationship between two premisses which had already been determined, an attempt was made to draw a conclusion. This technique of formal logic was also used of the problem of predestination. The basic biblical text was 2 Peter 1.10: ".... Brethren, give all diligence to make your calling and election sure:

for if you do these things, you shall never fall." Because the fruits of faith are good fruits, piety by virtue of this text implies that one's own election can indeed be sure. One of the chief spokesmen of the English Puritans, William Perkins, used 2 Peter 1.10 as the motto of his famous book 'A Treatise Tending unto a Declaration whether a Man be in the Estate of Damnation or in the Estate of Grace' (Breward 1970:85ff, 353). Perkins argued that this particular text implied that one should determine oneself whether one was elected or not. By looking at the fruits of belief (i.e. piety), such a question could indeed be answered for oneself. According to Perkins, that kind of knowledge should be obtained with the help of the so-called practical syllogism, a way of reasoning in accordance with the rules of logic. The practical syllogism was as follows: Every believer is a child of God - I believe - Therefore I am a child of God (Kendall 1979:8, 70 ff).

On the basis of this argumentation, it is perhaps not immediately obvious that Perkins regarded the progress of sanctification and the practice of piety so important for attaining assurance. Nevertheless, this is the aim of the syllogism. Anybody who denies himself, and has his only joy in Jesus Christ, anybody who tries to live piously, can assert on the basis of his pious deeds that he believes. Because faith manifests itself in pious deeds, the assuredness of faith, and thus of election can be obtained. This approach, however, means a transition in Puritan thinking towards an increasingly greater individualization of piety as an essential in the Christian life (see Staples, this volume). The main difference between Calvin and Puritan theologians as Perkins and Ames can be seen in their dealing with Paul's Epistle to the Romans. In this most fundamental charter of the Reformation Luther's profoundest concerns are articulated: the relationship between Law and Gospel, between Sin and Grace.

In the development of Calvin's theology, the relationship between Law and Gospel also had a central place. In the first edition of the 'Institutes' of 1536, the first two chapters are devoted to this issue (Calvini O.S. I:37-96). Moreover, a lecture dating from 1533 has been preserved - the rectorial lecture of Nicolas Cop, which was almost certainly written by Calvin himself - containing an exposition of the Beatitude from the Sermon on the Mount which deals with the 'poor in spirit' (Calvini O.S. I:4-10). What is striking about this speech is the fact that it is thus dominated by Luther's fundamental distinction between Law and Gospel. The 'poor in spirit' are believers who have no confidence at all in their own abilities. They know that, in the presence of God, they have nothing which they can invoke in their own defence. Nevertheless, the blessing which accrues to the 'poor in spirit' is that they shall see God. This is the essence of divine Grace. Later, however, Calvin's theology has another starting-point, namely the doctrine of the sole Sovereignty of God. The final (i.e. the fourth) edition of the 'Institutes' is totally dominated by it.

Yet, the polarity between Sin and Grace continued to play an important part in Calvin's theology. The first biblical commentary which he produced was on Romans, the Pauline epistle which is characterized by this particular theme. Romans is quoted abundantly in the 'Institutes'. He used it for instance as a starting-point for his treatment of Christology. But he appeals to Paul's letter time and time again in the 'Institutes' when he is dealing with the manifold ramifications of the doctrine of election. As for the incarnation, he stated that redemption was the sole purpose of the incarnation (Inst. II, 12, 2-4, in: Calvini O.S. III:438-442). In other words, Calvin links together the doctrines of election and salvation in order to show those who were anxious about their sins how to find comfort and assurance. Salvation had already been promised to the believers, because Christ had offered himself as a sacrifice for repentant sinners. In the 'Institutes', Book III, 24, 5 he worded his famous sentence: 'Christ, then, is the mirror where in we must, and without selfdeception may, contemplate our own election.' In his explication of this pronouncement, Calvin appealed explicitly to Rom. 8. 32. The point which he was making is that Christ and the believers are one body. Therefore, it is possible to know that Christians are indeed in communion with Christ. 'Now He gave us', says Calvin, 'that sure communion with Himself, when He testified through the preaching of the Gospel, that He had been given to us by the Father to be ours with all His benefits' (Inst. III, 24, 5, in: Calvini O.S. IV:415 ff).

Despite this emphasis upon redemption, however, Calvin did not believe that the polarity between Law and Gospel actually is the abrogation of the Law by Grace. Calvin taught the three-fold use of the Law of the Ten Commandments (Inst. II, 7, 6-15, in: Calvini O.S. III: 332-340). He agreed with Luther that the Law is the norm by which human conduct must be measured. The Law makes sin manifest and reveals to men that they are sinners. Secondly, the Law must be accepted as the basis of civil Law. This is its public function, an argument Calvin shared with Luther too. Finally, Calvin went beyond the latter when he stated explicitly that the Ten Commandments have a special function for believers. This so-called third use of the Law is very important. Thanks to God's Law believers have a standard which they can apply in order to stimulate the right kind of christian behaviour. Calvin actually borrowed the notion of the third use from

Melanchthon and Bucer. It is remarkable that Calvin was already emphasizing the third use of the Law in the first edition of the 'Institutes' (Calvini O.S. I:61-63).

Calvin devoted much more attention to the third use of the Law than to the first two. He insisted that this is its principal use (Inst. II, 7, 12, in: Calvini O.S. III:337ff). But he still regarded the first as highly significant. Time after time, he argued that if human conduct were to be measured against the requirements of God's Law, it would still fall short of what is required. According to the Law, averred Calvin, God demands a righteousness which is so complete that nobody can attain it. But in Christ, God was full of grace and mildness towards miserable and unworthy sinners who loved Christ. Nevertheless, Calvin firmly rejected the view that this entailed the assumption that the Law had no more relevance to believers, because the abrogation of the Law, to which Paul himself referred, only touched upon the ceremonial laws in the Old Testament, which were now unnecessary, thus dispensing Christians from their obligation to observe them. The Law condemned believers no longer. The lament of Paul in Romans 7, moreover, that he had a perpetual conflict with the vestiges of his flesh, meant that Paul realized that sinners always remain sinners. Believers could, therefore, derive some comfort from the thought that they are no longer subjected to the Law absolutely (Inst. IV, 15, 12, in: Calvini O.S. V: 293 ff; vcp. Inst. II, 7, 14ff, in: Calvini O.S. III:339 ff). Yet the Law still remained as the best means for teaching believers what God's will is. So they must strive to keep the Ten Commandments to the best of their ability because they are the will of God. For God's willingness to forgive sinners did not absolve Christians from their duty to seek after righteousness.

Calvin also taught the assurance of faith. If the believer was not fully convinced that the death of Christ had reconciled sinners to God, he would always be anxious. So believers should only try to triumph over their fears by seeking communion with Christ. It was, therefore, quite possible for a believer to be assured of his salvation or even to be assured of his election. Calvin justified his stance by appealing to the work already accomplished in Christ and its significance for mankind. The faithful could rest assured in the promises already made in Christ (Inst. III, 13, 14, in: Calvini O.S. IV:218 ff; op. Inst. III, 2, 16, III, 2, 32, III, 24, 6, in: Calvini O.S. IV:561 ff, 579, 971 ff).

In Puritan circles, however, Calvin's theology of Sin and Grace, Election and Assurance, was developed in a rather different direction. Obviously Puritans did not underrate the significance of the Redemption by Jesus Christ. Yet the doctrine of Assurance in the theology of a Puritan such as William Ames had a different slant. According to Ames, the believer should examine his own practice of piety, the fruits of his own faith in order to attain certainty. This explains why he emphasized the importance of sanctification. Like Calvin, Ames also used Paul's Epistle to the Romans, but he stressed different points. He was struck, for example, by the importance of Rom. 8:13: 'but if ye through the Spirit do mortify the deeds of the body, ye shall live' (Marrow 1, 29, 20, in: Eusden 1968:170). The 'Marrow' includes examples in abundance of this stress upon the process of sanctification, even at the expense of other aspects. Naturally, Ames still accepted the axioms of the Reformation, especially the notion that one is justified by **faith** and not by works. But he also insisted that if the fruits of Grace are indeed visible in the saints this provides an assurance that grace is actually working. The assurance of faith played an all-important role alongside faith in his theology. So the believers were encouraged to practise piety, because their piety assured them of their election.

Not so with Calvin. His main point on assurance would seem to be that it is objective and external rather than subjective. A believer obtained assurance not by self-examination, by examining his own piety, but by looking at the promises of Christ. Puritan theology was indeed 'Calvinistic', and the Puritans were indeed 'Calvinists' if we look at their theology as a whole. But, if we look at their theology in detail, their ideas demonstrate that there is a world of difference between Calvin and the Puritans (Hall 1966; cp. Broeyer 1984).

Conclusion

From his arrival in Geneva until his death in 1564, Calvin held the view that piety was supremely important. Right from the start, he intended to transform Genevan society into a pious community, because God's honour demanded an onslaught against sin. Glory was given to God by piety. Above all, it was his ideas about God's honour, table-fellowship with Christ in the Lord's Supper, and his appeal to the third use of the Law which supplied Calvin with the theological legitimation which were needed to justify the fervent quest for purity in Geneva. His talent for organization supplied him with what he needed to realize his aims.

The connections between Calvin and the Puritans begin at the level of theology. Calvin wanted Christians to live in accordance with the Ten Commandments. He demanded piety, because he believed that God also demanded piety and God was insulted by sin. Calvin, however, did not give his spiritual followers the extra stimulans to practice piety which the Puritans would later supply. Calvin's version of piety did not yet guarantee assuredness of the believer. But Calvin's dire warnings that sin provokes the divine wrath performed the same function.

Calvin did much to further religious education in Geneva. For example, when several men were found to be ignorant of the Creed in 1557, they were banned from participation in the Lord's Supper, and ordered to take lessons in the articles of religion (Roget V 1879: 101 ff). The main means of mass-communication was the sermon. The younger generation had the catechism drummed into them. In this connection it is even possible to speak of indoctrination (Monter 1967: 100, 103). Undoubtedly many people were socialized in such a way, that they began to internalize the doctrine which Calvin had emphasized. They began of their own volition to do their best to seek the glory of God along the way of piety. Genevan piety became, thus, less and less dependent upon external coercion (Monter 1967:101ff; Plomp 1969:247ff). Nevertheless, the Consistoire still possessed the means of coercion if they were required. In the time of Calvin, therefore, Genevan society underwent a moral transformation: first as the result of pressure from above, then from below: but still influenced from above by preaching and teaching.

The Lord's Supper always remained the starting-point, because those who partook of it had to comply with the required norms of conduct. In 1550, moreover, a plan was broached in order to ensure, by means of the regular visitation of private houses, that pastoral supervision was intensified, in the hope that, thus, the quality of the Christian community gathered around the Communion Table improved still more. This was eventually institutionalized in 1561 when such provisions were included in the revised version of the 'Ordonnances Ecclésiastiques'. In 1555, the church obtained from the Council the right of excommunication. In this way, Geneva ultimately became a uniquely important centre of European Christianity. Visitors from elsewhere were absolutely amazed to see how its citizens actually lived (MacNeill 1962:78ff). Though Geneva was not a Puritan city in the strict sense of the word it still embodied the 'Puritan' ideal.

References

Ammann, H.
 1954 Oberdeutsche Kaufleute und die Anfänge der Reformation in Genf, in: *Zeitschrift für Württembergische Landesgeschichte*, 13, 150-193
Bergier, J.F.
 1972 Zu den Anfängen des Kapitalismus - Das Beispiel Genf, in: *Kölner Vorträge zur Sozial- und Wirtschaftesgeschichte*, Heft 20
Berry, L.E.
 1969 Introduction, in: (ed.) *The Geneva Bible*, 1-24, Madison, Milwaukee, London: University of Winconsin Press.
Breward, I. (ed)
 1970 *The work of William Perkins*, The Courtenay Library of Reformation Classics, vol. 3. Abingdon, Sutton, Courtenay Post.
Broeyer, F.G.M.
 1984 Der Einfluss Calvins auf Whitaker und den Englischen Puritanismus, in: W.H. Neuser (ed.) *Calvinus Ecclesiae Genevensis Custos*, 213-220, Frankfurt, Bern, New York, Nancy: Peter Lang
Calvin, John
 1973 *Institutes of the Christian Religion*, J.T. McNeill (ed.) F.L. Battles (transl.), 2 Vol., Philadelphia: Westminster Press
Calvinus, J.
 1964 *Opera quae supersunt omnia*, T. XI, XIII, XLIX, W. Baum, E. Cunitz, E. Reuss (ed.), Corpus Reformatorum, T. XXXIX, XLI, LXXVII, New York, London, Frankfurt am Main: Johnson, Minerva
 1926/ *Opera Selecta*, P. Barth, W. Niesel, D. Scheuner (ed.), 5
 1952 Tomi, Monachii in Aedibus: Chr. Kaiser
Collinson, P.
 1967 *The Elisabethan Puritan Movement*, London: Jonathan Cape
Eusden, J.D. (transl. & ed.)
 1968 *The Marrow of Theology, William Ames 1576 - 1633*, Boston, Philadelphia, Pilgrim Press.
Garrett, C.H.
 1966 *The Marian Exiles. A Study of the Origins of Elizabethan Puritanism*, Cambridge: Cambridge University Press
Hall, B.
 1966 Calvin against the Calvinists, in: G.E. Duffield (ed.), *John*

Calvin, Courtenay Studies of Theology, Vol. 1, Abingdon: Sutton Courtenay Press

Hedtke, R.
  1969   Erziehung durch die Kirche bei Calvin. Der Unterweisings-
          und Erziehungsauftrag und seine Anthropologischen und
          Theologischen Grundlagen, *Pädagogische Forschungen*, Bd.
          XXXIX, Heidelberg: Quelle und Meyer.

Kendall, R.T.
  1979   *Calvin and English Calvinism to 1649*, Oxford University
          Press

Kingdon, R.M.
  1962   (éd.) *Registres de la Compagnie des Pasteurs de Genève au
          temps de Calvin*, t. II, 1553-1564, Avec la collaboration de
          J.F. Bergier et A. Dufour, Travaux d'Humanisme et
          Renaissance, Vol. 55 II, Genève: Droz.
  1984   Calvin and the Government of Geneva, in: W.H. Neuser (ed.).
          Calvinus Ecclesiae Genevensis Custos 149-67, Frankfurt am
          Main, Bern, New York, Nancy: Peter Lang.

Köhler, W.
  1939/   *Zürcher Ehegericht und Genfer Konsistorium*, 2 Bde, Quellen
  1942   und   Abhandlungen   zur   Schweizerischen   Reformation
          Geschichte, Ser. II, Bd. 7, 10, Leipzig: Heinsius

McKee, E.A.
  1984   *John Calvin on the Diaconate and Liturgical Almsgiving*,
          Travaux d'Humanisme et Renaissance, Vol. 197, Genève:
          Droz.

McNeill, J.T.
  1962   *The History and Character of Calvinism*, New York: Oxford
          University Press

Monter, E.W.
  1967   *Calvin's Geneva*, New York, London, Sydney: John Wiley
  1976   *Witchcraft in France and Switzerland: the Borderlands
          during the Reformation*, Ithaca, London: Cornell University
          Press

Morgan, I.
  1965   *The Godly Preachers of the Elisabethan Church*, London:
          Epworth Press

Parker, W.R.
  1968   *Milton. A Biography*, Vol. I, Oxford: Clarendon Press

Parker, T.H.L.
  1975   *John Calvin. A Biography*, London: Dent

Perrenoud, A.
  1979   *La Population de Genève du XVIe au début du XIXe siècle.*
         Etude démographique. T.I. Structures et Mouvements.
         Genève: Jullien.
Peter, R.
  1984   Genève dans la Prédication de Calvin, in: W.H. Neuser (ed.).
         Calvinus Ecclesiae Genevensis Custos, 23-48, Frankfurt am
         Main, Bern, New York, Nancy: Peter Lang.
Pfisterer, J.
  1957   *Calvin's Wirken in Genf. Neu Geprüft und in Einzelbildern
         dargestellt, Zeugen und Zeugnissen*, Bd.I, Neukirchen:
         Neukirchener Verlag
Plomp, J.
  1969   *De kerkelijke tucht bij Calvijn*, Kampen: Kok
Ritschl, A.
  1880   *Geschichte des Pietismus. Bd.I, Der Pietismus in der reformi-
         scher Kirche*, Bonn: Adolph Marcus
Roget, A.
  1870/ *Histoire du Peuple de Genève depuis la Réforme jusqu'a
  1883* *l'Escalade*, 7 Tomes, Genève: John Jullien
Thomas, K.
  1970   *The Relevance of Social Anthropology to the Historical
         Study of English Witchcraft, in: M. Douglas (ed.),
         Witchcraft, Confessions and Accusations*, A.S.A. Monographs,
         Vol. 9, London: Tavistock
Wallace, D.D.
  1982   *Puritans and Predestination. Grace in English Protestant
         Theology 1525-1695*, Chapel Hill: University of Carolina
         Press
Wendel, F.
  1950   *Calvin. Sources et Evolution de sa Pensée religieuse.* Paris:
         Presses Universitaires

Patterns of purification: the New England Puritans
Peter Staples

Patterns of purification: the New England Puritans
Peter Staples

When Richard Rogers, a seventeenth-century English Puritan, was told
that his conduct was too 'precise', he replied by observing that he
served a 'precise' God, thus confirming that there is at least a modicum
of truth in predicates such as 'precisionist' (or Puritan) which were
first used by the opponents of radical Protestantism (Greven 1977: 141).
But it would surely be quite misleading to presuppose that Puritans
simply tried to identify a certain ontological 'something' called 'purity'
and then strived for it. As Perry Miller rightly observed, the Puritans
originally set out to purify an **institution** (Gilmore 1980:23). The main
purification was to be a purging of the Church of England from all
the remnants of medieval Catholicism which had survived the partial
reforms of Henry VIII, Edward VI and Queen Elizabeth: e.g. the wearing
of the surplice during divine worship; the use of the sign of the cross
in the baptismal liturgy; and the ring in marriage. Originally, Puritanism
was a protest against the 'half-way' measures which were prescribed
(and enforced) by 'Anglican' and Lutheran Princes,: both in England
and in Northern Europe. Its stated intention was to return to the **pristine purity** of the original Christians, as described in the Acts of the
Apostles, and to establish a society or polity based upon the Ten Commandments, which would be preached by properly appointed Ministers
of the Word and enforced by the local magistrates and the godly elders.

'Insofar as a religious motivation propelled Englishmen to emigrate to
New England, that impulse was not theological but ecclesiastical. The
colony intended first of all to set up a New Testament polity, to follow
the New Testament prescription of how a pure church should be instituted, and to the realization of this true Christian polity, all other

purposes, political and social, were to be subordinated. Hence the major literary productions of the first generation in New England are **treatises on polity** - those of Cotton, Davenport, Richard Mather, Norton, and above all Thomas Hooker's *Survey of the Summe of Church Discipline* Miller, in Gilmore 1980:23).

The Puritans sought for a life of purity: churches that were pure, and communities bound together in unity, harmony, and purity (ibid. 141). In their quest for purity (in this specific sense), the Puritans tried to follow a God-given pattern of life which permitted no deviations from the path laid down for them in the Holy Scriptures, and taught to them by their parents and their properly appointed ministers.

The Puritan pattern of purification is probably best presented as a quest for **simplification:** i.e. the removal of all unbiblical features from both public institutions and one's personal life. The most important aspects of the basic pattern are:
- the Order of Salvation, as conceived by Puritan theologians such as Perkins and Ames; this showed how the lives of the visible saints could eventually be brought into strict conformity with God's divine plan for His creation;
- the **church-orders**, which showed how the saints could be organized into 'pure' churches (i.e. local congregations);
- the **'covenants'**, individual or collective **contracts** to walk in the ways of the Lord;
- the patterns of biblical interpretation, preaching and pastoral ministry;
- the patterns of worship;
- the patterns of childrearing, socialization and dicipline;
- the pattern of Puritan migration.

Obviously, is not possible to describe the whole of the pattern here in sufficient detail. Nevertheless, an attempt can at least be made to outline its main features before proceeding to identify some of its excesses, its local variations, and its unintended consequences: e.g. witchcraft and the Spirit of Capitalism.

The pattern of migration: from old to New England

In order to relate the basic pattern of Puritanism and some of its variations to the historical trajectory of the Puritan Movement, it is necessary to begin with the pattern of migration: i.e. the Errand into the Wilderness. This process involves both the migration of ideas as well as the migration of those who held them. Whatever the **material** causes of the Puritan Revolution in England (e.g. Fulbrook 1982), contemporary students of Puritanism are unwilling to deny or delete the religious (i.e. ideological) factor (Sperry 1945:27). The process of Puritanism began when some of the Protestant exiles fled from the Counter-Reformation in the time of Queen Mary (1553-1558) to the bastions of Reformed Christianity in Geneva and Frankfurt. There, their radically Protestant identity was further reinforced by their contacts with the Calvinists. When they returned to England in 1558, they were determined to complete the reformation which was temporarily postponed by the persecutions of 'Bloody Mary'. However, they found that Queen Elizabeth was equally determined to revive the earlier compromise between the political theory of the Lutherans and Roman Catholicism. She emphasized the prerogatives of the Crown in matters affecting the Church and at the same time wished to maintain many Catholic traditional institutions: such as the celibacy of the clergy and the use of crucifixes and statues, alongside the Book of Common Prayer which was reintroduced in 1559. Although the more critical of the Protestants were able to force the issue on such matters as celibacy, it was impossible to obtain consessions on episcopal government in the church and the **ritualia**. Nor was it possible to meet the Puritans even half-way when their grievances were aired at the Hampton Court Conference in January 1604 in the time of King James I. This explains why English Puritanism began as a conflict on ritual. In fact, Puritans were free to practice their own form of discipline unofficially and preach Puritan sermons without undue harassment until the advent of William Laud in 1628. Until them, the radical Protestants were not systematically harassed at all: some of them even became prelates of the Church of England, whilst others taught divinity in the Universities of Oxford and (especially) Cambridge.

When Laud became Bishop of London (1628) and Chancellor of the University of Oxford (1629), he began to enforce stricter conformity to the Book of Common Prayer, and to use his powers of censorship in order to suppress radical Protestant literature. When he finally became Archbishop of Canterbury in 1633, he also made increasing use of the powers vested in the Court of High Commission, which was reconstituted by Queen Elizabeth in 1559. With these powers he attempted to enforce ritual conformity and to suppress Puritan preaching in the parishes (Tyacke, 1973). The Puritans not only wanted freedom to preach and practice their ideals: they also intended to place the whole of the English people under Puritan discipline. Their ideal was to prescribe puritanism by law and to give the local magistrate the necessary legal authority to enforce it. After the advent of Laud, however, the larger ideal receded. Many Puritans refused to 'tarry' any longer for the coming of such a magistrate and swarmed to New England. There they attempted to establish Biblical Commonwealths, in which the visible saints would subject themselves (and others) to a strict form of Puritan discipline.

In England, however, the struggle between the radical Protestants and the Crown (which governed and protected the Church of England) continued unabated between 1630 and 1660. The result was a civil war during which the militant Protestants defeated the royal army (thanks to Cromwell's New Model Army) (Aylmer, 1972); executed the King and the Archbishop; abolished the Book of Common Prayer and the Episcopate; and finally established a **dictatorship** (Russell, 1973; Aylmer, 1972). Even this did not satisfy all the militants, many of whom were now advocating a Congregational form of church government (forbidding all outside interference in the life of the local congregation, even from Parliament) instead of the more 'hierarchical' synodal system of the Presbyterians (Pearl, 1972). Most Puritans wanted neither the bishop nor the 'classis' (Miller 1956:2). Furthermore, the Puritans who did remain in England were now confronted by a new kind of radical apocalyptic sect (e.g. the Fifth Monarchy Men) (Hill, 1975); as well as by proto-communistic movements such as the Levellers and the Diggers (Lewy 1974). Even the Puritan Divines (Protestant theologians) began to differ fundamentally from each other on 'the designs of the Zion which they wanted to establish' (e.g. Tai Lui 1973). They also began to consult rival eschatological time-tables. Ultimately, the Puritans fought against each other, as well as against the central political authority and the 'reprobates'. Something like ten percent of the English people perished during these conflicts.

The result of the chaos was the restoration of the monarchy, the Book of Common Prayer and the episcopate in 1660-1662. Charles II could then take firm steps to prevent the Puritan preachers from propagating their political creeds (e.g. no state interference in the life of the local congregation) as well as the most distinctive parts of their religious ideology. For example: 'None are in their sermons to bound the authority of sovereigns, or determine the differences between them and the people; nor argue the deep points of election, reprobation, free will etc'. (Royal Decree of 14 October 1662 in Cragg 1950:33). Puritanism then went underground in the two overlapping subcultures of millenarianism and 'dissent'. It emerged again in more tolerant times (thanks to the more liberal thinking of John Locke) in the form of 'Free Churches'. By the 1690's, it was even possible for the London Parliament to reassert some of its authority and control over the colonies in New England, most of which were 'planted' by the Puritans.

Meanwhile, thousands Puritans had already set sail for North America in order to escape from the tyranny of the monarchy and the prelates of the Church of England (before civil war) as well as from the **anomie** generated by the revolution; because the saints themselves had fragmented the original Puritan Movement into competing and warring sects (Murrin 1972). The initial intention of the colonists was to build the right kind of Biblical Commonwealths in which Puritan discipline would be strictly enforced by the local magistrate and godly elders. Their City on the Hill was deliberately intended to be an exemplary model or pattern to be followed by those whom they had left behind and, indeed, by the rest of the world in its totality. By the end of the seventeenth century, there were no less than 77 congregational churches (i.e. autonomous local churches) in Massachusetts alone; and another 35 in Connecticut, 6 in New Hamshire, and 2 in Maine (Gaustad 1962:14). Many of the expatriate Presbyterians, Baptists, and the Quakers (some of whom - if not actually all of them - were also practitioners of a Puritan form of piety) were also engaged in this kind of exemplary community-building. Because political rivalry exclusively demanded the attention of the London Parliament throughout most of the seventeenth century, the colonies which were 'planted' were virtually free from political interference until the restoration, by which time they were firmly established in their New Zion.

Most of the original colonists were members of trading companies. They either paid their own passage or held substantial shareholdings in these companies. Those who were too impecunious to finance their own voyage usually contracted their services to the company until their arrears had been fully paid off. Indeed, if many of the colonists enjoyed voting rights in New England, this was (in the early years) simply because share-holders were entitled to vote at their meetings. If the colonists were able to buy out their share-holders and financial backers in England, they were more or less completely free to establish their New Zion in any way they liked. Provided, of course, that they could defend their settlements from the incursions of the Indians and receive regular supplies of stores and new recruits from the old world (Sperry 1945:30).

Thus, the colonists had the maximum amount of political, social and geographical 'space' in which to fulfill their original intentions. There were no established interests to challenge. Apart from the Indians, it was an institutional void which facilitated the maximum range of social experimentation; and also offered unprecedented stability for those whose values were communal (Murrin 1972:231).

The original migrations consisted of mainly self-selected groups of Puritans. Whole families, indeed whole congregations, followed 'charismatic' leaders such as William Bradford through the North Atlantic storms to havens like Plymouth Rock and Massachusetts Bay. Puritan masters brought their faithful servants and apprentices. Wives and children followed their fathers and husbands. Together they undertook what they themselves called a 'pilgrimage' to their Promised Land. Their quest for the New Zion was even described by Puritan historians (e.g. Cotton Mather and Edward Johnson) as if it were a **New Exodus**: i.e. a repristinization of the Sacred History of Israel. The battles fought by the New England soldier against the **Indians** were described in the traditional language of the **Holy War**: as in the Books of Samuel and Kings (Ferling 1981). Their pilgrimage seems to bear all the essential hallmarks of a ritual process. It reinforced their communal solidarity and confirmed their ideological expectations: e.g. the firm belief in a providential deity whose divine intentions were being fulfilled by their migration. (The last thought of those who perished during the perilous voyage are not, of course, recorded). Even if the dangerous voyage untimately failed to reinforce group unity, non-believers and deviants could always be banished to Rhode Island: or sent home on the next vessel bound for England. In this way, fully 75% of those who eventually declared their independence in 1776 could rightly claim to have come from a Puritan background: and no less than 85 - 90% of the 'rebels' bore in some way what Ahlstrom calls 'the stamp of Geneva' (1972:124). It was indeed a 'tribal' migration, but, within the Puritan tribe, there were many different clans.

Purity and Church order

Purification of institutions had been one of the original motives of Puritanism, so the establishment of and differences between church-orders are important (Walker 1960). Each town or settlement had its own local pattern, many of which have been reconstructed by local historians (Murrin 1972). Two factors are important here: the jealously guarded **independence** of the local congregational churches, and the fact that the traditional English 'county system' was not originally imported into New England. There were no **provincial towns** and consequently little centre-periphery conflict in New England. Conflicts, of which there were many, were usually fought out **within** the towns themselves, between neighbours and local factions, rather than between towns and provincial capitals, or even with the metropolis. Many local 'fractures' have now been exposed by local historians who have examined litigation procedures (e.g. Demos 1970) and the witchcraft trials (e.g. Boyer and Nissenbaum 1974; Demos 1982).

Probably the group unity originally generated by the perils of the dangerous Atlantic crossings did not long survive in New England, despite the fact that, in practice, town and church were virtually synonymous (Murrin 1972:234). Nevertheless, the colonists did not try to lessen these high levels of local conflict by moving elsewhere. In some places, geographical mobility was no greater than one percent per annum, which is considerably lower than the four percent levels recorded in some English villages in the same period (ibid.). Such mobility was probably curbed by three factors: the activity of the Indians in the outback; the need to obtain permission from the local congregation to move elsewhere and the necessity of presenting a satisfactory testimonial of good conduct before taking up residence in a new congregation; and the sheer longevity of the original New England patriarchs. Life-expectancy was of the order of seventy years for both men and women. Indeed, twenty percent of the first two generations of patriarchs in Andover seem to have survived well into their eighties (Murrin 1972:230). Which means that the sons had to wait for a considerable time in order to obtain their inheritances and lacked the necessary capital to establish themselves elsewhere.

The settlements were established around the church-building. On arrival, the saints entered into a 'covenant' to walk in the ways of the Lord. Then they elected a minister to preach the Word of the Lord, and officials to supervise the local congregation, parcel out the land, and build (and maintain) the roads and pathways. They also fixed the local prices. Originally, they combined the functions of magistrate or sheriff (i.e. civil functions) together with those of the ruling elders (i.e. an ecclesiastical office), though the two 'powers' were gradually separated. In any case, the civil 'arm' was generally expected to enforce the first 'table' of the Ten Commandments by punishing blasphemy, heresy, profane language, and the desecration of the Sabbath (i.e. Sunday).

The purification of self: beliefs and piety

Perry Miller's now classical descriptions of the New England Mind (1939 and 1953) can rightly be called 'a self-contained study of the most inclusive and carefully articulated belief system in the history of American ideas' (Sobczak 1982:45). Schneider had pointed out that North American Congregationalism was 'a social reform movement with a complete ideology' (1946:3). Despite its not inconsiderable short-comings (e.g. Miller's unfortunate tendency to synthesize Puritan thought as though it were the product of a single intelligence by riding rough--

shod over many a question of context and chronology), *The New England Mind* is still the best reconstruction of the Puritan pattern of thinking, despite more than forty years of detailed criticism (see Hoopes 1982).

The most typical features of the New England Mind are:

1) the basic assumption that God's sovereignty, will and power really are **sovereign**;
2) the assumption that the visible saints (i.e. the converted) should organize themselves into Biblical Commonwealths, in which God's sovereignty is acknowledged and divine laws enforced;
3) the assumption that individuals, families, local congregations and, ultimately, the whole nation must stand in a **covenant** relationship with the Almighty.

Hence the absolute necessity of walking in the ways of the Lord as prescribed in Holy Scripture. Indeed, the relationship between ideology and ethos is so intimate that patterns of thought (or belief) and patterns of behaviour (i.e. piety) must always be examined together. The task of the Puritan theologian, as stated by their most authoritative teacher, W. Ames, is to teach people how to live 'unto God' (**Deo vivere**). This can only be done by following consistently the basic Puritan Pattern (the **Ordo Salutis**) which was described in great detail in the **Medulla** (= The Marrow of Theology); and earlier by Perkins in *The Golden Chain*, (e.g. Graafland 1961; de Groot 1978; and Eusden 1983, who includes an English translation of all *The Marrow*). The Marrow was undoubtedly the most influential source of Puritan thinking in New England throughout the whole of the seventeenth century. As late as 1717, Increase Mather could still think of no better handbook of theology to recommend to aspiring Ministers of the Word and Sacraments in New England. Every Puritan student in Europe and New England who 'aspired to the Puritan Way' was expected to work his way through the Marrow.

Ames spent most of his life teaching in the Netherlands, in the now defunct University of Franeker. From Peter Ramus (a Hugenot) he borrowed the notion that theology is a practical rather than a speculative discipline. After all, Puritans needed to know how to live in accordance with the Will of God, so that, ultimately, the life of Jesus Christ could be manifested **in their bodies** (2 Cor. 4.10). He finally defines theology in terms of 'that good life whereby we live to God' rather than in terms of living to oneself (see Eusden 1983:1-38; and Marrow 1.1.1.ff.), As Ames himself averred:

'This practice of life is so perfectly reflected in theology that there is no precept of universal truth relevant to living well in domestic economy, morality, political life or lawmaking which does not rightfully pertain to theology' (Marrow 1.1.12).

In more sociological parlance: theology is important because it provides the legitimation for living this kind of life. The most important practice in Puritanism is, therefore, the practice of this kind of piety.

Both Perkins (e.g. Hindson 1976) and Ames (in the Marrow) codified the various stages of this highly complicated discipline, i.e. the basic Puritan pattern, as a kind of rite de passage,: or as a pilgrimage (compare John Bunyan's popular presentation of it in the *Pilgrim's Progress*. Thus conceived, salvation begins with the Eternal Decrees of God. They are, in principle, unchangeable because God's will is indeed sovereign. Hence the implication (confirmed by a whole catena of quotations from the Holy Scriptures) that God's human creatures are all predestined either to salvation or damnation (Marrow 1.25.1 - 41). The final goal of God's elect (but not the reprobates) is Glorification: i.e. perfection in this life and eternal life thereafter (Marrow 1.30.1 - 34). This goal was to be archieved in several distinct stages: i.e. Justification by Faith (alone) and not by good works, as the medieval Catholic Church affirmed, and Conversion (Marrow 1.27.1 - 27; and 1.26.19 - 34). Justification by faith alone was the corner-stone of Lutheran theology; whilst the emphasis upon Election and Predestination is much more typical of Reformed, or Calvinistic, theology. Characteristic emphases of this kind of Puritan theology are:
1) the ever-increasing enphasis upon the need for conversion;
2) the crucial role of the covenants: especially in the process of community-building;
3) the view that the human will is free rather than determined. Conversion, from the early writings on, was crucial.

It would be wrong, however, to understand the experience of conversion at this stage in terms of its more spectacular psychological overtones from later times, like rolling over the floor in anguish (i.e. the 'holy rollers') or 'fits'. For Puritans, conversion generally means the **total surrender** of the human will to the will of God: which was confirmed by signing the covenant and living in accordance with God's laws. However, it was indeed accompanied by weeping on some occasions. Conversion can be regarded as the necessary transition from external to internal discipline.

In fact, only those saints who had already manifested the external signs of regeneration and conversion could be recognized by the local congregation as visible saints and receive the privileges and benefits of sainthood; the right to vote in the local council; to partake of the Lord's Supper and to present one's as yet unconverted children for baptism. Only the 'converted' could participate in the Covenant of Grace, which was the only way to attain Sanctification, Glorification and Eternal Life. The original Covenant of Works had already been annulled by God following the disobedience of Adam and Eve in the Garden of Eden. Henceforth, the only way in which a covenant relationship could be established with the Almighty was on on the basis of one's faith, modelled on the covenant made by Abraham and his family with God in Genesis 17. This was the basis of the National Covenant which was made between the sons of Abraham (i.e. Israel) and their God. The Covenant of Grace was made possible by the life, death and resurrection of Jesus Christ (Eusden 1983:51-55). The main difference between Puritan covenants and the covenants of the Old Testament is that the latter also entailed certain ritual observances, e.g. circumcision and sacrifices. But these ritual observances were abolished by Christ when he inaugurated the New Dispensation; hence the strong anti-ritualistic tendency in Puritanism (see below).

The orginal Puritan covenants were very 'open-ended'. For example: the essence of the now famous Mayflower Compact is that the Plymouth pilgrims covenanted themselves 'to walk in His ways made known, or to be made known unto them, according to their best endeavours, whatsoever it should cost them, the Lord assisting them' (Miller 1956:5f). The terms of the original Salem covenant are equally vague;

'We covenant with the Lord and with one another, and do bind ourselves in the presence of God, to walk together in all His ways, according as He is pleased to reveal Himself unto us in His blessed work of truth'. (Ahlstrom 1972:143)

The contents of the New England 'group mind' emerged, therefore, in a rather gradual way as the saints experimented in order to discover the right kind of church-order and discipline which was most suited to their needs. Important in this experiment were the conflicts that arose with the deviants, such as Anne Hutchinson and the 'antinomians' (who, like the Quakers, also appealed to the 'inner-light' for further guidance alongside the Holy Scriptures); the Quakers; and the witches (Erikson 1966). Puritan covenants were most probably expressed in simple terms because relatively few of the original Pilgrims (i.e. the ones who drafted the foundation covenants) had received any formal theological education. As Ahlstrom rightly indicates, the original representatives of separatism in the Plymouth colony were not theologically minded 1972:238). In other words, the ever-increasing sophistication and complexity of New England theology (e.g. the massive output of Jonathan Edwards) was not quite typical of all the Puritan congregations especially at the beginning of the seventeenth century. But the situation soon changed once a theological academy was established at Harvard, and when theological debate was intensified by conflicts with the dissidents.

The Covenant of Grace invariably demanded a total reformation of character, hence the traditional rejection of all idle recreations such as sport and games, the theatre, and the typically English May-Day celebrations. In the same vein laws against 'vain' display and ostentatious clothing were the strictly enforced. The 'plain' style of the Puritans (and especially the Quakers), the continual meditation upon God's divine laws (which not only involved reflection upon the content of the Sunday Sermons, but also learning to read the Bible for oneself) and the constant recollection of the basic sinfulness of the unregenerated human condition after the Fall constitute part of the same picture. Such duties were continually reinforced during the customary household prayers, during divine worship, and during the Fast Days which were prescribed by the public authorities whenever it was believed that an angry God was punishing His people for their sins. This happened with some frequency: when the crops failed; when the Indians went on the war-path; whenever the London Parliament tried to reassert its political authority and, above all, when it was believed that witches were active. Many of the more literate Puritans also recorded in their spiritual diaries (of which many have survived) their daily progress (or otherwise) towards the goal of perfection, salvation and eternal life. This process of critical self-examination virtually replaced the medieval practice of confessing to a priest. If such self-scrutiny failed, and if the example of the already-converted saints was insufficient to prevent back-sliding amongst the others, the magistrates and the elders would intervene by reimposing external discipline. If necessary sanctions were used. These included a private-warning, followed by a public-warning if their voice were not heeded. And, if a public warning failed, more powerful sanctions could be applied, such as banishment, the withdrawal of the right to carry a gun, imprisonment or eventually even death by hanging in cases of murder and witchcraft. Internal discipline, which was always preferred to external coercion, was attained during the process or experience of conversion in the case of adults.

This internal discipline has become the hallmark of a Puritan. Of course it has been ridiculed often. Epithets such as 'puritanical' are consistently used by many Americans to denote people who are simply afraid of life. People believe that once Puritanism had taken firm root in American soil it just grew 'like some poison ivy from whose roots stifling tendrils have coiled around the American soul' (Miller, in Gilmore 1980:22). Puritans, however, were not afraid of life, but wanted simplicity. Even if Puritans like Thomas Hooker did reject painting (for example) as the mere addition of paint and varnish to wood and canvas, the poetry and prose of the Puritans, together with their sermons and their histories, are of great depth and scope. Its proper value should not be dismissed on the basis of a crude comparison with the convoluted and more 'baroque' style of their 'Augustan' contemporaries in Old England, such as John Donne and Launcelot Andrewes (Miller 1956 in Gilmore 1980:22-23). After all, especially in literature 'plain' could well be beautiful (e.g. Hooker's point). Such simplicity, however, was actually demanded by the exigencies of the wilderness situation in which Puritans found themselves in their New Canaan. Amongst the Quakers, 'simple' was virtually a shibboleth. Despite the prejudices of the popular pundits, Puritans in New England cannot simply be treated as Philistines. Nor were they iconoclasts in North America, as their colleagues on the other side of the Atlantic undoubtedly were. In their New Canaan there were no decorated churches polluted by 'images' to purify.

Futhermore, Puritans rejected neither the world (and, hence, science) not their bodies as such,; because both were conceived as 'creatures' of God. But they did indeed assume that if they were eventually to pass from this world into the life everlasting their love of this world would ultimately have to be tempered with considerable self-restraint; hence the well-known tendency in Puritanism towards the practice of what is now known as 'inner- worldly asceticism'. Perry Miller calls this: 'loving the world with weaned affections'. This latter term was not only applied by Puritan ideologists to the right way in which to love one's property and one's worldly possessions, but also to the right way in which to love one's wife, husband, children, parents, and even one's country. This was the razor's edge along which all Puritans were required to walk. That was their true intention, their original aim, even if many (if not most) of the Puritans ultimately failed to live up to such unbelievably high standards. Some did become fanatics and hypocrites. Others (e.g. John Wise and Benjamin Franklin) do seem to have 'transported the Puritan ethic of Christian industry into a secular context' (Miller 1956:171 ff.).

The 'weaning of affections' should not be exaggerated however. Even those who fervently believed that the love of God must always take absolute precedence over the delights of this world were not automatically incapable of appreciating both its delights and (above all) its lawful uses (Daley, in Gilmore 1980:45). Thus, Puritan teachers never insisted that 'Brother Body' should be despised and therefore rejected as such. Though neoplatonic in some respects, the Puritans saw the body as something more than a prison from which the soul should happily escape at its first opportunity (ibid.) Indeed:

'...nowhere is the distance between the Puritan and the Gnostic or Manichaean or Catharist dualist greater than in their attitude towards the death of the body. The **Catharists**, for example, believed that the proper life of man on earth consisted of the endura ritual suicide by starvation. But the Puritans did not despise the body, nor were they half in love with easeful death' (ibid.).

Puritans were not, generally speaking, obsessed by sexual purity in the strict sense that this is all that matters; the general view is mistaken in this, too. Certainly they did not condone sexual promiscuity, but purity implies a great deal more than sexuality. Still, its mattered for them. Michael Wigglesworth, for example, a Tutor at Harvard, did indeed record in his diaries that he was perpetually troubled by nocturnal emissions, experienced severe sexual problems throughout the whole of his married life, and never completely liberated himself from the fear that sexuality is always associated with filthiness and sin (Greven 1977:131ff.).

Abolishing outward sacredness

Puritans dispensed completely with all notions of sacred time and sacred place (Walsh 1980). The traditional Christian Calendar was completely abolished. Only the Sunday 'meeting' remained, together with the irregular Fast Days (see above). Even Christmas was abolished in England during the time of Oliver Cromwell. To this very day, it is still not a public holiday in Scotland. Because Easter invariably fell on a Sunday, this was always a problem for Puritan preachers who were consistent in their repudiation of the traditional calendar. The usual solution was to preach on a theme which had no direct connection with Easter. When Christmas also fell on the Lord's Day, the same tactic could again be employed. It is even possible that many Puritans in New England had forgotten how to compute the right date for Easter. They also consistently ensured that none of the new place names in their New Zion would bear the traditional overtones of sacred space, like Holywell. They also ensured that their church-buildings did not have 'sanctuaries', altars, images and even steeples (the 'classical' New England church building with steeple only began to appear in the eighteenth century (Noll et al. 1983:76ff.). Actually, they were 'meeting-houses' in which 'secular' business was also routinely transacted (e.g. H.G. Turner 1979). Particular places were simply not sacred for the Puritans. Their meeting-houses were indeed the centre of their towns and settlements, but a meetinghouse is not a sacred centre. (Winslow, 1972) Paradoxically, however, by describing their 'pilgrimage' to the New Zion in terms of the Sacred History of Israel (see above), they ascribed to New England as a whole the sacred status of a Holy Land. It had no shrines and holy places, but the people who lived there was believed to be a people 'holy unto the Lord'. Its temple was the law of God. Indeed, their pilgrimage to their Holy Land does seem to bear some of the typical hallmarks of a ritual process (cf. V.W. Turner 1969).

There was always a strong anti-ritualistic tendency in radical Protestantism. Hence the purification of medieval Catholic worship and the protests against 'Anglican' and Lutheran ritual which characterized the first generation of Puritans (see above). In New England, there was no temple, no priest and no sacrifice, because there can be no intermediary between God and the local congregation except the Bible, the Holy Spirit and Jesus Christ. The sacraments of Baptism and Holy Communion were generally regarded as a 'sign' or 'seal' of election (Holifield 1974). They confirmed the status of visible sainthood which had already been achieved by conversion, by signing the covenant, and by walking in the ways of the Lord. For Puritans, sacraments are never the means by which salvation can be appropriated and regeneration achieved, (as is the case in Catholic sacraments). This is precisely the reason why the right to participate in the sacraments (see above) is always strictly reserved for the saints who have already manifested 'in their bodies' the signs of regeneration (Marrow 1.36.1 - 34). In other words, Puritans did not seek ritual purity at all but, rather, a spiritual re-birth without any ritualia.

Puritan patterns of child-rearing

Greven (1977) has described three different patterns of child-rearing in early America. He relates them to the two dimensions of religious experience and the self: i.e. to the individual psyche rather than to the hypostatised 'group mind' reconstructed by Perry Miller. Greven calls these three patterns (or types of temperament) the self suppressed; the self controlled; and the self asserted. They are subsumed under three different categories of Protestants: i.e. the Evangelicals, the Moderates, and the Genteel. But only the moderate constitute a logical class based solely upon the criterion of temperament, as the evangelicals constitute a basically religious category. The latter seems to include many typical New England Congregationalists, whilst the former seem to be mainly covenant-minded Puritans (May 1979).

The evangelicals (i.e. Puritans) were generally authoritarian parents, because they believed that the total authority of God is always reflected in the authority of human parents (especially the fathers). In the

Puritan family the father not only represented God, but also had the duty of enforcing His divine authority in the home over both wife and children. (In practice, however, much of the pre-school instruction of the children fell to the mother). In order that the children might have at least some chance of attaining eternal happiness after death, and achieve the status of visible sainthood here on earth, no effort should be spared in the breaking of the child's will. Indeed, intolerance towards oneself (i.e. the self suppressed) left no room for flexibility towards the back-slidings of others, including one's children. For Puritans such as these, the status of the newly-born child was always highly ambiguous. The logical consequence of the stricter interpretation of the doctrine of election was that every unformed child must be either a potential saint or a potential devil.

By contrast, moderates (who were also Puritans) were authoritative rather than authoritarian parents who believed that the will of the unformed child needed to be 'bent' instead of 'broken'. So they usually emphasized exhortation and example rather than corporal punishment and psysical chastisement. Their pattern of religious upbringing is, therefore, based upon the need for growth in grace rather than upon a sudden and dramatic conversion like St. Paul's on the road to Damascus. Nevertheless, the moderate approach does not exclude conversion though this is a much less traumatic experience without psychological symptoms.

The moderates were more conscious than the evangelicals of the sheer ambiguity of divine and human power. They feared that total power and unlimited authority 'would be destructive of their own carefully nurtured sense of self and of liberty' (Greven 1972:234). So how did the moderates reconcile the basic contradiction between absolute divine sovereignty and the milder medicine of moderate piety? They resolved this paradox by appealing to the doctrine of the **Covenant of Grace** (see above). Because God and His covenanted saints had made a mutually-binding contract, salvation was always assured for as long as the visible saints kept their part of the bargain. 'By virtue of the Covenant, moderates of the Federalist persuasion were able to acknowledge the ultimately absolute power of God while resting assured that, in practice, even His power was limited' (ibid. 236). In this way, God's love and justice were ultimately able to prevail over His 'tyrannical' power. God would now be conceived as a benevolent, reliable, and trustworthy being who governs His creatures in accordance with just laws accessible both to the powers of Reason and to those who acquaint themselves with His divine will as revealed in the Holy Scriptures. For the moderates God's Will is no longer totally unpredictable and completely inscrutable.

The Genteel, finally, disapprove of both introspection and fervent piety. They accept the self and society without much question (May 1979:107ff.). So they cannot be regarded as Puritans in any sense.

Contradictions and aberrations

It has already been noted that New England Puritans consistently assumed that the will of the unformed child must be either 'bent' or 'broken'. This basic assumption appears to contradict the logical consequence of the Eternal Decrees when stated in their strongest form: i.e. the sheer 'unfreedom' of the unregenerated human will. Eusden has already (correctly) maintained that the stance of Ames on this highly controversial issue was somewhat closer to that of the Dutch Remonstrants than it was to the more typical (i.e. Reformed) stance of the Contraremonstrants. If the human will is completely determined by God's Eternal Decrees (which predestined either to salvation or to reprobation), then God seems to be responsible for human sins. Although Ames always insisted upon the sole-sovereignty of God, he seems to have been aware of the force of this kind of objection. So he qualified the more typical Calvinistic stance by stressing man's response in the drama of salvation. This is the starting-point of the typical New England doctrine that aspiring Puritans should prepare themselves actively to be converted, rather than passively and anxiously awaiting the process of regeneration expected by the elect. If grace were eventually to be experienced, then spiritual preparation was not only helpful but also necessary (Eusden 1983; Pettit 1966). Even Ames tells his readers in the Marrow (1.3.5 - 6) that faith cannot be received without a genuine turning of the will towards God. But his attempt to reconcile the basic freedom of the human will with the absolute power of God is formulated very unclearly. He is obviously wriggling on the hook:

'An unclear and remote inclination toward God precedes faith, a certain shadow of which is found to some degree in all creatures. ...But since this is inefficacious it is an ineffectual 'woulding' (as they say) to love God, rather than true love' (Marrow 2.7.4 - 5).

The basic inconsistency is rather obvious here: for it is logically quite impossible to assert the absoluteness of the Eternal Decrees (and, hence, God's unlimited sovereignty) whilst setting free the human will to choose between good and evil, for or against the Gospel. Ames still believed that Arminianism (i.e. the view that Christ died for all, rather than just for the elect) is heresy; but he also rejects the stricter Calvinistic view that a sweeping syllogistical declaration of the sufficiency of God has solved the problem of salvation (Eusden 1983). Later, Methodists would employ the arguments of the Remonstrants to assert that God, of His own Free Will, bestowed upon all enough grace to allow them to make a free choice for or against the Gospel.

An intermediate solution eventually emerged in New England in the dispute between the Puritan theologian John Cotton and a certain Dr. Twisse, who had already played a considerable part in the drafting of the (Calvinistic) creed now known as the Westminster Confession. Dr. Twisse attempted to defend the typically Reformed assertion that God elects or rejects His human creatures merely in accordance with the good pleasure of His divine will, i.e. in an arbitrary fashion. Cotton's riposte was as follows: Dr. Twisse was allowing God's sovereign power to take precedence over His Grace and Justice. Puritans who attempted to walk in the ways of the Lord in accordance with their covenant promises (see above) would not be rejected arbitrarily by God because all covenants with the Almighty were unconditionally binding on both sides for as long as they were kept by the saints. God had bound Himself in a contractual way not to behave in a way which is totally capricious. Thus he limited the capricious will of God whilst simultaneously demonstrating how the wicked world could eventually be liberated from the disorder caused by human sin.

Puritans did not yet believe that Christ died for all rather than just for the elect, but they did believe that he had already 'paid the price' (i.e. his atoning death); **ergo**, either God is unjust (a **reductio ad absurdum**) or God must 'set thee free from all iniquity'. Thus, the Covenant of Grace guarantees that those who fulfil its conditions will not miss their just reward: an argument whose logic is quite incompatible with the stricter interpretation of the Eternal Decrees defended by the Calvinists. Hence the fact that Dr. Twisse cannot endorse the doctrine of the Covenant of Grace. And hence his immediate rebuttal: 'since the Fall of Adam all being born in sin, there is no place for such a Covenant' (In Miller 1939:404ff.). Whilst still remaining loyal to the official Reformed doctrine of reprobation and election, Cotton was ultimately driven to soften it by 'smuggling in' what Miller calls 'elements of abstract justice' (ibid. 405).

There were no magical means of obtaining salvation in New England, but there were many binding covenants. Puritans did not necessarily have to panic except, perhaps, during the uncertain period preceding their conversion (Against Weber 1971:104ff). If New England Puritans were afraid, their fears were due more to the **anomie** unleashed by sin and wickedness than to Weber's alleged 'salvation panic'. Indeed, even Ames taught Puritans how to live in this certainty: i.e. how to be assured. Greven's 'moderates' could pave the way towards the more optimistic and tolerant society proclaimed by John Locke and the more 'genteel' contract society presupposed by the advent of mercantile and even capitalistic aspirations. By this time, reason (rather than a totally capricious God) was sovereign and dicipline was no longer a strict Puritan one. But it was revived (especially on the new frontiers) in a milder form by the Methodists. Is also survived in Liberal Protestantism: which stressed the need to live a 'good life' (albeit in a bourgeois form) but legitimated it now with much less theological baggage and coupled it with the need to practice religious tolerance (Parsons 1984).

Superficially, the practice of witchcraft and the prosecution of witches seem to be the most serious 'deviation' from the basic Puritan Pattern. There is some truth in this argument but, again, we must take care not to allow ourselves to be beguiled by popular prejudices. In any case, witchcraft, for the Puritans a Covenant with the Devil, is the opposite of the Covenant of Grace. It is also the ultimate denial of the sovereignty of God. But the prosecution of witches is neither a deviation from the Puritan Pattern nor an 'excess'; for in the quest for the purity of public life, Puritans followed the laws laid down in the Holy Scriptures. In Exodus 22.18 it is clearly stated that: 'Thou shalt not suffer a witch to live' (cf. Dt. 18.10). Those who prosecuted and executed witches were simply not acting ultra vires, for those were the laws which New England had accepted. Hence the hundreds of cases documented by Demos (1982) and the witch-craze of 1692 in Salem Village analysed by Boyer and Nissenbaum (1974) and popularised by Arthur Miller in *The Crucible*. Boyer and Nissenbaum did indeed expose the fault-lines in local society: family feuds and the struggles between a dying agrarian society and the mercantile style of Salem Town, from which the Village was trying to extricate itself. But this is not the whole story, nor a completely satisfactory explanation. The pattern of settlement in the village was a radical deviation from the normal Puritan pattern of migration and settlement in which the first priorities are the building of a meeting-house, the signing of the covenant, the calling of the minister and the establishment of Puritan discipline in the centre of village life. The Salem study amply demonstrates that this was simply not the case here. (The only comparable case of the separation of a settlement from an already-established congregation is the separation of Cambridge Town and Cambridge Village, where the meeting-house was the first priority). In Salem Village, the inhabitants had already run three ministers out of Town before the meeting-house was built and the covenant was late in coming.

Salem Village is neither a deviation from normal Puritan discipline nor an example of the excessive use of power. One should recall that witches had to be exterminated and Puritan discipline had never been established in Salem in the first place. We can only think in terms of a deviation if the basic pattern of discipline had already been established. When all the apparatus of Puritan discipline had been formally established by the signing of the covenant in November 1689, the minister could see that it was merely a formality. The covenanted saints did not fulfill their contractual obligations (attending worship, living in harmony, paying the minister's regular stipend, delivering his firewood etc.). Behind the social and economic conflicts (correctly) exposed by the Salem study, there also lies a more fundamental conflict (unique in the annals of New England) about minsterial authority and the establishment of Puritan discipline. The authors have demonstrated this, but they do not seem to be aware of its significance. Instead, they look for 'revealingly idiosyncratic' glosses in the minister's sermons (ibid. 161ff.). He did compare his betrayal by the villagers with the betrayal of Jesus by the High Priests and Judas: but what should one expect of a conventional Puritan minister who had been taught by Ames and others to scrutinize his life and his immediate situation to see whether the life of Christ were being manifested in his body? The most that can be alleged against such a conventional Puritan minister is that he never learned to love the things of this world 'with weaned affections', a fault which he shared with all of his parishioners. This is demonstrated by the severe financial demands which the minister made on his appointment and his refusal to vacate the parsonage following his dismissal. The first really successful minister in the village was actually an easy-going 'hunting, shooting and fishing type' who fits perfectly into Greven's Genteel category, i.e. not a Puritan (Boyer and Nissenbaum 1974:217 ff.). When Green restored Salem Village to 'normal', it must be conceded that its earlier normality had never been characterized by proper Puritan discipline at all.

Nevertheless, his predecessor had made a desperate last-ditch attempt to introduce such discipline. When he lashed out against the witches, some of whom had been delated by his own adolescent daughter and her friends, he did so by invoking the ultimate Puritan sanction against what Puritans generally took to be the most 'diabolical' manifestation of human wickedness: i.e. not simply the assertion of self-will, but the total surrender of the will to the will of Satan. This presupposed that New England society (and its juridical apparatus) knew what witchcraft was and what kind of evil deeds were believed to be perpetrated by witches. Otherwise, there was a real danger (recalled by some of the 'witches' during their trials and before their executions) that innocent blood was being shed (which also was forbidden by the Holy Scriptures). Neither an uninterpreted bible, nor a vaguely worded

covenant, nor yet the precedents recorded by Demos were then judged
to be sufficient to pronounce upon such issues. Theological 'experts'
like Increase Mather were called in from outside to reexamine both
the concepts and the juridical procedures. He ultimately produced a
coherent biblical and covenant interpretation that recognized witches
but gave no theological charter to witch hunts and trials (ibid. 10ff.).
Hence the growing tendency to give the accused the benefit of the
doubt: especially when the evidence was intangible and unempirical (e.g.
the sighting of 'spectres'). Still more tangible evidence (e.g. the 'witches tit') was sufficient to secure a conviction, e.g. a wart or an over
izedlitoris. The delation of notables such as the wife of the Governor
of Massachusetts also served to put an end to frivolous accusations.
Later, as the Salem study acknowledges, some of the psychological
symptoms of bewitchment would be interpreted as the onset of a conversion experience ('fits').

Future studies of New England witchcraft will have to pay more
attention to theology and popular beliefs, as well as relate them to
'fractures' in local Puritan society (Demos 1982, Boyer & Nissenbaum
1974). Recent studies have too exclusively linked the witch craze with
local politics and economic developments (Greven 1984). One must also
discover why (e.g.) sick cows and 'bewitched' people were regarded as
evidence of witchcraft rather than the punishments of an angry God
who does not tolerate sin and wickedness in any shape or form. Weisman's thesis (Weisman 1984) that - contrary to general witchcraft theory - not the lower but the higher strata in society were dominantly
involved in the witch craze, sheds an interesting light on the whole
issue. Anyway, Salem should not be seen as Puritanism 'gone mad' but,
rather, as an aberration due to insufficient grounding in the Puritan
way of life.

References

Ahlstrom, S.E.
    1972   *A Religious History of the American People*, New Haven: Yale
            University Press.
Aylmer, G.E. (ed.)
    1972   *The Interregnum: The Quest for Settlement 1646-1660*. Lon-
            don: Macmillan.
Boyer, P. & S. Nissenbaum
    1974   *Salem Possessed: The Social Origins of Witchcraft*, Cambri-
            dge Mass.: Harvard University Press.

Cragg, G.R.
1950   *From Puritalism to the Age of Reason: A Study of the Changes in Religious Thought within the Church of England 1660-1700*, Cambridge: Cambridge University Press.
Davidson, J.W.
1977   *The Logic of Millennial Though; Eighteenth-Century New England*, New Haven: Yale University Press.
Daly, R.
1980   'Puritan Poetics', in: Gilmore 1980: 34-45.
Demos, J.P.
1970   *A Little Commonwealth; Family Life in Plymouth Colony*, New York: Oxford University Press.
1982   *Entertaining Satan; Witchcraft and the Culture of Early New England*, New York: Oxford University Press.
Erikson, K.
1966   Wayward Puritans: A Study in the Sociology of Deviance, New York: Wiley.
Eusden, J.D.
1983   *The Marrow of Theology: William Ames (1576-1633)*, Durham, North Carolina: Labyrinth Press.
Ferling, J.
1981   'The New England Soldier: A Study in Changing Perceptions', in: *American Quarterly Review*, 33: 26-45.
Fulbrook, M.
1983   *Piety and Politics; Religion and the Rise of Absolutism in England*, Württemberg and Prussia, Cambridge: Cambridge University Press.
Gaustad, E.S.
1962   *Historical Atlas of Religion in America*, New York: Harper
Gilmore, M.T. (ed.)
1980   *Early American Liturature; A Collection of Critical Essays*, Englewood Cliffs, N.J.: Prentice-Hall.
Graafland, C.
1961   *De zekerheid van het geloof; Een onderzoek naar de geloofs-beschouwing van enige vertegenwoordigers van reformatie; een nader onderzoek*, Wageningen: Veenman.
Greven, P.
1977   *The Protestant Temperament: Patterns of Child-Rearing, Religious Experience, and the Self in Early America*, New York: Knopf.
1984   Review of Demos (1980), *History and Theory*, 23:236-251.

De Groot, A.
  1978   'Amesius, Guilielmus (William Ames)', in: *Biografisch Lexicon voor de geschiedenis van het Nederlandse Protestantisme*, part I, Kampen: Kok.
Hall, D.D.
  1970   'Understanding the Puritans', in: (ed.) Bass, H.J. *The State of American History*, Chicago: University of Chicago Press.
Hill, C.
  1975   *The World turned Upside Down: Radical Ideas During the English Revolution*. Harmondsworth: Penguin.
Hindson, E.
  1976   *Introduction to Puritan Theology; A Reader*, Grand Rapids:Baker.
Holifield, E.B.
  1974   *The Covenant Sealed; The Development of Puritan Sacramental Theology in Old and New England,1570-1720*, New Haven: Yale University Press.
Hoopes, J.
  1982   'Art as History: Perry Miller's New England Mind', in: *American Quarterly Review*, 34: 3-25.
Lewy, A.
  1974   *Religion and Revolution*. Oxford University Press.
Tai Lui
  1973   *Discord in Zion; The Puritan Divines and the Puritan Revolution 1640-1660*, The Hague: Nijhoff.
May, H.F.
  1979   'Philip Greven and the History of Temperament', in: *American Quarterly Review*, 31: 107-115.
Miller, P.
  1939   *The New England Mind; The Seventeenth Century*, New York: Macmillan.
  1953   *The New England Mind: From Colony to Province*, Cambridge Mass.: Harvard University Press.
  1976   *The American Puritans; Their Prose and Poetry*, New York: Doubleday.
  1980   'A Colonial Dialect', in: Gilmore 1980: 22-33.
Murrin, J.M.
  1972   'Review Essay' in: *History and Theory*, 11: 226-275.
Noll, M.A. (et al)
  1983   *Christianity in America: A Handbook*, Lion Book, UK. edition, Iring: Lion Publishing; USA. edition, Grand Rapids: Eerdmans.

Parsons, G.
    1984   'Pietism and Liberal Protestantism: Some Unexpected Continuities', in: *Religion*, 14: 223-243.
Pearl, V.
    1972   London's Counter Revolution. in: Aylmer 1972: ch.1.
Pettit, N.
    1966   *The Heart Prepared: Grace and Conversion in Puritan Spiritual Life*, New Haven: Yale University Press.
Russell, C. (ed.)
    1973   *The Origins of English Civil War*. London: Macmillan.
Schneider, H.W.
    1946   *A History of American Philosophy*, New York: Columbia University Press.
Sobczak, M.
    1982   'Hoopes's Symposium on Perry Miller', in: *American Quarterly Review*, 34: 43-48.
Sperry, W.L.
    1945   *Religion in America*, Cambridge: Cambridge University Press.
Turner, H.W.
    1979   *From Temple to Meeting House; The Phenomenology and Theology of Places of Worship*, The Hague: Mouton.
Turner, V.W.
    1969   *The Ritual Process: Structure and Anti-Structure*, London: Routledge & Kegan Paul.
Tyacke, N.
    1974   Puritanism, Arminionism and Counter-Revolution, in: Russell: ch.4.
Walker, W.
    1960   *The Creeds and Platforms of Congregationalism*, Boston: Pilgrim Press.
Walsh, J.P.
    1980   'Holy Time and Sacred Space in Puritan New England', in: *American Quarterly Review*, 32: 79-95.
Weber, M.
    1971/3   *The Protestant Ethic and the Spirit of Capitalism*, London: Unwin.
Weisman, R.
    1984   *Witchcraft, Magic and Religion in Seventeenth Century*. Massachusetts: University of Massachusetts Press.
Winslow, O.E.
    1972   *Meeting House Hill 1630-1783*. New York: Norton & Co. 2nd.

Puritanism and the Second Reformation in the Netherlands
Anne van der Meiden

Puritanism and the Second Reformation in the Netherlands
Anne van der Meiden

Preliminary observations

Firstly a personal remark as the reader has to right to know who is telling this 'story'. I do feel a duty to explain to my readers my former - and present, to a certain extent - involvement in this very interesting phenomenon in Dutch religious life.

I grew up in a Church and a family where the heritages of Puritanism were fostered in a special, 'accommodated' way. The church was one of the many denominations which emanated in the 19th Century from the Netherlands Reformed Church, the 'official' Church of the Reformation of the 16th Century. In the 19th Century two important Separations, the Separation ('Afscheiding') of 1834 and the so-called 'Doleantie' (1886) alienated many people from the Church; many of those were both historically and spiritually deeply rooted in Puritanism or - as the Dutch themselves prefer to put it - in the piety of the Second Reformation, a term that is explained later in this article.

The family had its origins on the father's side in the pietistic wing of the Netherlands Reformed Church (many pietists did not leave the Church!) and on my mother's side in the piety of the 'Separation' and the 'Doleantie'. Moreover, from her side I inherited a mild chiliasm and a strong congregationalism, which will be dwelled on later. After 20 years I left this Church and made a move in the direction of liberal theology. I had the opportunity to serve a very little congregation (in the weekends) as pastor in a part of the Country where the so-called 'black-stocking-churches' (extremely orthodox and very strict) dominated religious life. It has been a remarkable experience to serve a liberal island in a pietistic ocean: and I realize that this inspired me to reflect on the past more profound than I did before, in my book *De Zwarte Kousen-Kerken* (the Black-Stocking-Churches) (1981).

So the reader is warned (as I am myself), that I am not a purely objective observer, viewing this phenomenon from a distance. I have the words, thoughts, feelings and spiritual experiences of this Reformation under my skin; in my case distance only means a judgement and an evaluation: to discern better what was real and authentic. Thus, for me any objectivism is only legal on the basis of subjectivism. But that would be another chapter.

Some concepts

First, the concepts to be used in this article need to be clarified. **Puritanism** was originally used for the movement in the Churches of the Reformation which aimed at the purification of the Church (the eradication of all Roman heresies); in later developments of the Reformation the term was used for all the activities of converted people to purify their lives from worldly concerns. Puritanism became an important aspect of the **sanctification** of life, including an aversion to sin, segregation and separation. Puritanism became the overall-term for 'the way of life of converted people, including their restless endeavours to create an immaculate church on earth' (Reedijk 1938:1).

Piety indicates the inner processes of implementation of belief and religious experience. In Dutch theoretical jargon, we distinguish between 'voorwerpelijkheid' and 'onderwerpelijkheid', which mean more or less 'objectivism' and 'subjectivism'. In the 1930's many discussions on this subject where held in the Synod of the Christian Reformed (Gereformeerde) Church in the Netherlands: Is it enough to offer the gift of Salvation in the blood of Jesus Christ in objective terms, or do preachers have the duty to explain to the congregation how this salvation becomes a reality in the hearts of human beings?   Pietists are 'subject to' (onderwerpelijk), which could lead to the characteristic expression I heard many times: 'It might be true that Jesus was born in Bethlehem but even if he was born there a thousand times, but never in my heart, I am lost'.

The term **fundamentalism** characterizes, among other things the way Christians think about the reliability of the Scriptures and the way life must be founded on the guidelines laid down for us in the Bible: i.e. for personal, spiritual and social life (see Post, this volume). These three terms nearly always come loose together in the doctrine and practice of the so-called 'black-stocking-churches'. Where one of them is missing, we find denominations and sects which - in the eyes of the

Second Reformation - are not fully fledged inheritors of the Reformation.

The roots

Although the term Puritanism can be used as an umbrella-term for many different tendencies and movements in Dutch religious life, we must realize that none of these movements ever used the term officially in their names, and that it was never even used as a 'nick-name'. Dutch church leaders and leading ministers in the second half of the 17th Century were influenced by the Scottish and English puritan movement in a specific way. The original use of the term Puritanism to denote a reform-movement in the Church of England between the two Acts of Uniformity (1559 and 1662), never found any response in the Dutch Church; simply because the Dutch Reformation of the 16th Century had been far more radically 'Geneva-oriented' from the beginning than was the case in many other European countries (see Broeyer, this volume). Puritanism was first and foremost an ecclesiastical ideal (Wood 1930). Its main goal was the abandoning of all 'popish' remnants. The ideal was a church with a pure structure, according to the Scriptures, with people who dedicated themselves to a pure life (the eternal fight against sins) and with a mission toward the State, to follow her vocation to be a pure State, dedicated to the service of the Lord and his commandments. Puritanism always had at least three main options: church-life, personal life and society (see Staples, this volume).

It must be clear that the meaning of the term Puritanism evolved in 17th Century England in the direction of 'a greater sobriety of life', with one-sidedness in the explanation of the commandments, a pious, devout and godly life (Bunyan 1680). The ideal of a pure Church lost its importance in Great Britain, mainly because many of the Puritans found a new religious home in the smaller non-conformist denominations (Baptist, Methodists). Consequently, the original aim, i.e. the reformation of social life and political reform, melted away and made way for an ego-centered religious life, where personal conversion, the experience of God's work in man's soul as well as a strict and 'narrow' life were the central themes. It was mainly this move from ecclesiastical ideal to individualistic experience that made Puritanism so attractive to Dutch theology (cf. Breen 1980).

The Second Reformation (Nadere Reformatie)

The term 'Second Reformation' usually refers to a typically Dutch movement in the official Netherlands Reformed Church, shortly after the official foundation of the Church (the Synod of Dordrecht, 1618-1619). Strongly influenced by Scottish and English reformers like Perkins and Hayward, and by the mystical writers of the Middle Ages (Bernard, Ruusbroeck, Fauler and Thomas à Kempis) young ministers and theology-professors in the first half of the 17th Century (The Dutch Golden Age) created a new movement. To them, the reformation of the Church was not complete when new church-laws, confessions and hymnbooks were available. Reformation could only be a real reformation with a sanctification of heart and society. Theology is not a mere rationalistic science, but - as Voetius (one of the fathers of the Second Reformation) expressed it in his inaugurational lecture in Utrecht, 1634 (*De pietate, cum scientia coniganda*) - only a conversion, a godly life and a continuous *exercitia pietatis* can create a fruitful theology. And secondly, the Church should be an instrument to sanctify society and public life. This is the main framework of the movement. The theological implementations will be discussed later on.

The Second Reformation started, according to Fieret (1981), with William Teellinck, a minister in Middelburg (1600), to find her last witness in Witsius (1636-1708). This is only true, if - like many church historians do - one restricts the movement to the official church. However, one should not neglect the fact that the leading principles of the Second Reformation were taken over by smaller groups, non-conformist churches, 'conventicles', congregationalists and other dissidents.

Admirers of the Second Reformation movement tend to forget that this movement caused separatism: and any separatism always generates more separatism. As long as little groups claim the truth and nothing but the truth they must, consequently, banish all members who deviate from the approved paths. Algra (1966) gave his book on the separatistic movements in the 19th Century in the Netherlands a remarkable title: *The miracle of the 19th Century*. However reading the sad story of the endless troubles, theological conflicts, un-christian quarrels and human failures, the word miracle does not appear very apt; unless it is considered a miracle that the church still exists!

Theological and social aspects

It is impossible within the framework of this article, to describe Puritan theology as it developed in the Second Reformation. The main reason is that in the later phase of the Second Reformation the pluralistic reality of church life generated a variety of theological strains. Different groups emphasized different theological aspects. The only thing which can be done now is to identify certain 'generalizations' in theological thinking. Wood (1930) finds the roots of Puritan theology in the five tenets of Calvinism:
- election and reprobation;
- the limited scope of the atonement;
- total human depravity;
- irresistible grace;
- final perseverance.

Puritans emphasized the sovereignty and the justice of God and, thus, the sinfulness and all-pervading character of sin. The mortification of sin is one of the central duties of the Christian life. This is one way to describe the theological tenets of Puritanism. Let me try to rephrase this. In its later development, Puritanism closely connected with pietism, influenced by the German piety of the 18th Century. Especially in the smaller churches, the theology of Puritanism emphasized the following items:

1) Election as the irreversible decision of God as to who will and who will not be accepted.
2) Strong separation between converted and non-converted people, which must be made clear in the sermon (separating preaching).
3) Religious experience, strictly personal, as a fruit of conversion. The word "bevinding" (experience) is the most common term to indicate this personal experience (Brienen 1978).
4) Passivity as confession of the total impotence of human beings to participate in the process of their salvation.
5) Quietus and acquiesence under the government of God and his absolute providence.
6) Submission under the inspiration of the Holy Spirit and recognition of the fact that faith is a **datum**, something which is given; not an act of the human will.
7) The bible as the eternal word of God, mechanically dictated and untouchable by human knowledge.

People who live in this mixture of old Puritanism, piety and more or less romantic religious experiences, developed their own life-style. To them, theology is very practical. This means that it preaches claims for personal life and political life. It must be said that the mystical tendencies of the second reformation survived in smaller groups through the 18th and 19th centuries right-up to present day. Their leaders exhausted themselves in micro-psychological research of human souls and committed to paper all their daily religious experiences. They are called 'the old fathers'.

In the Netherlands we still have about 300,000 people 'who never bowed the knee to Baal', who refuse to watch Television, as one of Satan's most successful instruments for destroying the world, who do not take out insurances (they prefer to bear their own risks). They are very strict in the sanctification of life (a narrow life gives a broad entrance!), observe Sunday as a holy day, protect their children against a profane world, working at their own salvation with fear, tears and doubts. These people are tenderly shocked by a deep-going mystical sermon; avoiding this world's enjoyments they hope to find a place in heaven. They are still there! Just in a forgotten corner of life? Some of them yes, but others do not hide themselves **cum libello in angello**, but present their thoughts and principles on different levels in society. These groups may be almost unique in the world, though they are comparable to some groups in the immigrant-churches in the United States like the right-wing of the Amish people.

They preach their lifestyle in their own primary schools, highschools, schools for social work, schools for journalism and, more recently, their own university. They have their representatives in Parliament, they have their own newspaper and several magazines. This is the active 'image' of Puritanism and piety in our days (see Post, this volume). In my book on these groups (1981), I mentioned some examples of sermons gathered over many years. There might be no other place in the world where sermons like these are preached. The language the preachers use (converted, not learned ministers!) is almost incomprehensible for outsiders, as their concepts and phrases are deeply rooted in ancient times (see V.d. Ketterij 1972). They enriched the Dutch language and still use words that are not used in 'normal' conversations. On the other hand: words that are normally used have a different meaning in such preaching. For example: When you meet a friend, you say: 'How are you?' In the language of what is sometimes called the 'heavies' this means: 'What was your last religious experience, what station did you pass on the way recently?' The 'way' then is the totality of religious experience, the believer's process of communication with God. God has a way for his elected people. Everybody has his or her own way, passes the stations of calling, election, justification, conversion, etc., along private patterns. God never makes ready-to-wear clothing.

Converted people love to speak in little select groups (conventicles) about their experiences.

The conventicles

The term **conventicle**, which is characteristic in the language of the Puritan movement in the Netherlands, is hard to translate into English. It is not a company or a party, nor an assembly, but a small congregation without any structure or organization. The Dutch word company ("gezelschap") for conventicle expresses the deeper meaning of the word: a group of people that come together during the week, mostly in the house of one of them, to speak about the spiritual experiences of the previous week. In the early days of the reformation, the official services in the church did not apparently satisfy the religious needs of converted people. Not even the sermons of the ministers of the Second Reformation in the 17th Century could replace the close and sometimes mystic communication of converted people in small groups. 'Companies' (gezelschappen) are still held in the Netherlands, but one must be an insider to be invited to such a meeting. The birth of the phenomenon appears to be legal. In the first decennia after the official Reformation, also in the years of reconstruction and restoration of the church, new means and methods had to be introduced to teach people the basic concepts of the new doctrine, to teach them to speak freely and spontaneously about their own religious experiences. To achieve this aim, the Synod of Dordrecht legalized the conventicles as useful instruments.

Later, during the Decline of the Second Reformation, in the period of overruling piety, the 'companies' (gezelschappen) sometimes degenerated into 'sultry' and mystic groups with Puritan excesses: a totally pure life, a sharp control of the lives of the participants, extreme high standards for 'holiness' and even dangerous exclusivism. At least in two cases this extreme type of 'company' lead to religious murders (Schotman 1941 and Tolsma 1945). But these are extreme cases. Most of the time these 'companies' were (and still are) peaceful and friendly meetings of like-minded people who want to meet each other and talk about everything the Lord did unto their souls. In 1972, Wiegeraad proposed to stimulate the 'companies' in Church-life, not in order to create separate islands of little brothers and little sisters (the 'heavies' in the Netherlands prefer like to speak in diminutives: little blessing, little signal of mercy, little touch of the Spirit and the like a tendency for which the Dutch language is well suited) but to train a 'cadre' of laity (Wiegeraad 1972).

In conventicles we hear people speaking about the present state of their religious life. The notion of 'state' is important, not to be equated with 'status quo'. In the theological jargon 'state' is discerned from 'stand', separating what you **are** (converted) from what you **feel** or are at this given moment. Let me give a banal example: being an American citizen (your state) you can live for many years in a foreign country (your stand). The state is fixed, the stand fluctuates. The best a human being ever can reach in this life is the conviction that one is a Child of God. This religious possession is very valuable, untouchable and finally decisive. The rest, outside, is the world, the flesh, the temporary shelter we live in. But one should take life on earth seriously. In a pure Calvinistic sense, the believer is bound to work hard, to live at peace with God, family and neighbours. Home discipline should be strict and the rod should not be spared, as Bunyan said. Working hard and working in an honest way are closely connected. It is well known in Holland that workers from this extraction are most reliable; they are honest, punctual and demonstrate a steady application to work. They have been educated to control themselves and are not seldom gifted with the spirit of enterprise.

Here, we touch on the connection with the American Puritanism (New England), where, in the eyes of the real Dutch Puritans, the Calvinistic basics were accepted in a rationalistic way, but never 'internalized' in a pious life. Be that as it may, it is clear that in Puritan life, where it coincided with early capitalism, the roots of a disastrous double-morality were laid. Without doubt, Puritanism influenced ethics and has found a willing partner in liberalism. But this again is the root of a morality, where the impossibility of the application of the rules, given by God in his commandments, was rationalized into an accepted double-morality.

Daily life: complex and paradoxical

Trying to describe the modern daily life of this group, we must be very careful because the temptation is very real to draw a caricature, by either overstressing or underestimating certain aspects. As for Puritan elements: they try hard to live a holy life, to act always according to the Scriptures and their consciences. They avoid everything that could mislead them: e.g. worldly pleasures in movies, television, books and theatre. The touchstone is simple: where the Lord not is served explicitly, it would be better to avoid such places! Except, that is, for the place where one earns one's daily bread. People try to educate their children in the same way, but are confronted with the fact that children do not recognize any longer the external attributes of Puritan life: Janse clearly described in his recent research the difference between younger and older people in the churches with a strong tradition in the second Reformation (Janse 1985). Although the devilish world penetrates lifes and hearts, they try to protect themselves and their children courageously against undermining forces. There is not an absolute and definitive list of things one should or should not do. Some of these people avoid the use of bicycles or cars on Sundays. Others no longer have objections. Some of the women do not enter Church without a hat. Some do. There is not much tolerance among them on these questions and we still read in the newspapers from time to time remarkable stories about conflicts in certain church denominations, when a member of a congregation (or even a minster!) is caught watching television in secret on the attic of his house. Social control in some congregations is very strong. During my period in a region with many of the small congregations, I noticed that sometimes the male members of the congregation had many important meetings in other villages during the World Football Championship: they watched television in other places.

Here, I touch again that important aspect: the double-morality. It is amazing to see that the morality in these groups is very strict, on one hand, even in minute details; however, in matters of immediate profit in business, morality is much less strong. Commenting on a slightly irregular business transaction, an elder declared: 'That is not Gospel, that is business'. The ten commandments are not 'applied' in the same measure and weight: sexual intercourse before marriage is more severely punished than lies on the marketplace. These people fight for the rights of the unborn child, but you never find any explicit reference as to the rights of living children. They greatly value the soul of one single human being, but none of them is a pacifist. Pacifism as a conviction is not allowed in these groups. It is possible to sing at the same time the hymns on God's beautiful Creation and one day later to overspray your land with chemicals to promote the results. Here we see one of the weakest aspects of this puritanism; i.e. the simple fact that it is not applicable in all situations, for all people in all social and political circumstances. Preached as an untouchable truth and an uncontrovertible reality, in daily life it fails to be realized in all areas of human life. People in these groups suffer from it, but they do not feel this as the shortcomings of their doctrine, rather as their own incapacity to obey God's commandments.

We must not forget that the basic criterion in these groups is whether one is converted or not. Leadership in these circles is only accepted from converted people. Even in families it occurs that although fathers are dominant (which is a creation-given construction) mothers rule the household because they are converted, while the fathers are not (yet) convinced that they belong to the People of God. There is no difference between men and women as far as religious affairs are concerned. In the conventicles, women are not simply passive listeners, they participate in the discussions in exactly the same way as men. The term 'Mothers in Israel' expresses the deep respect for converted women and in the literature on conversions (reports on the way God had chosen to bring Mrs. A. or Mr. B. to their Salvation), women participate on a par with men. Of course, women cannot lead congregations as ministers or elders. That is the prerogative of the men, who are regarded as the apex of the crown of God's Creation.

People in these congregations really do look after each other in times of sickness, disasters, death and misfortune. Of course, no thing in life occurs without the will and the providential hand of the Heavenly Father, but we as human beings are called to help our neighbours, especially within the religious community. This help never gets much publicity, it finds its way along secret paths and many people who receive help do not know where it comes from. Still, people in these congregations never try to replicate the situation of the first Christian community, described in Acts 2. There is no sign of repristinization: they read with respect and admiration the stories of the first congregation and then start to confess that the Church was driven so far from this ideal situation by the sins and disobedience of God's People. It is as simple as that.

Modern implications of the Second Reformation

Although Dutch Puritanism and piety was and will be petrified in the solid rocks of Calvinistic dogmas, there are many social and spiritual threats to resist. In spite of all endeavours to keep the church and family 'pure' and free form the infection of dangerous 'diseases', the outside-world will intrude irresistibly and undermine the unshakable fundaments. I will mention seven specific problems:
- Some types of Puritanism overextend themselves in activity and zealous organizational exhibitionism. The will of God must be demonstrated in all areas of social and political life! Sometimes young people feel they are entangled in a network of unavoidable duties and obligations. It is hard to endure confrontation with the same issues all the time, the same boundaries and the same claims everywhere. In my own experience, an escape form this small world can generate a feeling of liberation and (even) redemption.

- What hurts - especially young - people in this group most is the
political conservatism their representatives demonstrate in Parliament. These men are considered the best spokesmen of the extreme
right, which means that they nearly always vote against proposal,
to regulate social and moral renewals in society. They do not hesitate to confront the other members of Parliament with, what they
call, the Word of God. Recently, among young intellectuals in their
own group a serious opposition arose against this uncontrolled abuse
of multi-interpretable bible-texts. Yet this is but one field where
the dismantling of unquestioned beliefs and strictly obeyed principles
can be noticed.
- The early Puritan merchants, who made fortunes in trade, were
sober in their expenses for their own needs. They were deeply convinced that more money meant extra investments and extra investments meant more business, more wealth to share with other people.
A stone tablet at the facade of one of the rich merchant's mansions
in Amsterdam reads as follows:

> 'piper peperit pecuniam
> pecunia peperit pompam
> pompa peperit paupertatem
> paupertas peperit pietatem'

Pepper made money, money caused luxury, luxury caused poverty,
poverty caused piety. But in the 18th and 19th centuries the merchants, although very strict in doctrine and discipline, demonstrated
their wealth in a brutal way. Ever since, the old ideal of sober and
modest life has only had few adherents!
- Family-life, the cornerstone of society, is still very important in
these groups. Having children means an 'order', a responsibility and
a blessing. My mother used to say that 'children are a blessing, but
one must learn to see that in belief'. The old family-life with strict
discipline and total obedience is loosing its grip on such society.
There are many reasons for this. The most important is that young
people have a much better education than their parents. They have
contacts with different beliefs and ideas and consider alternatives,
which their parents have never even dreamt of. Modern transport
enables them to break out of their isolated position and to cross
the boundaries of their areas. Social control will be less effective
in the future, which means that the younger generations learn to
make their own decisions, even if these oppose the moral codes and
rules of conduct of their protected environment.
- The theological concepts of what might be called neo-Puritanism,
shows a trend towards a rationalistic objectification of subjective

experiences. In his excellent book on the linguistic patterns in pietistic literature in this group, V.d. Ketterij (1972) covered this aspect, just by describing how objective, experienced truths are coagulated in petrified terms. This means that e.g. the mere use of the right terms and words in sermons and pastoral counseling is enough. The original terms, charged with tension and emotions, became hatracks to hang phrases on. They cannot be missed, but they are just frameworks, empty, used as 'shibboleths', hallmarks for authenticity; well trained believers are unshakable assayers and judges. Thus, religious experience risks to loose its spontaneity, and an important aspect of the old Puritanism will disappear.

- One of the most threatening processes, closely related to the developments above mentioned, is the 'continuous reformation' resulting in continious separations and schisms. It is sad to behold how small churches are split up into two or three groups and how these separations split up families and even marriages. The original concept of continuous reformation, (ecclesia reformata semper reformanda) pleaded for a mentality in the church that could protect against the 'petrification' and dangerous peace. The term should not be interpreted as a divine command to leave the old church, the 'horrifying terror of Egypt', in order to march into the promised land. It is almost blasphemous to claim that God Himself brought His own people out of slavery into freedom, when little groups leave other little groups to create new mini-congregations. Still, it is interpreted that way and people do claim divine marching orders. These continuously disintegrating forces will seriously endanger the power of the neo-Puritanism of the neo-Puritanism for many years to come.

- Deterioration of the old morals of Dutch Puritan piety will not only come from the outside, but also from a close relative, i.c. neo-piety. A good example is the rise of the Dutch Evangelical Broadcasting Corporation, which tries to unite groups in the orthodox wings of the different churches in order to create a strong instrument to preach the gospel in a modern way, without damaging the old and beloved truths. This movement was born when the older Christian Broadcasting Company (NCRV) became too secularized and critical, too involved in social and political comment. This new type of Christian broadcasting reshapes the old securities into new forms. The central doctrine is that a man's soul is the most important object of evangelical activity and, consequently should be saved and shielded from the needs and sorrows of this world, governed as it is by Satan himself, a breeding-place for sin and destruction. With music (gospel-rock as well as the old hymns), sermons, biblestudies and talkshows, the gospel is distributed in a world that is not changeable but just passing by, ready for the final judgement. Though one needs to fight the evil structures, the political and social disasters, the world cannot be saved; thus, fighting outside evil should always be secondary to striving for one's own life in heaven (see Post, this volume). Looking at the activities of this neo-Puritanism, the old individualistic pietistic-Puritan will shake his head over so much human pride. This Gospel is not his. It is too smooth, too fast, too loud, too easy, too superficial. It is talking 'about' not 'out of'. Those believers dare to sing words they can never live up to. How about that old song: 'The Lord is my shepherd'? Who dares to sing that? Only a few will ever learn to sing it. Is it not a dangerous imagination to convert deep and heavenly things to one's own use, to appropriate things that respectfully should be left alone? No wonder that many of the 'heavies' do not join the Evangelical Broadcasting Cooperation because they feel and fear the abuse of holy values.

Conclusion

Puritanism in the form of pietism characterizes the Second Reformation in the Netherlands. Although influenced by parallel English and Scottish movements, it has found its own, and in many aspects unique, expression in Dutch church life. Followers of this movement form a rather stable group in Dutch society. They do not hide themselves, but speak and act in public and are well organized. In fact, their organizational activities were revitalized during the last decades. Although many threats hang over the existence of this group (in fact they form a conglomerate of many different groups) there is no reason to assume that the Second Reformation will die out in our life-time. On the contrary: since modern times deprive people of their securities and perspectives, these groups will retain their attractiveness for many years to come. They offer a way to redemption, forgiveness of sins, security for the life hereafter, an inspired community, as well as the firm belief and high hope that they obey a living God by avoiding the world and its temptations. But the world they reject deprives them of their children. This is the paradox of Puritanism in the Netherlands, and this is where the end will begin.

References

Algra, H.
1966   *Het wonder van de 19e eeuw, Van vrije kerken en kleine luyden*, Franeker: T. Wever.
Breen, T.H., N. York, U.P. Oxford.
1980   *Puritans and Adventurers: change and persistence in early America*, U.P. Oxford.
Brienen, T.
1974   *De prediking der Nadere Reformatie. Een onderzoek naar het gebruik van de klassificatiemethode binnen de prediking van de Nadere Reformatie*, Amsterdam: Bolland.
1978   *Bevinding, Aard en functie van de geloofsbeleving*, Kampen: Kok.
Bunyan, J.
(1680)   *Life and death of Mr. Badman.*
Fieret, W.
1981   *Puritanisme en Nadere Reformatie*, unpublished doctoral essay, Institute of History, University of Utrecht.
Haitjema, Th. L.
1964   *De nieuwere geschiedenis van Neerlands Kerk der Hervorming*, Den Haag, Boekencentrum.
Janse, C.S.L.
1985   *Bewaar het pand. De spanning tussen assimilatie en persistentie bij de emancipatie van de bevindelijke Gereformeerden*, Houten: Den Hertog.
Ketterij, C. v.d.
1972   *De weg in woorden. Een systematische beschrijving van piëtisch woordgebruik na 1900*, Assen: Van Gorcum.
Linde, S. van der
1973   Mystiek en Bevinding, in: *Mystiek in de Westerse Cultuur*, Kampen: Kok.
Meiden, A. van der
1981   *Welzalig is het volk: een bijgewerkt portret van de zwarte kousen-kerken*, Baarn, Ten Have. First Ed.: 'The Black Stocking Churches, 1966, Baarn: Ambo.
Reedijk, Is. J.
1938   *De Zwijndrechtse Nieuwlichters*, Zwijndrecht, Wed. Plancken
Schotman, W.
1941   *De blinde vaart*, (A report on the religious murder on a trawler from Katwijk, 1914), Naarden, private publisher.

Tolsma, F.J.
  1945   *Inductie: religieuze groepsvorming en godsdienst waanzin.* (An analysis of the religious murder in a farmers' family in Meerkerk, 1944), Amsterdam.
Wiegeraad, B.
  1972   Article in *Reformatorisch Dagblad*, 8 januari.
Wood, H.G.
  1930   Puritanism, in: *Encyclopedia of Religions and Ethics*, Vol. 10, Edinburg, T.A.S.T. Clark, p.p. 507-515.

Purifying Holland: the Dutch Evangelicals
Piet Post

Purifying Holland: the quest for purity among the
Dutch Evangelicals
Piet Post

Introduction

'Holland no longer is a Christian country'; this is regularly heard in
Dutch evangelical circles. For them this is a clarion call to purify
Holland, reconverting it into the Christian nation it once was. So this
analysis of a Dutch puritan movement will focus on the purification
of society, in contrast to the purification of self, as described by van
der Meiden for the more pietist puritans of the Second Reformation
(van der Meiden, this volume).

The Dutch evangelicals form by no means a homogeneous group, but
are a puriform collective of many small denominations and churches
of orthodox protestant extraction. Though on many issues they fight
each other, they still unite against a common 'enemy' (often called 'the
world' or 'secularization'), bound together by a common ideology: i.e.
fundamentalism. In this article, I shall explore the way this ideology
and its ramifications serve as an instrument for purification, and what
the consequences of this quest for purity are for the people concerned.
The rallying point of the evangelicals is the 'Evangelische Omroep' (E-
vangelical Broadcasting Corporation, henceforth called EO), and our
discussion will focus on that institution: its theology, organizational
structure, connections with other institutions and its effect on Dutch
society in general and the Dutch evangelicals in particular.

A voice for purity: the Evangelical Broadcasting Corporation (Evangelische Omroep).

Holland since the beginning of the 20th century has been a 'pillarized' society, a unique socio-religious structure that has triggered off considerable research and evoked a lot of commentaries (Coleman 1978). 'Pillarization' is the development of parallel institutions for different sectors of the population. The main criterion for this peculiar division has been religious and/or ideological denomination. So, from the early decades of this century, the Dutch Catholics, the Gereformeerden (the Reformed Church in the Netherlands) together with the Hervormden (Reformed) as well as several other groups have had their own primary and secondary schools, their own university, their own health services and hospitals. Of these, the separate schooling historically and socially has been the most important. Before World War II, the broadcasting corporations for a large part followed the same model: a catholic and a protestant corporation emerged, as well as some based on non-religious ideologies. Among these pillars, Protestant Netherland has been well represented. Still, for the orthodox Protestants, which we regard here as Evangelicals, this was not enough. In their view the Protestant Corporation (NCRV) was not strict enough; secularization was encroaching upon the system.

The same media, however, were instrumental in the 'de-pillarization' of Dutch society that set in after the sixties. Some new, general public oriented broadcasting corporations were established, among which the TROS was important. Their programmes lacked any religious or ideological context and quickly gained a large following. The confessional corporations fought this tide by moving towards a less confessional profile, one of the less orthodox ones even becoming the haven of the left-wing intelligentsia. The Evangelicals in Holland were alarmed and shocked, in sofar anyway as they were allowed to watch TV. This dilution of the Reformed identity of the NCRV (the Protestant corporation) was for them a serious problem, and even amounted to a beginning secularization among their own brethren. Thus, in 1965 evangelicals took the initiative to start a new corporation with a 'positive christian' character. At first they tried, as a pressure group, to move the NCRV into a more orthodox course, but this soon failed. The de-pillarization proces had become a part of the Dutch social landscape. On 21 april 1967, the Evangelische Omroep (Evangelical Broadcasting Corporation) was organized in the juridical form of a 'Stichting' (Foundation). Two protestant ministers of the Reformed Church and the Moravian Brethren (Evangelische Broedergemeente) were central in this endeavour. Whereas most broadcasting corporations are associations, this juridical form of

a 'Stichting' is remarkable, and might aim at a centralization of power
(De Boer & Sondorp 1981:36). Two years later the EO was designated
a broadcasting authority (for an overview of the Dutch broadcasting
regulations, see appendix). Though most other corporations did not expect a bright future for the newcomer (Munters 1970), the number of
members and subscribers quickly grew from 15.000 (1969) to 100.000
in 1972 (Munters 1972:1). This is sufficient for a change from aspirant-
status to C-status. So the EO became a real presence on the Dutch
television screens. Ten years later the EO reached the 300.000 mark
and so received B-status, thereby growing larger than one of the original protestant corporations.

Given its history the EO has a distinct vocation in Dutch society:
'The EO wants to be a firehouse in a disturbing world, for our country
will wither away when the knowledge of God vanishes' (1), EO general
manager Dorenbos declared in a recent interview. So the EO sets its
goals much wider than its colleagues: the EO aims at saving Holland.
Its vocation is primarily an ethical and fundamentalist one:

'The EO beckons society to return to the Bible in order to follow
what the Lord God spoke to us in it. So I appeal to all Christians to
close their ranks. As Christians we should teach obedience to the standards of the Bible. Who else will do so?'(2)

This exclusivity is characteristic. The phrase 'we christians' embraces
but a tiny fraction of those Dutch calling themselves christians, and
should be read as 'we, the real or the pure Christians'. The voice is
that of a prophet calling society to repentance, appalled by the general
deterioration of moral standards. It is, in short, the voice of a puritan
minority.

In evangelical circles, it is hardly possible to distinguish between
theology and other activities; and that is exactly their intention. The
first and most prominent issue in both the founding of the EO and its
preaching is the purification of society by cleansing it of a great number of sins: a characteristic which it shares with its American counterparts. Reading fundamentalist writings, one is often confronted with
'sin catalogues' in which the ethical deterioration of modern society
is characterized. The EO too works with such lists, as the following
quote from their directory shows. In fact, this list of evils is their definition of the world surrounding them, the disturbing world they have
to live in:

'Abortion goes together with free marriage, streaking, the derailment
of youth and of their parents, massage-institutes, euthanasia, individualism, egoism, sex, materialism, fornication, the 'pill', unemployment,

decadence, drugs, action groups, lèse majesté, anarchism, environmental pollution, hunger, drought etc.'(3).

A strange list for an outsider who fails to see the connection between the various evils. But for an evangelical all items on the list stem from one and the same tree. Its name is secularization. The EO perceives itself as God's chosen instrument to stem the tide of secularization, both for its members and for the whole of the Netherlands. This, they feel, is a prophetic calling, to be a Voice for Purity:

'It (the EO) has a vocation to be a witness in the midst of our people....There is a link between national sins and the national plagues. Exposing those sins very precisely is part of the prophetic testimony. God himself calls an errant people back to 'the Law and the Testimony'(4).

The legitimation is divine, in evangelical belief. This broadcasting corporation is founded on a prophetic calling from God. This holds for the general attitude of the EO members and leaders; it can best be compared with the famous picture by Chagall of Mozes descending from Mt Sinai with the two tables of the law under his arm. Likewise, the EO descends from the TV screen in the rooms of the Dutch: with the law of God in its hands.

Success, however, is not very evident. Not only does the EO represent a minute fraction of the Dutch (ca. 3%), programmes, sermons and its exhortations are heard by a small minority top. Non-evangelicals hardly ever watch the EO, several viewing surveys demonstrate. Furthermore, Dutch society has not changed noticeably. The few non-evangelicals who hear the broadcast testimonies may sympathize with the feelings, but inevitably define the way of expression and the charted course as a christian fossil. Still, the call to purification cannot be compromised as it is God's work. The apparent lack of success does not deter the evangelicals. For them, there is no way around God's word. They see their human efforts for purification as but a part of God's work to purify society. So, rationalizing their lack of success, society has to run its course towards the End of Time. The stubbornness of the unrepentant is too great for any purification to succeed. The failure to change society means then that one is still fighting on the right side. This rationalization, which serves as an important means of legitimation of the EO activities, easily leads towards overstatements and an exaggeration of the message. In a desperate effort to be heard, the EO exaggerates, for example, the ills and evils of society:

'Hospitals become abortion-clinics and euthanasia institutions. Soon, one will not even know whether the physician is a healer or a killer. ...... The EO wants to be your voice, calling for a return' (5).

Another way would be participation in the democratic parliamentary procedures. However, this inevitably leads to compromises in the complicated Dutch political situation. Straying from the straight and narrow path is detestable, even if a larger following could be gained (6).

Theology: purifying doctrine and morals

At the turn of the century in the United States, a group of theologians arose that wanted to halt the secularization of theology. They postulated the truth of a limited number of dogmas - e.g. the Virgin Birth of Jesus - and claimed the Inerrancy of the Bible as an inviolate principle. This movement, calling its dogmas the Fundamentals of Faith, was dubbed fundamentalism (Warfield & Orr 1910). James Barr characterizes this doctrine thus:
a. A very strong emphasis on the inerrancy of the bible. The absence of any sort of error in the Bible.
b. A strong hostility to modern theology and to the methods, results and implications of modern critical study of the Bible.
c. An assurance that those who do not share their religious viewpoint are not really 'true Christians' (Barr 1977:1).
The EO in fact is the Dutch exponent of this theological movement. As such it has no clear affiliation with one or several denominations; its very fundamentalism tends to exclude the evangelicals from the mainstream Dutch protestants, even from the ones considered orthodox. Their resistance against any critical interpretation of the Bible is based on the fear that the biblical precepts will be undermined and relativated. However, the discussion with the other protestants hardly ever deserve the term discussion. The evangelicals operate from an exclusivist viewpoint with a strong in-group orientation:

'Though discussion may be held, they are often sham discussions, tended in fact not to give equal hearing to a variety of positions but to create opportunities for the rehearsal of the normal fundamentalist viewpoint.' (Barr 1977:320).

As a case, illustrating the way the EO creates for itself a minority position, the EO reaction to one particularly authoritative orthodox protestant theological document may serve.

In 1981 the report **God met ons** (God with us) was issued by the Synod of the Reformed Church in the Netherlands, dealing with the nature of scriptural authority. The report embodied the result of a long discussion in these churches, the preliminary end of a long process. Modern critical biblical research is selectively accepted. The EO proclaimed itself to be an opponent of this report, mobilizing all forces at its disposal: radio and TV as well as conferences and publications. Three points were crucial in the war the EO engaged against the report.

First of all, the evangelicals do not want to relativize in any way the concept of truth. **God met ons** is written with a relational concept of truth, in which truth emerges in a relation, within the interaction of a human being with something else. The evangelical reaction:

'In the biblical concept of truth any truth comes from above, from God....As we possess in the Bible the absolute truth about God, the believer can defend himself against the enemy with a "It is written."'(7).

The fierce reaction is typical: the other Protestants are defined as enemies; thus strengthening the sense of exclusivity and exclusiveness of the movement.

The second issue is its view of biblical inspiration. The report uses an organic vision of inspiration, as a result of a decennia-long discussion on the topic. This has the advantage of avoiding the mechanical and fundamentalistic use of Scripture. This, of course, is gist to the fundamentalist mills. The EO denounced this view in its heavy handed terms: 'The main error of the report is the denial of literal, complete inspiration of the Bible' (8).

The third topic is just as important. The report advised against using the Bible as an ethical blueprint, because the Bible in ethical issues does not have 'a system of unhistorical, objective and ever valid truths' (9). In this vein, christians must assume the burden of responsibility to interpret the Bible for their own time, their own ethical issues. The EO fears thus that, the foundation of a biblical ethics will disappear.

'We believe that Scripture does indeed contain absolute, divine norms, also for problems such as divorce, the role of woman etc, that are valid without change in all eras' (10).

In this way, the evangelicals not only emphasized their own position and closed their ranks in doing so, they also isolated themselves from one of the main currents in orthodox protestant circles, the Dutch Reformed Church (Gereformeerde Kerk). For it was these calvinist churches, an ever strong and influential part of Dutch society, that were defined as the enemy. For their part, the 'Gereformeerde Kerken' integrally denounced fundamental teachings and purification claims.

This 'discussion' highlights all main fundamentalist issues save one. A clear chiliasm pervades the theology, a millenarianism that belongs to the core of the doctrine.

'Faith in an inerrant Bible as much as an expectation of the second coming of Christ has been the hallmark of the Fundamentalist' (Sandeen 1970:103).

The correlation between both doctrines is evident: without a millenarian vision the biblic prophecies would be pointless and void. So our times are interpreted as the End of Time ('Eindtijd'), the last days of this wicked world. Preaching is 'Second Coming'-oriented, which in fact may add another challenge to the task of the EO: little time remains to preach and purify Holland and oneself.

Organization

The EO is organized, as we have seen, in the legal form of a 'Stichting'. This was originally chosen as a means to lessen the risk that the members take over its management and leadership. A hierarchical, topdown type of organization is not in itself unusual among broadcasting corporations, but nowhere is the trend as clear as in the EO. Their organization is authoritarian and pyramidical. A few people, almost all preachers/ministers, are still in the position of power. They command the deep respect of the evangelical constituency, its members and associates alike. The members see them as pillars of faith for whom one should pray regularly. They are the ones who should pray regularly. They are the ones who hold the frontline against the enemy. Nearly all of them are ministers, in that they are the ones who lead the services: they preach the Word ('bedienen het Woord'). Usually they have some theological schooling in the form of an evangelical Bible school. Academic theological schooling is scarce, and not very much sought after. In fact, that is some what frowned upon. Especially the older leaders are the patriarchal figures, who, in the eyes of the members, have given their lives for the service of the Lord. When in doubt or in trouble, one should look up to them, and, inspired by their example and precept, follow the right way again. A few of the older leaders have and have had a distinct personal charisma. The transition from personal to positional charisma (see Thoden van Velzen & van Beek, this volume) is quite clear. The younger ones, except maybe one, have not yet reached that personal stature; e.g. the son of one of the founders, who was expected to become an important figure, has never quite possessed the same charisma as his father. Still, the fact that the new leaders hold the positions is sufficient to command a great respect. Being functionaries of the EO implies the full backing of the orthodox. Thus, leaders have a virtually unlimited credit based on a solid doctrinal foundation. The leaders and their associates are known mainly from the mass meetings. At the yearly rallies they are the ones that preach the 'Word'. For social mobility in the movement the meetings are the main channel.

On the whole, the leaders enjoy the same kind of respect with their associates. On the basis of their calling, they demand an unquestioning obedience from their associates. This is given, as obedience is viewed as part of one's respective calling. Through the specific form of the foundation, the associates do not have the same kind of labour rights as is normal in Dutch society. They are much less protected by law than their colleagues in other broadcasting corporations. Their influence on policy-making is also much more restricted. Yet, the personnel of the EO on the whole does its work with a remarkable amount of love and idealism, taking the authoritarian structure in its stride. Still, this kind of system runs counter to the usual Dutch way of organizing either broadcasting corporations or foundations and, consequently, the EO has had more than its share of internal conflicts. Many associates have been fired because they did not fit into the system, or strayed from the doctrine and the fold.

In 1979, one of the leading socio-economic magazines in Holland issued the 'EO dossier'. In that issue they unfolded the mismanagement of the leadership, amounting to a kind of tyranny by the few top leaders. They could hire and fire their personnel whenever any criticism on their policy was raised. In 1981, an action group of former EO personnel published an account of 'concentration camp-like experiences'. One of them told that he still had trouble sleeping from Sunday night to Monday, as on each Monday morning a prayer meeting in the EO chapel was (and still is) always held. He thought these sessions hypocritical against the background of the daily excoriation of personnel. One example is a well-loved presentator, a minister who was fired in 1982. He had forgotten to congratulate Princess Juliana on her birthday. Of course, there was more to it than that. The employee remained silent till the case was publicized. Then he furiously lashed out in print:

'I have been put out like a dog. I still endorse the EO, which has always had all my heart. But there are people in the EO who do not belong there (12).

The typical reaction of the leadership is to see any labour conflict in terms of a doctrinal struggle and to resort to moral and biblical arguments to solve a conflict in management. It is the false conscience of the ex-employees that rouses them unto this mud-slinging. Faults may be made where ever people work. A critical reaction towards the leadership, however, is a form of persecution, and as such a proof that the leader is still on the right path. In a letter to the publisher, one EO member stated:

'Is it not deplorable to that the SEM (the magazine in question) tarnish the standing and reputation of the EO and its named associates? I do deeply respect the dignified tone in which the EO counteracts this mud slinging, and simply want to add what has been written in John 15:20: As they have persecuted me, so they will persecute you too' (13).

The membership of the EO has a very strong bond with the organization. It is by no means a cross-section of the Dutch population. A large proportion is older than the Dutch average (14). Their denominational background is quite diverse. The EO has no special bond with a specific church or group of churches. But they do have a definite church adherence, in sharp contrast with the majority of the Dutch people. More than half of the EO membership belongs to the more liberal mainline 'Reformed Church' (Hervormde Kerk), often among the 'Gereformeerde Bond' (a small ultra-orthodox subgroup within the 'Hervormde Kerk'). The remainder comes from other churches on the far christian right, such as the 'Christelijk Gereformeerd' (Christian Reformed), 'Vergadering van Gelovigen' (Darbists), Baptists, Pentacostals, Gereformeerde Gemeente, 'Gereformeerd Vrijgemaakt' ('Free Reformed', two ultra-Calvinist groups), 'Vrije Evangelie Gemeente' and 'Vrije Evangelische Gemeente' (two Pentecostal groups), the Salvation Army. Surprisingly, 2% of its membership is Roman Catholic: an unexpected phenomenon where there is such a pronounced Reformed ethos. This may be explained by the appeal the EO programmes have in the conservative Catholic circles, esp. on ethical issues.

One astonishing fact is that, despite the strong bonds between organization and membership, a considerable part of the membership does not watch TV. About 7% of the members do not even own a TV set! Of the members that do own, a smaller proportion regularly watches TV than an average Dutch viewer. This (15) reflects an ambivalent attitude towards TV and radio that is inherent in orthodox Protestantism and evangelicals. At least one wing of the evangelicals views TV as an instrument of Satan that entraps the youth in ways of falsehood, deceit and moral decadence (see van der Meiden, this volume). Still, they are members of a broadcasting corporation, because they see a positive influence in the EO. Even when the media have a more positive appeal, people view them with misgivings that are eventually superseded by the notion that the call for purification should be heeded.

These denominations are represented in the Foundation Council 'Stichtingsraad' as well as in the Board, the Catholic Church and the Salvation Army excepted. The small ultra-orthodox protestant (Reformed) groups are overrepresented in the Council. The total spectrum of churches and denominations, however, is in no way a step towards ecumenism, but simply a practical, opportunistic bond between fissioning minorities, on the basis of shared ethical concern (Berger 1975:158).

The political preference of the membership is not well known, but with a high probability to the right of the political spectrum, where several minute 'Reformed Parties' form a haven for evangelicals. One indication is that in the EO programs only representatives of these parties (SGP, RPF and GPV) are allowed speaking-time. Only those parties are allowed to advertise in the EO TV and radio guide.

The evangelical pillar

A 'pillar' is, as we have seen, the complex of institutions, covering if possible all aspects of social and religious life, which is organized on the basis of religious or ideological denomination. In a sense, a 'pillar' is an attempt to generate a non-secular society. When not the entire society can be saved from secularization, at least a part of it, one section, can be retained pure. A 'pillar' aims at the doctrinal, ethical and social purity of a particular segment of the population. The EO, having been formed in an era where the de-pillarization of Dutch society had already set in, has every reason to strive to become such a pillar, replacing the crumbling pillars of mainstream Protestantism.

The evangelical pillar, though in no way completely organized yet, is constituted by an intricate network of evangelical organizations and corporations active in politics, education, publishing, record companies, travel agencies and in social welfare services. All these organizations, together, may be viewed as an evangelical pillar. The EO, then, is at the center of the network, being the nodal point where the strands of power and publishing come together.

The various links that tie the EO to other organizations are, on the whole, not well institutionalized. Usually all kinds of joint appointments of individuals form the core of those links. The EO is the podium for all kinds of activities, so the officials, leaders and precentors of the EO are in a good position to sit on other boards and councils. Sometimes a more direct link can be traced. The Director of the EO once challenged the evangelical publishing world to publish a christian Family Magazine to counter the increasing 'poisoning' of the Christian Family by non-christian media. The 'Reformatorisch Dagblad' (Reformed Journal), one of the two dailies that advertises in the EO TV-radio guide 'Visie' took up that challenge and issued the magazine 'Terdege' ('Solid').

A very important link is the one between the EO and the 'Evangelische Hogeschool ('Evangelical University', henceforth called EH). This university started its courses in 1977, teaching subjects that in other, long established Universities can be followed as well. This doubling of institutional supply is one of the dominant characteristics of pillarization (van Doorn 1956: 41). This evangelical tertiary education was the answer to - inevitably - the secularization of Dutch education. The existing Reformed University (The Free University in Amsterdam), the Theological University in Kampen and the Catholic University of Nijmegen were viewed as thoroughly de-christianized.

'Many students from christian families through their studies at the Universities have lost their faith in the salvation through Jesus Christ. Others may have stood fast, but they have, in and through their studies, arrived at a separation of belief and knowledge.'(16)

The EH takes the Bible as, the 'inspired, unerring Word of God', as its charter. For them, the Bible 'speaks with absolute authority, both where it speaks about salvation and where it speaks about history, the cosmos and nature.'(17) Its relations with the EO are evident. Much of the documentation published by or through the EO is used as texts. Personnel of the EO often have a joint appointment at the EH. EH lecturers often appear in EO programmes. Two EO board-members also have a controlling seat in the EH board. On the whole, the EH, serves as a think-tank for the EO, following the American example of Pat Robertson's 'Electronic Church.

Another very important link is the one with the publishing world. The EO has similar personalized links with the main evangelical journals and magazines. A considerable amount of attention is paid to youth and children magazines and publications. This is easily understood in their quest for purity of their own segment of the Dutch population, but it is quite characteristic of any pillar. In fact, the pillarization of Dutch society started with the so-called 'School Struggle', the battle of the denominations to win the constitutional right to educate according their own religious convictions. Several publishers have one EO board member on their board of directors.

A pillar, however, should broaden its appeal to the people, and control many aspects of social life. From this angle, the EO as broadcasting corporation is by no means a run-of-the-mill one. Its general policy is to strive for a dense network of close relations with its members and listeners. It goes to great pains - leading to substantial financial sacrifices from its members - to organize numerous mass activities, rallies and excursions beyond the scope of usual broadcasting activities. Each year the EO organizes a large conference of members, the Family Day, at which some 20,000 members show up. The youth are engaged in similar massive rallies, the 'Youth Days'. Besides, the youngsters can become members of the 'Ronduitclub', the youth club of the EO.

A spectacular part of the activities is formed by the travel-programme, in which Israel features prominently. The chiliasm, so dominant in the message and calling of the EO, generates a lively and deep interest in Israel. They are organized by the EO employees, and led by important EO associates and precentors, the managing director even showing up as a tour guide. Recently, the Dutch government forbade broadcasting corporations to organize this kind of 'branch alien' activity. Nowadays, EO Travels is a 'separate' organization, which - of course - can count on ample space in the TV guide. This interest in Israel is expressed also in a great number of commercial activities: e.g. the sale of Israel postage stamps, advertized in a brochure as follows: 'These stamps really illustrate the prophetic destination if this country and people'. In another endeavour, buying Israeli bonds, the wording was similar: 'In the coming days Jacob will take root, Israel will flourish and sprout, so that they fill the world with fruits.' This legitimation surely helped the purchasers to accept a much lower interest than they would have had in Holland. The idea that Israel was supported was a huge recompense. So, even the evangelical notion of furthering the Second Coming of the Lord is important in promoting EO activities and strengthening the evangelical pillar.

Of course, not all activities are so inner-directed. It is the purification of Holland that is the main issue. The evangelicals organize huge evangelization campaigns, like the one called 'There is Hope'. Every single address in the Netherlands was given some evangelization material. The costs of that large project were shouldered by the evangelicals themselves, stimulated and coordinated by the EO. However, any activity vying for the attention of the EO must start from the dogma of the inerrant Word of God. Ecumenical or public services, organizations and actions that have a more liberal theological base, have nothing to expect from the EO (except much criticism). Thus, all fund raising agencies which aim at the evangelical purse show their fundamentalist background in their brochures and publications. They may have to stress their christian profile in contrast to other similar - but secular - agencies. Sometimes, they use the purported communist tendencies in rival agencies to ensure a good reception in evangelical circles. As an example the evangelical organization 'Christian Help to those who are Persecuted for their Conscience' may serve. This is the evangelical equivalent of Amnesty International. Anti-communism, in any case, is a persistent theme in evangelical organizations; a number of them are engaged in sending evangelical materials to communist countries, bibles, brochures, tracts, as well as clothing and medicine. The foundation 'Answer' (Antwoord) is one of them; one of the EO board members happens to be on their board too.

As a body the evangelicals are very generous. They readily contribute to any cause they deem worthy, especially if the purification of Dutch institutions is aimed at. This generosity in giving is all the more remarkable when compared to the usual thriftiness that not only is routinely associated with Calvinism, but in fact with the associated soberness is a pervading asset of the evangelicals as well as of other orthodox Protestant groups.

Problem solving and social work is traditionally an important aspect of any pillar. Helping people in social or psychological distress should not be left to secular institutions. Thus, the foundation 'De Hoop' (Hope) tries to fill in that perceived void, focusing especially on drug addicts. Quite regularly they place a call in 'Visie' (Vision), the EO guide, for financial support, clearly stating as their explicit aim: 'For the christian social worker ... the paramount goal is to restore the broken relationship with God, as this is of eternal value'. (18) A similar organization, 'Schuilplaats' (Sanctuary), aims at the prevention of abortions. One of its policies is placing pregnant women in a family whenever needed. They also battle against euthanasia in order to 'protect life, that depends on Gods blessings, from the very begin till the end of it'. (19)

Any pillar tries to become a complete way of living within the framework of those public and civil institutions that cannot be duplicated. A pillar, like the evangelical one, thus aims to cover as many walks of life as possible, striving to become an all-encompassing institution. In this way, it becomes a greedy institution too (Thoden van Velzen, van Beek, this volume), regulating many aspects of daily life in the private sphere. Of course, this falls outside the reach of the EO proper, but the constituting churches do provide some control in these areas. Problems connected with birth, death, marriage and chastity are considered to be under jurisdiction of the churches. Whoever transgresses the Word, can count on a visit from the minister and a few elders in order to preach to the culprit the right way. This form of social control, in a situation where help is much more needed than sermons, often results in the 'transgressor' leaving the church community. The purification of sinners usually amounts to purification from sinners. The EO does, however, offer a platform on which to discuss these issues. Problems of and norms for sexuality e.g., are freely and frequently discussed in the TV programmes and the associated clubs for the youth. Of course, the message is the proscription of pre-marital sex and abstaining from the use of contraceptives. The general rule is that sexuality is a way to beget children for the Lord.

Conclusion

The quest for purity among the Dutch evangelicals is dominated by their ideology which has been characterized as fundamentalist. It is definitely a 'greedy ideology'. It claims to offer precepts for the right kind of living in all circumstances, and stresses the absolute need to follow only that narrow path. It defines anyone straying from the fold as 'not a real christian'. Turning outwards it is an ideology that opposes mainstream society and mainline churches. Adhering to the norms they perceive to have inherited from of old, the ideology defines itself continually in relation to the sins and evil of the larger world. It is an anti-ideology, more than a self-contained and autonomous one. Thus, in dealing with the 'World', the adherents continually have to tune their actions to the reactions prescribed by the ideology. The effect is quite dialectical. On the one hand, being a reaction to the world, the ideology and the movement are never in isolation, always responding to outside pressures. On the other hand, the anti-ness of their stance does, in fact, isolate them more and more from mainstream Dutch society. The ideology defines itself and its members as continuous marginal members of Dutch society, while striving to reshape society after its own image.

The movement has a strong geographical base in some rural areas of Holland (the Veluwe, e.g.) but, characteristically, never uses that stronghold as such. They are, in fact, afraid to be dubbed a 'Veluwe'-movement, as this clashes with their professed aim to cleanse all Holland. Isolation is not sought, and is even avoided. The evangelicals are a - very vocal - minority, which without secularization would have little 'raison d'être'. They are knights who would wither away without the dragon.

The media as such are a moot point in this movement, as many of them look with distrust at radio and TV. The paradigmatic way to purify people is preaching the Word (het Woord verkondigen) and any medium is judged by that yardstick. The arts, for instance, are treated with reserve. Painting is all right, provided the painter glorifies God's creation with his work. Meticulous representation of nature and - whenever possible - biblical scenes are called for. Rembrandt, with his precision and biblical inspiration is the paragon of painting. Van Gogh is tabu, because of his subjects and technique of painting, and for his lifestyle. He may be used in a sermon to exemplify a person 'who has

not yet really met the Lord'. Poetry should be clear, pure and oriented
to the Word. Any use of language should direct people towards the
Lord. Someone who speaks before an audience should lift the people
up to meet the Lord. Cabaret - culturally important in Holland - is
thus definitely 'out'. The only art that is really developed is singing
in choirs, considered the choice option to raise the hearts of the believers and touch the hardened hearts of those not yet reborn.

Television and radio bear the same characteristics: their programmes
should proclaim the Word. The 'message' is so central that the 'medium'
is secondary. The EO is well-known in Holland for its amateuristical
broadcasting, a fact recognized by the evangelicals. They do not resent
it. When preaching in front of the camera, things may go wrong. If
the minister looses the reference for his citation in front of the camera, no problem: the Word is preached. They do make a virtue out of
this mishaps. The anti-professional stance in the media tends to isolate
the evangelicals somewhat. It seems to appeal to the very young, but
their programmes become rather a laughing stock to the more mature
viewers. This anti-professional attitude ties in with their opposition
to some aspects of the electronic Church in the USA. Those gospel
shows and Television presentations are too smooth, too slick for the
Dutch evangelicals. The Gospel is not that easy, conversion is a hard
process. 'Ordinary' is well enough: too much beauty and show detracts
from the real thing. Thus, there is no tendency to invite renowned
preachers from abroad to address Dutch audiences. They do use in the
EO many films from e.g. the Moody institute; yet only those in which
the professional quality is beyond doubt, but very functional. The
American evangelical preaching is not even broadcasted.

A preacher/minister does not have to be overly professional: he
should state the truths in simple words, without making the implementation of his sermon look easy. Theology, then, is simple. A formal
theological schooling, e.g. at one of the official Dutch Universities,
is frowned upon. Though schooling is generally highly appreciated (using
your God-given talents), formal theology is bending the knee to
scholarship instead of to the Lord. Exposing oneself to the onslaught
of critical Bible commentaries is hazardous. Just take the Bible and
teach from it. The Bible, by the way, is considered to be accessible
to everyone. The same 'simple is pure' idea holds for the hymns they
use. Those of the Protestant Hymnbook are deemed too complex and
intellectualistic. They prefer the more pietist simplicity of Johannes
de Heer, a famous preacher/poet from the first half of the century.

They like to recognize their own language in hymns and sermons.
Like any movement, they have created their own 'jargon'. Whenever
a preacher uses the words 'zoenbloed van Christus' (the atoning blood

of Christ) and especially if he uses the soft pronunciation of the guttural in 'Christus', then one has tuned into the EO. If he then warns his listeners that they 'will come with empty hands at the foot of the cross', recognition is beyond doubt. As anywhere, such a 'Tale Kanaans' (i.e. the Language of Canaan) serves to generate recognition as well as to create and sustain a boundary: it is a means to preach and a means to protect.

The evangelicals feel that no compromise is possible. An absolute truth is absolute; the preaching of absolutes leaves no way for a soft touch. Still, the goals may influence the means. They remain wary of the use of the weapons of Satan to purify Holland. In this view, the EO is not a broadcasting corporation: it is a mission-network. The main mission field is Holland, and that field should be evangelized. They do give attention to any corner of the world where the Word is preached, like some Third World countries; but their main focus of attention is on the Netherlands. One should clean up one's own yard before cleaning someone else's. Thus, the turning inward for purification of their own circles and the purification of the larger society is part and parcel of the same process. The failure of the latter is essential in the success of the former. As long as Holland remains impure, the evangelicals can look forward to a purer future.

Thus, the Dutch evangelicals are caught between the conflicting goals of purification of self and that of society, between raising their voice in protest and being marginalized into a dark corner of society, between the call to preach the Word and the danger of rendering society immune to that preaching. No compromise means the loss of appeal and the absence of bargaining chips. So, their own ideology, greedy by virtue of its uncompromising stance, ties the evangelicals to an impure world with the call to be pure themselves; thus creating an ever growing abyss between evangelicals and society. They shout the Word louder and louder to an ever-receding and deafer ear.

Appendix: the Dutch broadcasting system

About the 1920's, when most of the Dutch broadcasting corporations were organized, Holland was still a pillarized society. In fact, four pillars, i.e. complexes of institutions organized along ideological lines, were discernible; one Protestant, one Roman Catholic, one liberal Protestant, and one Socialist. Every pillar received its own broadcasting corporation, and received broadcasting time on the government-controlled network. Until the Second World War, each Dutch listener had his own corporation, and one generally listened only when one's own pillar was 'on'.

After the War deconfessionalization set in and people listened to what they liked. The coming of television enhanced this proces, though the TV-programmes were as pillarized as radio was, being part of one corporation. Thus, the broadcasting structure gradually became an anachronism: a pillarized corporational structure serving a de-pillarizing society. The last decennia some 'general' corporations appeared on the scene which, through their rapid growth, underscored the loss of pillarized appeal for the Dutch public. Still, the system as such remains friendly and open for new 'pillars'. Every social group that bases itself on a religious or quasi-religious foundation can opt for time on the network. If they can show that their following is large enough, they receive a proportional amount of time on public TV (there is as yet no purely commercial network in Holland though there is indeed some advertizing. What is missing here, is direct sponsoring. Characteristically, one non-denominational corporation is flirting with fully sponsored TV). Thus, after the initial 'aspirant' status for which 60,000 members must be shown, if the group can boast 150,000 paying members it acquires C-status, with 300,000 B-status and with 450,000 A-status, at each phase receiving more time on the network. The broadcasting time will be at the expense of the other corporations, as the total amount of network time is limited. The cost for the broadcasts as well as the costs for making the programmes is paid by the government, financed by the broadcasting tax (kijk- en luistergelden), paid by everyone with a radio or TV-set, plus - more recently - the profits of advertizing. This system is regulated and fixed by law, and is and has been the subject of heated debates among the representatives; one particular government fell on the issue of public broadcasting.

Notes

1) 'De EO wil in deze verwarrende wereld een baken in zee zijn, want ons land verkwijnt als de kennis Gods verdwijnt'. *Trouw*, 2 april 1986, p. 13.
2) 'De EO roept de samenleving op tot terugkeer naar de Bijbel en de handhaving van wat de Here God ons daarin zegt. Daarom roep ik alle christenen op zich aaneen te sluiten. Wij christenen moeten in gehoorzaamheid spreken over de normen van de Bijbel. Wie anders zou dit moeten doen'. J. Schreur, *Visie* 13 (1982), 2, p. 6.
3) L. Emmink, Leven in het Ik-tijdperk, in *Visie*, 12, 1981, 10, p. 8. 'Abortus hoort bij vrije huwelijken, naaktloperij, ontsporing van

de jeugd en van de ouders, massage-instituten, euthanasie, individualisme, egoïsme, seks, materialisme, ontucht, de 'pil', werkeloosheid, decadentie, drugs, actiegroepen, majesteitsschennis, anarchisme, milieuverontreiniging, honger, droogte en ga zo nog maar even door'.

4) J.C. Maris, De EO en het Volksleven, in: *Visie* 13, 1982, 29, p.3. '... zij heeft een getuigende roeping in het midden van heel het volk. ... Er is verband tussen nationale zonden en nationale plagen. Het behoort tot het profetisch getuigenis dat dit wordt aangewezen, heel concreet. God Zelf roept een afgeweken volk terug 'tot de Wet en de Getuigenis'.

5) 'Ziekenhuizen worden vernederd tot abortusklinieken en euthanasiehuizen. Men weet straks niet meer wanneer de dokter de 'healer' of de 'killer' is ... De EO wil namens u spreken en oproepen tot terugkeer'. Advertisement in *Visie*, 12 (1981) nr. 45, p. 33.

6) An example of this process can be found in a conflict within the ranks of the RPF (Reformed Political Federation). The two representatives split on the issue of opportunism versus orthodoxy. The orthodox line prevailed.

7) 'In het bijbelse waarheidsbegrip komt de waarheid van boven, van God... Juist omdat wij in de Bijbel de absolute waarheid over God bezitten, kan de gelovige zich tegenover de vijand verweren met een 'er staat geschreven', *De Bijbel in de beklaagdenbank*, 1981: 47.

8) 'De kerndwaling van het rapport is de loochening van de woordelijke, volledige inspiratie van de Bijbel'. *De Bijbel in de beklaagdenbank*: 32.

9) 'Een stelsel van onhistorische, objectieve, altijd geldende waarheden'. *God met ons*: 51.

10) 'Wij geloven dat de Schrift wel degelijk absolute, goddelijke normen bevat, ook voor problemen als echtscheiding, de plaats van de vrouw, enzovoort, die onveranderlijk voor alle tijden gelden'. *De Bijbel in de beklaagdenbank*: 28.

11) *Sociaal Economisch Management*, March 31, 1979.

12) 'Ik ben op straat gezet als een hond. Ik sta nog altijd achter de Evangelische Omroep, die steeds mijn hart heeft gehad. Er zitten echter mensen bij de EO, die er niet horen...' *Zwolse Courant*, May 27, 1982.

13) 'Is het niet dieptreurig dat SEM de goede naam en eer van de EO en met name genoemde medewerkers aantast? Ik heb respect voor de waardige wijze waarop de EO deze vuilspuiterij weerspreekt en wil hieraan toevoegen wat geschreven staat in Joh. 15, vers 20:

'Indien zij Mij vervolgd hebben, zij zullen ook u vervolgen'. *Trouw*, 5 april 1979.
14) The figures on *Visie* (EO-TV/radio guide) subscriptions show less specific EO profile:

age	Visie-subscriptions	Dutch average
18-34 y	24,0%	31,4%
35-49 y	28,6%	29,7%
50-64 y	29,9%	23.4%
65 +	17,5%	15,5%

Thus, young people may subscribe to *Visie* without viewing the programmes, while old viewers view the programmes without subscription.
15) Average viewing time per day (viewers survey NOS)

	EO	Dutch average
less than 75 minutes/day	53%	35%
75 - 135 minutes/day	30%	31%
more than 135 minutes/day	17%	34%

(This survey excluded people without a TV set)
16) 'Veel studenten uit christelijke gezinnen hebben tijdens hun studie aan de universiteit het geloof in de verlossing door Jezus Christus verloren. Anderen zijn staande gebleven, maar zijn door en in hun studie gekomen tot een scheiding van geloof en wetenschap'. *Studiegids Evangelische Hogeschool*, 1983-1984, p. 5.
17) 'De Bijbel spreekt met absoluut gezag, zowel waar hij spreekt over het heil, als waar hij spreekt over de geschiedenis, de kosmos en de natuur'. Article 2 of the Statutes of the EH.
18) 'Voor de christen hulpverlener ... is het belangrijkste doel de verbroken relatie met God te herstellen omdat dit van eeuwigheidswaarde is'. Definition of therapy of the Foundation "Hope" (De Hoop) in Dordrecht.
19) 'In afhankelijkheid van Gods zegen het leven te beschermen vanaf het stricte begin tot aan het einde daarvan'. *Visie* 14, (1983), 49: 34.

References

Barr, J.
1977   *Fundamentalism*, London
Berger, P.
1975   *The Sacred Canopy*, New York: Free Press
Boer, E. de & O. Sondorp
1981   *Meer of minder dan een Evangelische Omroep?* Unpublished
        MA thesis, VU Amsterdam.
Coleman, J.A.
1978   *The Evolution of Dutch Catholicism, 1958-1974.* Berkeley: U-
        niversity of California Press.
Doorn, van, J.A.A.
1956   Verzuiling: een eigentijds systeem van sociale controle, *De
        Sociologische Gids*, III: 41-49
Marsden, G.M.
1980   *Fundamentalism and American Culture: the Shaping of Twen-
        tieth Century Evangelicalism, 1870-1925.* Oxford University
        Press.
Munters, Q.
1970   *Recrutering als roeping.* Meppel
1972   Recrutering en polarisatie, *Intermediair*, 8,3: 1
Sandeen
1970   *The Roots of Fundamentalism*, Chicago
Warfield, B.B. & J. Orr
1910   *The Fundamentals: a Testimony of the Truth.* Des Moines.

Puritans in Arabia: the Wahhābī movement (18th–19th c.)
Jacques D.J.Waardenburg

Puritans in Arabia: the Wahhābi movement (18th-19th c.)
Jacques Waardenburg

This contribution concentrates on the movement which arose in response to the religious call of Muḥammad ibn ᶜAbd al-Wahhāb (1703--1787) which is known as the Wahhābī movement. We concentrate on its history until the 20th century, leaving out of consideration its influence on regions outside Arabia. The first part provides some biographical details about the founder and sets out the substance of his call, which led to the foundation of the Wahhābīya community in Nejd in Central Arabia. Subsequently the way in which the Saᶜūd family exercised leadership of the community and gave a powerful impetus to the movement in the 18th and 19th centuries is described, and the political consequences of their actions are mentioned. Finally, attention is paid to the infrastructural factors which, together with the effect of the religious call and astute political leadership, can help to explain the rise and success of the movement.

Secondary material, that is to say studies previously published which are based on doctrinal and historical writings by Wahhābī authors is the main source for this paper. We have no records left by outsiders who could have observed the Wahhābī movement in Nejd itself during the period treated here. This is only possible in the 20th century when ᶜAbd al-ᶜAziz II (1879-1953), the founder of the modern Saudi Arabia, renewed the Wahhābī call.

Muḥammad Ibn ᶜabd Al-Wahhāb (1703-1787)

Muḥammad ibn ᶜAbd al-Wahhāb was born at al-ᶜUyaina in Nejd in 1703 into one of the families of Banu Sinan of the Tamim tribe. He came of a Hanbali family with a tradition of learning. His grandfather, Shaikh Sulaimā-n b. Muḥammad, had been Mufti of Nejd and had had a great number of pupils, and his father, ᶜAbd al-Wahhāb ibn Sulaimān,

Muḥammad Ibn ᶜabd Al-Wahhāb (1703-1787)

Muḥammad ibn ᶜAbd al-Wahhāb was born at al-ᶜUyaina in Nejd in 1703 into one of the families of Banu Sinan of the Tamim tribe. He came of a Hanbali family with a tradition of learning. His grandfather, Shaikh Sulaimā-n b. Muḥammad, had been Mufti of Nejd and had had many pupils, and his father ᶜAbd al-Wahhāb ibn Sulaimān was Qadi at al-ᶜUyaina, teaching in the local mosque. Al-ᶜUyaina at the time had a certain prosperity but no particular intellectual resources. After having received religious instruction from his father, who had himself written a tract against the veneration of human beings (saints) to which the Hanbali tradition had been opposed since its beginnings, Muḥammad went as a young man to Medina to pursue his studies further in this centre of religious learning.

Historians report that two teachers in Medina, Sulaimān al-Kurdi and Muḥammad Hayāt al-Sindī, discovered in the young man's religious ideas traces of 'heresy'. It may be assumed that already at that time he was strongly opposed to all forms of veneration of human beings, whether Shīᶜi Imams or Shīᶜi or Sunni 'holy men' or saints, to whom miracles were often ascribed. This attitude may have been reinforced by what he saw in Medina of 'pious' practices around the tomb of the prophet Muḥammad, who is buried there, and what he must have seen in both Mecca and Medina of the exploitation of pilgrims by the   inhabitants of these cities who indulged in an ostentatious and materialistic way of life painful to anyone who took the religious precepts seriously. It is known that already in his youth Muḥammad also had been struck by 'primitive' religious practices of the Bedouin related to the veneration of trees and rocks. Such practices must have been current in Central Arabia at the time, and it may be asked whether this relatively inaccessible region of the Peninsula had been islamized at all since the Prophet's death in 632 AD apart from the Bedouin's nominal conversion to the Islamic faith.

As a student in Medina Muḥammad ibn ᶜAbd al-Wahhāb was a faithful pupil of Shaikh ᶜAbd Allāh Ibrāhīm al-Najdī (al-Madanī) who stressed the decadence of Islam in Nejd and the need for serious religious reform there. The Shaikh's teaching was in the Hanbali tradition and inspired in particular by the ideas of Ibn Taimīya (1262-1328), the great 'puritan' reformer along Hanbali lines, and Shaikh ᶜAbd al-Bāqī al-Hanbalī (d. 1661) a great authority on Tradition (**Sunna**). Muḥammad ibn ᶜAbd al-Wahhāb received permission by means of a diploma to continue Shaikh ᶜAbd

Allāh's teaching, which means that he was also considered by him to be a trustworthy transmitter of his ideas. Another important teacher with whom he studied was the above mentioned Muhammad Hayāt as-Sindī, who was well versed in the knowledge of Sunna and equally keen on reform of current Islamic practices. He also advocated a re-opening of **ijtihād**, i.e. the independent 'free' interpretation of the sources of religion, in particular Quran and Sunna.

After his studies in Medina, Muhammad ibn ᶜAbd al-Wahhāb studied for some years in Basra with Shaikh Muhammad al-Majmūᶜī, an authority in the fields of Arabic language and Sunna; he is said to have been a tutor in the house of the local Qadi Husain. As a port city with a considerable Shīᶜi population Basra must have increased the young man's zeal for reforms. According to his Arab biographers the local ᶜulamā' pressed him to leave the town since the existing order was somewhat disturbed by his attacks on 'idolatry' (**shirk**) and veneration of human beings. They report on travels which the young man is said to have made to Baghdad, where he married a wealthy woman who subsequently died, and further to Kurdistan, Hamadan, Isfahan, Qumm and even Damascus (where he is supposed to have become a true Hanbalite) and Cairo. Such accounts, however, may have been meant to enhance the image of the founder as a widely traveled scholar rather than to render facts truely. More certain is that he was in al-Ahsā', on the Gulf coast, for studies.

Around 1739 Muhammad ibn ᶜAbd al-Wahhāb joined his father in Huraimla where he must have written his most important book, the **Kitāb al-tawhīd** (Book on the Oneness sc. of God). Now that his ideas had cristallized, he started preaching and acquired pupils and adherents. His biographers speak of a certain animosity of his brother Sulaimān towards him; Sulaimān is said to have written a tract attacking his ideas, while his father warned him to be more prudent in proclaiming them. After his father's death in 1740, Muhammad succeeded him in teaching but seems to have been urged to leave Huraimla shortly afterwards. He went back to his birthplace, al-ᶜUyaina, where he could spread his ideas for some years. He even succeeded in convincing the local Emir ᶜUthmān b. Bishr (of the Banū Muᶜammar) to cut down some sacred trees and destroy some domes over graves of 'holy men'. Through his preaching he became known in the whole region and his religious zeal gave him much prestige with the population. Biographers mention, however, the animosity of his cousin ᶜAbd Allāh b. Husain. His stay in al-ᶜUyaina came to an end because the Emir of the whole region up to the coast requested that Muḥammad ibn ᶜAbd al-Wahhāb be expelled since religious feelings of (presumably Shīᶜī) people in al-Aḥsā' had been hurt. He was able to leave then with his family and his property which must have been considerable at the time.

He was received in 1743 by a pupil of his, Shaikh Muḥammad ibn Suwailam, who lived in the town of Darᶜīya, reported to have had about 70 houses at the time. Here he also met Shaikh ᶜĪsā ibn Qāsim, received visitors and could preach. The oasis was ruled by the Emir Muḥammad ibn Saᶜūd, of the Bedouin dynasty of the āl Saᶜūd who were part of the large tribal confederation of the ᶜAnāza. Two brothers of the Emir, Mushārī (who was reported to have destroyed some funerary monuments, following the dictates of the new call) and Tanayān, as well as his wife, arranged the Shaikh's introduction to the Emir, who accepted his call and doctrine and took upon himself its defence and further propagation as well as the protection of the Shaikh himself. A simple mosque was built and instruction in the new doctrine as it was elaborated on the basis of the Shaikh's **Kitāb al-Tawḥīd** became obligatory for everyone. It is told that all the inhabitants accepted the new doctrine except four who left the place. Darᶜīya thus became the first stronghold of the Wahhābī movement spiritually, politically and even militarily, its inhabitants receiving training in the use of fire-arms. Historians speak of a formal 'pact' of allegiance concluded between the Emir Muḥammad ibn Saᶜūd and the Shaikh Muḥammad ibn ᶜAbd al-Wahhāb in 1744 AD (1157 AH). Such an allegiance (**baiᶜa**) had existed in former times, when the representatives of the Community recognised a new Caliph as its worldly leader. Through this pact the Bedouin principality became an Islamic nomocracy (a political entity based on the authority of religious law), the political sovereignty exercised by the ruler being distinct from the authority of the scholars of religion (ᶜulamā'). This construction has been the foundation of the Wahhābī state which has existed up to the present day. On a personal level the destiny of Muḥammad ibn ᶜAbd al-Wahhāb and his family (āl al--Shaikh) and that of Muḥammad ibn Saᶜūd and his family (āl Saᶜūd) were to be linked to each other, as they have remained up to the present day, the continuity of political leadership and of the Wahhābī character of the state being guaranteed accordingly.

When the Shaikh died at the age of 89 years in 1792 he had seen the successful expansion of the new state and the increasing acceptance of the call which he had proclaimed since the age of about 35. He is reported to have died poor, not having sought wealth for himself, and to have been buried anonymously in Darᶜīya as prescribed by his own doctrine. He appears never to have had ambitions for temporal power or desire for a particular spiritual status, just keeping to the simple title of **Shaikh**. It seems to have been the Shaikh who insisted that the ruler of the Wahhābī state should be not only **Amīr** but also **Imām**, head of the new Islamic state, or even **Imām al-Muslimīn**, the leader of the true Muslim community (which had been the classical title of the Caliph). In fact, the Shaikh had been the real power behind the throne, but after his death the Emir ^CAbd al-^CAzīz I (1766-1803) was to be considered both the spiritual and temporal chief of the Wahhābīs, as would be his successors. There were to be intermarriages, however, between the al-Shaikh and the al Sa^Cud, and the descendants of the Shaikh would continue to play an active role in the state, maintaining and propagating the doctrine, occupying important functions for which knowledge of religion was required and seeking to remain the conscience of the community and the nation-state (Laoust 1939: 506-510; Philby 1930:8-13, 54-56).

Doctrine

From the beginning Wahhābīs called themselves **ahl al-tawḥīd**, that is to say those who profess the Oneness of God. They called their movement the call from Nejd, or the call for Oneness of God, or simply the Call (**al-da^Cwa**). They considered themselves to be within the confines of Sunni orthodox doctrine. The doctrine and moral practice of **tawḥīd** (Oneness) indeed has been central to the movement from its beginning. God is absolute and cannot be compared to anything else. His most important attribute or quality is his oneness. He is absolutely one in the sense that there is no division within Him, and there is nothing divine outside Him as the profession of faith (**lā ilāha illā'llāh...**) expresses, i.e. He is also absolutely unique. As a logical consequence the movement has always been fervently opposed to anything infringing on the oneness of God, whether it be idolatry or the veneration of 'holy men', or states of mind in which anything other than God acquires an absolute character. All of this is considered the sin of **shirk**, associating anything with God. This in itself is good Sunni doctrine, but Muḥammad ibn ^CAbd al-Wahhāb rigorously advanced it as the absolute norm for any Muslim. It was the very essence of his call and it led sometimes to violent political action and always to a strengthening of the moral fibre so that people would refrain from anything which might infringe **tawḥīd**.

Theology

In points of theological doctrine, the movement wanted to keep to Quran and Sunna as the only valid sources of religious knowledge, very much as Aḥmad ibn Hanbal (780-855) had proclaimed centuries earlier. It was out of his teaching that the so-called Hanbalite legal 'school', within which Muḥammad ibn ᶜAbd al-Wahhāb should be situated, had developed. Muḥammad (d.632) is of course recognised as the Prophet but the Wahhābīs do not declare him to be infallible. His precepts should be obeyed and his example followed but any veneration or cult of him is strictly forbidden. Consequently, Muslims should not make pilgrimages to the tomb of Muḥammad in Medina, though they are free to visit it. Muḥammad can have an interceding role but only with the authorisation and agreement of God himself. The 'Companions' of Muḥammad should be respected in good measure but not honoured; they can be criticised for certain of their actions.

Among the founders of the four Sunni legal 'schools' Aḥmad ibn Ḥanbal occupies a privileged place because he followed the Sunna most scrupulously, but the other three founders are also highly esteemed. Muḥammad ibn ᶜAbd al-Wahhāb did not say, as Ibn Taimīya (1262-1328) had done, that all Muslims should go back to the doctrine of the Salaf, the pious contemporaries of the Prophet. He considered that beyond these contemporaries the first three generations of Muslims (up to the third century of Islam) provided the model for right thinking and behaviour. He vigorously combatted all non-Sunni schools of thought and rejected philosophical theology in whatever form. Muslims were to adhere strictly to Quran and Sunna. Only in later times was the movement to accept analogical reasoning as a way of interpreting these sources of religion permitted alongside the consensus prevailing in the third century of the hijra (9th century AD). Quranic exegesis along Wahhābī lines is literalist and rejects innovations after the classical Quran commentaries, just as it has rejected innovations in other religious domains as well, at least as they have occurred since the third century of Islam. Its attitude to mysticism has been less clear-cut: the tārīqas (brotherhoods), the zāwiyas (schools with their communal life), forms of asceticism and liturgies were forbidden as far as they were contrary to the Sunna. But the mystical intention of 'interiorizing' acts of worship, and of devoting oneself totally to God, has been accepted and applied as the basis of the moral life of the community.

Community

The ideas about communal life largely follow from the tenets just mentioned. For Muḥammad ibn ᶜAbd al-Wahhāb, the Muslim community's aim is to apply the sharīᶜa (sacred Law), prescribing what is religiously good and proscribing what is religiously bad. He stresses even more than Ibn Taimīya the equality of all Muslims. No special respect should be paid to descendants of the Prophet; and, on a very practical level, marriages between members of the community should be exempt from the conditions of social equality current in Muslim societies at the time. On the other hand he is more inclined to excommunicate people from the Muslim community than any of his predecessors of the Hanbalite school. As soon as someone infringes the **tawḥīd** and does not respond to the subsequent appeal to repent, he or she can be excommunicated. In fact according to strict standards the majority of Muslims are not true Muslims at all but have lapsed into forms of **shirk**, and this legitimates the carrying out of **jihād** against them. In doctrinal treatises different kinds of **shirk** are distinguished, just as different kinds of unbelief are.

The Wahhābī territory was called land of the Muslims and there was a marked tendency to consider all the outside territory (of Bedouin who had not submitted, the Ottoman Sultan and other Arab rulers than the Saᶜudis) as the domain of **kufr**, that is the land of war against which **jihād** could be waged, and was waged in fact, when circumstances permitted. Muḥammad ibn ᶜAbd al-Wahhāb and the Wahhābīs after him regarded themselves exclusively as the one and only rightly-guided Islamic community. The **umma** (Muslim community) takes precedence over any other social ties, in particular tribal particularism, but also individual rights and privileges. There ought to be complete solidarity among members of the movement, and any trace of secession or civil disturbance has to be eliminated for the sake of the community. All the (male) members share equal rights and responsibilities, and unity and equality are stressed again and again. Only within the community can Islam be practised as it ought to be. One of the consequences drawn from this is that Muslims should emigrate from any country or region in which shirk and **kufr** are manifest and Islam cannot be professed properly and settle in Islamic territory (**dār al-islām**), which then acquires the name of **dār al-hijra**.

The Wahhābīs, however, interpret this **hijra** ('migration') also on a moral level. ᶜAbd al-ᶜAzīz II was to use the doctrine of **hijrat al-uhramāt**, the 'abandoning of all that is forbidden by God and the

Prophet Muḥammad', in the 1910's and 1920's as an incentive to
settle the Bedouin in new agricultural communities. This is nothing
less than a complete conversion both personal and social, the
Islamic community being of another kind than the naturally-given
ties of family, clan and tribe.

Leadership

In the community leadership belongs to the **Imām,** who should be
strictly obeyed as long as he does not order disobedience to God.
Muḥammad ibn ᶜAbd al-Wahhāb describes the function of the **Imām**
in the same terms as Ibn Taimīya did in the 14th century. His
duties included ensuring that the principles and practices of
religion are well preserved. The imamate and emirate of the
Wahhābī state were created 'in order to force the people, in their
own interest, to obey God and his Prophet' (Laoust 1939:527). Thus
the **Imām** can regulate the behaviour of his subjects down to the
smallest details and he is obliged 'to consecrate to God in the **jihād**
the persons and property of the Muslims' (Laoust 1939:528). Perhaps
even more than that of Ibn Taimīya, Wahhābī doctrine has
strengthened the position and power of the **Imām** as the more or
less absolute leader of the community. It is thereby presupposed
that the ᶜ**ulamā',** those who know the precepts of religion, and the
imām as the leader of the community, cooperate. The state is not
absolute in itself. It is only a temporal rule organizing things to
give the **sharīᶜa** the most effective sanctions and coercive power.
Interestingly enough, Muḥammad ibn ᶜAbd al-Wahhāb does not speak
at all of the caliphate which, during his lifetime, was assumed to
be embodied in the Ottoman Sultan. The Wahhābīs' feeling was that
one could accept the rule of anyone who followed the Sharīᶜa' like
the Wahhābī **Imām** and they probably saw the Ottomans as usurpers
of the caliphate, but they never preached open rebellion against the
Ottoman rulers.

Jihād

More than any other Sunni thinker, including Ibn Taimīya,
Muḥammad ibn ᶜAbd al-Wahhāb elevated the **jihād** to one of the
principal activities in Islam. He directed it against all Muslims who
had forsaken the cause of Islam, not only against non-Muslims.
Three kinds of **jihād** are distinguished: against apostates who leave
Islam altogether, against dissenters who still recognise the
authority of the **Imām,** and against secessionists who sow disorder

or desert from the Islamic communty. 'Any Muslim who, for whatever reason, fell into conflict with their (the Wahhābīs') interpretation of Islam or challenged their authority was generally considered to be an apostate unbeliever, and was liable to the severest sanctions, although these were not clearly defined' (Helms 1981:99). Jihād was to be waged against all those who had committed **shirk**, infringed one of the cultic or moral prescriptions of Islam, and indulged in the cult of 'holy men' (Laoust 1939:529). But for the Wahhābī Muslim jihād is more than an incidental armed struggle; it represents a continuous endeavour:

As a member of the Islamic community, he struggles for an internal spiritual reform in the path of God against the profane aspects of his human existence while at the same time waging an external struggle against those who oppose his goal or the well-being of his religion (Helms 1981:96).

This holds true for other Muslims as well, but the Wahhābīs have taken the command very seriously. When jihād slackens Islam will degenerate. The Wahhābīs wage jihād, moreover, against dissension in the community, which they consider a basic evil and ascribe to the introduction of innovation in religion after the models established in the third century after the Hijra. The aim of jihād is to bring about the rule of the Word of God and it can take many forms besides that of armed conflict. Every Muslim in the Wahhābī community has the obligation to practice 'good council', that is, to correct his brothers (and sisters) fraternally if they have committed an infraction against religion, and to do his utmost to improve and strengthen the community. Among the tasks which the Imām must perform in the name of jihād are also the development of education, the issuing of decrees concerning communal life, the prevention of reprehensible actions or damage to people's property or honour.

   The conception of jihād just mentioned implied that superstitions and the cult of holy men were to be proceeded against with radical, violent methods appropriate to the rooting out of evil. Superstitions in Arabia covered in particular cultic practices related to trees, stones and caves. Already the prophet Muḥammad in the 7th century had called for all remnants of the pagan time of ignorance before him to be destroyed. Muḥammad ibn ᶜAbd al-Wahhāb did the same and his followers, too, speak of the time of ignorance before his reforms in the 18th century. The cult of 'holy men' was considered to be **shirk**, 'associationism', as the cult of idols instead of God. The holy men were defined not only as

those whom people considered saints and to whose tombs they
would go to implore blessings, but also Shaikhs of mystical brotherhoods claiming to have charismatic powers, and the **Imāms** of the
Shīᶜites and other descendants of the Prophet as the case might
be. Ridding the graves in cemetries of ornaments, domes or even
inscriptions, and the eradication of all forms of cult except the
worship of God were practices which spread the fame of the
Wahhābīs, besides their regular warfare in which women and
children were not necessarily spared. Thus they became known and
feared for the violence which they committed with religious zeal.

The **Imām** has to ensure that the Quranic punishments are
applied and that the religious rituals and obligations like worship,
fasting and religious taxation (**zakāt**) are well performed. Muḥammad
ibn ᶜAbd al-Wahhāb is unique in prescribing obligatory attendance
at public prayer and payment of **zakāt** even on windfall profits, for
instance in trade. Among Wahhābī ᶜulamā' voices have even been
raised to make the performance of the pilgrimage to Mecca obligatory for all those who have the means to perform it, an obligation
which should be enforced by the **Imām**.

Religious ethics

Of particular interest for the purity-orientedness of the movement
is the moral aspect of the doctrines of Muḥammad ibn ᶜAbd
al-Wahhāb. When preaching **tawḥīd** (Oneness, sc. of God) he had
two things in mind. It was in the first place the 'objective'
recognition of the oneness and almighty character of God, or the
acknowledgement that oneness in the proper sense only belongs to
God. In the second place it was the subjective 'appropriation' of
this objective oneness: the recognition of the oneness of adoration.
In this the believer subjectively accepts nothing and no one else
but God as his master, thus achieving both devotion to God alone,
and a unified moral consciousness proper to a person who takes the
utmost care only to serve God in his actions. This devotion of
oneself to God and this requirement of a devotion of life from the
community as a whole could and did lead to an intransigeant moral
rigorism as the dominant tone in Wahhābī society (Laoust
1939:31-532).

There is a rigid element in this religious devotion. Whereas
certain sūfīs have considered tawḥīd to be the continuous endeavour to realise mystical union, Muḥammad ibn ᶜAbd al-Wahhāb
taught in the 'puritanical' Hanbalite tradition that Oneness should

be understood subjectively as oneness of adoration: a complete abandonment, worship and glorification of God alone. For this reason Henri Laoust stresses the importance of the notion of ᶜibāda in the call of Muḥammad ibn ᶜAbd al-Wahhāb, which indicates total obedience to God, a free and methodical serving of God. God has created man to serve Him; and man, consequently, should continuously render a disciplined service to God alone, following the precepts which God himself has ordained and revealed through his Prophet. This service of God implies resignation of oneself to the sovereign will and decision of God, devotion through appropriate words and actions to the community, and avoidance of major sins. Above all, man should guard against any possible 'infiltration' of the heart by a hidden 'associationism' with the risk of something gaining an importance which is only due to God himself. Life becomes a continuous training, which is part of jihād, in sincere and total devotion to God, combined with meticulous observance of the prescriptions of the sacred Law (Laoust 1939:514-533).

In his doctrines Muḥammad ibn ᶜAbd al-Wahhāb stands in the line of a whole range of reformist thinkers along Hanbalite lines. Apart from Muhammad the Prophet himself, we may mention here the names of Ibn Taimiīya (1262-1328) and his pupil Ibn Qaiyim al-Jawzīya (d. 1350), of Abū Yaᶜlā al-Farrā' (d. 1066), Ibn Tūmart (d. 1130), Ibn ᶜAqīl (d. 1120), and the legal works of al-Hujawī and al-Mardāwī. Wahhābī doctrine has been severely criticised by a number of Sunni and Shīᶜite authors (Karout 1978). In the 20th century Muḥammad Rashīd Ridā came to its defence (Ridā 1344).

Achievements in the 18th and 19th centuries

Expansion

The first decades of the Wahhābī state of Darᶜīya were a period of endless struggle to bring Bedouin tribes under Saᶜūdī and Wahhābī authority. In 1755 the Emir and Imām ᶜAbd al-ᶜAzīz I (ruled 1766--1803), who is considered to have been the real founder of the first Wahhābī empire, occupied Riyad, driving out a bitter enemy of the Wahhābīs. After each conquest a garrison was installed consisting of well-paid leaders who showed religious zeal for the Wahhābī cause, while teachers and preachers were appointed to instruct the new subjects in the call. In larger places a Qadi and Mufti would be installed, in smaller places only a Qadi. In 1786 Nejd was under Wahhābī control and the Emir could think of building a larger Arab Sunni state where Islam was restored in its original purity, over against the eïsting Ottoman and Persian empires. The state expanded eastward with the submission of the Banū Khālid in al-Ahsā' on the Gulf, southward with the conquest of Nejran and northward with incursions into Iraq, often as reprisals against punitive expeditions sent from Basra and Baghdad at the order of the Ottoman authorities but which failed. On 21 April 1802 the Wahhābīs took Kerbela on a Shīᶜite religious holiday, profaning the shrine of Imām Husain, which was pillaged, and carrying out a massacre among the inhabitants.

The Hijaz.

With the Sherifs of Mecca, who since the Turkish evacuation of the Hijaz at the beginning of the 18th century had been masters of this important part of Arabia, relations were complex. Muḥammad ibn ᶜAbd al-Wahhāb had sent a deputation to Mecca to discuss his doctrine with the Meccan scholars of religion, claiming that the Call was not a heresy, that the destruction of domes over graves was a product of piety, and that intercession by saints (denied by the Wahhābīs) was not orthodox doctrine. As a result of this discussion the Wahhābī doctrine was recognised as in accord with the school of Ibn Hanbal and consequently had to be tolerated. Yet sometimes the Holy Places were forbidden to Wahhābīs or even to pilgrims who had traveled through Wahhābī territory at a time when the Wahhābīs were still declared to be enemies of true religion. In 1798, however, the Sherif of Mecca, Ghālib, was obliged to drop his ban simply because no pilgrims could reach Mecca overland except through Wahhābī territory. The situation and way of life of the inhabitants of Mecca and Medina has been described aptly by Alois Musil (1928:65):

'The profit derived from the numerous pilgrims and from the rich gifts they brought enabled the inhabitants of Mecca and al-Medina to live in luxury. These townsfolk had become accustomed to beautiful dress, many ornaments, and gay entertainments and could afford to smoke tobacco and drink not only coffee but intoxicating liquors. The Wahhābites intended to purge the holy cities of such dissipation and to train their inhabitants in modesty and simplicity. By accepting Wahhābite guidance the inhabitants of Mecca and al-Medina would have lost not merely their income and comforts but the respect with which they were regarded by the pilgrims. Loath to consent to such humiliation, they were, naturally enough, ready for war to protect their earthly well-being.'

It should also be borne in mind that the Hijazis, living in a province where agriculture was possible and where an urban culture existed in and around Holy Cities considered to be the centre of the Islamic world, tended to look down on the Bedouin of Nejd. They considered them little better than barbarians, lacking proper culture and adhering to a form of Islam which was either riddled with paganism or so rigidly puritanical as to frighten off anyone who enjoyed a more comfortable lifestyle and a higher level of education. Muslims living in towns, villages and oases could not but fear the prowess and lust for riches and power of Bedouin, Wahhābīs or not.

Subsequent events are well-known and need only be mentioned in a few words. In 1803 ᶜAbd al-ᶜAzīz took Mecca, which had been evacuated by Ghālib. Idolatrous practices were rooted out and persons suspected of being associated with them were killed. The garrison which ᶜAbd al-ᶜAzīz had left in the town was then in its turn largely massacred by the inhabitants. The new Emir, Saᶜūd (1803-1814), took Medina by the end of 1804 and retook Mecca in February 1806 after a siege. Mecca was now pillaged and Medina, which had tried to revolt, underwent the same fate.

In the Hijaz the practices of the Wahhābites were forced on both the inhabitants and the pilgrims. The holy sepulchres were destroyed or locked up, pilgrimages to them stopped, gold, silver, and silk ornaments forbidden, music silenced, and both coffee and tobacco proscribed. The beautiful Mahmal litters, which had arrived every year from Egypt and Syria accompanied by a band of music, were denied admittance lest they incite the pilgrims to idolatry and remind the inhabitants of the supremacy of the sultan in Constantinople (Musil 1928:266-267).

Reaction

The fact that the Ottoman government no longer exercised actual authority over the Holy Places, that Wahhābī doctrines were now officially recognised in the Hijaz, that the Friday sermon was no longer said in the name of the Sultan or Caliph in Instanbul, and that pilgrim caravans organised by the Ottoman authorities were forbidden to enter Mecca demanded a reaction. The new state was growing dangerously. In April 1806 an attack on another Shiᶜite holy city, Nejef, could just be thwarted, but in July 1810 the Wahhābī army stood at the gates of Damascus and in the same year took Asir south of the Hijaz. The energetic Sultan Maḥmūd II, who had come to power in Istanbul in July 1808, coordinated his action with Muḥammad ᶜAlī who had been the strong man in Egypt since 1811, and two major expeditions from Egypt to the Hijaz and from there to Nejd, respectively in 1811-1815 and 1816-1818 crushed the Wahhābī state. On 9 September 1818, after a siege of more than five months, Darᶜīya was taken and completely destroyed, as were other towns and villages of the Wahhābīs including their natural resources of palm-trees. Many people were killed and all the members of the Saᶜūd and the Shaikh families were brought to Egypt as prisoners; only a single person succeeded in escaping. The Imām ᶜAbd Allāh ibn Saᶜūd together with some close collaborators were beheaded in public in Istanbul on 17 December 1818.

Infrastructural foundations of the Wahhābi state

The history of the Wahhābī movement in Arabia is not only that of Muḥammad ibn ᶜAbd al-Wahhāb's doctrines and their impact but also that of the āl (family of) Saᶜūd. In the foregoing we paid much attention to Wahhābī ideology and its expansion. It is time now to consider the power base and the expansion of the Saᶜūd family, in alliance with Wahhābī ideology. We follow here in broad lines the analysis offered by David A. McMurray in an unpublished paper (McMurray 1983).

The first hypothesis is that there had been for centuries long-distance trade between the Gulf coast and the Hijaz through the Arabian desert as a result of which a large settled population had built up in Nejd. When the Europeans, however, in the 16th and 17th century started to transport goods from the East, either by the sea route or overland via Basra and Baghdad to Aleppo, the trans-Arabian trade declined rapidly. Money shortage brought about a decline of the oasis towns and the possibilities of the nomadic tribes, in response to which Nejd fell back on the elementary sources of production. These were oasis-agriculture and pastoralism (with a certain interdependence), together with the well-known bedouin raiding of each other and the oases. This raiding probably increased to the extent that trade decreased. Nejd was divided into a number of petty Emirates based in the various towns which were ruled by powerful families. There was no central authority and the power of the Emirs was no longer based on tribal connections but on the settled population and on their control over the existing trade and agriculture in the region. These Emirs gradually increased their military force in order to maintain control over their regions.

The second hypothesis is that the āl Sa^{c}ūd succeeded in establishing a state capable of monopolizing the use of force to extract the available sources of income by agricultural and pastoral surplus, by tributes, and by direct appropriation through raiding. It was military power which was at the basis of the Wahhābī state, and conversion to Wahhābism meant in fact economic and political subservience to the state of Dar^{c}īya.

Dar^{c}īya expanded its authority in three ways: first of all by open warfare; expeditions were financed through the confiscation of all booty. Secondly the oasis dwellers were terrorized. If they submitted and gave their allegiance to Dar^{c}īya they only had to pay taxes; but if they resisted their date groves were cut down and they were deprived of their livelihood. And in the third place propaganda was made among the nomadic tribes. They had to be convinced of the advantages of submitting themselves, paying tribute but then also joining in the division of spoils after 'razzias', which had become a state enterprise.

Consolidation of the state

The āl Sa^{c}ūd succeeded in building up and centralizing state power and consolidating the state, at the price of disrupting tribal structures. They managed to do this in various ways:

1) There was no standing army which might have become an opposing power. After each campaign the army was disbanded and only at the outset of a new campaign did a conscription of soldiers, both from the oases and all the tribes, take place. Besides this, the Sa^{c}ūd family established a private militia of volunteers from the tribes which was at their disposal.

2) Local forms of power and control were broken up. Shaikhs who resisted were simply sent to Dar^{c}īya and replaced by an appointed kinsman; the military leaders had to reside in Dar^{c}īya; local Qadis were replaced by trained appointees paid solely from state funds; local treasuries were placed under the administration of clerks from Dar^{c}īya. Dependency on Dar^{c}īya was enhanced by the fact that the tax collectors were all sent out from Dar^{c}īya, and that through the appointed Qadis there was a uniform dispensation of justice.

3) The fact that leadership remained in the āl Sa^{c}ūd through inheritance guaranteed continuity of leadership and accumulation of power. It also meant a break with traditional tribal practice where a new Shaikh was chosen only after the death of the last one, so that continuity could not be anticipated.

4) All the territory under Wahhābī control was pacified by means of measures like collective punishment, fines imposed on all parties involved in a conflict, and the substitution of the payment of blood money for revenge as far as possible. Such measures were applied.

5) The state assured internal security with rigorous means, maintaining law and order. This created an almost unheard - of situation of peace, which may have been an impetus for many a conversion of groups who would be able to live without fear of raiding or attack.

6) The state established dependable sources of revenue. Treasures were brought in as booty; zakāt was collected everywhere; taxation was levied in the conquered territories. Areas on the periphery of Wahhābī control paid tribute to be left in peace, while dues were levied on commercial traffic and even on pirating in the Gulf. Commerce was encouraged in several ways (except that trading with non-Wahhābīs was prohibited). But above all, the state was economically based largely on the expropriation of agricultural land. All territories that revolted were confiscated by the state and there was an immense expansion of state lands in the oases, which were agricultural. This must have provided the main source of income of the Wahhābī state.

The state, however, did not only take; it also gave. There was a sophisticated system of revenue collection from pastoralists as well as settled agriculturalists, but also of redistribution not only for the tasks of the state but also to relieve the hardship of the poor, to compensate losses suffered by soldiers, and so on. Even if Nejd did not reach a very high level of development there was a huge improvement in living conditions compared to those of fifty years earlier. The British envoy Capt. Sadleir, who crossed the desert at the time of Ibrāhīm's pitiless devastations (ca. 1819), describes how much cultivated land (not only date palms) there had been and how the ruins witnessed to extensive buildings in the towns. The state of the āl Sa^cūd had an economic basis which was self-sufficient and lent force to the spread of Wahhābī ideology.

McMurray (1983) concludes by saying that the Wahhābī movement arose in reaction to the decline of international trade routes through Nejd. It developed its social structure in opposition to the tribal current in Arabia: tribal loyalty was replaced by loyalty to the state and to the Wahhābī creed. There was mass conscription and the Sa^cūds' private guard was not kin-based. State law was enforced over tribal law and state collection of tribute was enforced over local tribute arrangements. Finally, thanks to the rule of inheritance, leadership within the Sa^{C}ūd family was institutionalized. As a result the new state was able to dominate both oases and tribes.

Survival

From 1818 to 1821 there was nothing left of Wahhābī rule or religious authority. But in 1821 Turkī, a cousin of the late ^{C}Abd Allāh ibn Sa^{C}ūd, succeeded in restoring the Wahhābī state round the new capital, Riyad, which had not been destroyed by the Egyptians. Turkī was assassinated in 1834. His successor, Faisal ibn Sa^{C}ūd, succeeded during his second period of rule (1843-1865) in reconquering the major part of Nejd and establishing his authority over the greater part of the Gulf. As in former times this meant acknowledgement of Wahhābī rule and payment of an annual tribute. Faisal ibn Sa^{C}ūd gave ^{C}Abd Allāh b. Rashīd (r. 1834-1847) the governership of Hail where he established another Wahhābī state, the Shammār confederation.

A long rivalry between the Banū Rashīd in Hail and the Banū Sa^{C}ūd in Dar^{C}īya ended when the former took Riyad in 1884 and when the last members of the Sa^{C}ūd dynasty sought refuge with Shaikh Mubārak of Kuwait after an unsuccessful insurrection in 1891. The Banū Rashīd applied the Wahhābī precepts less rigorously and more selectively than the Sa^{C}ūds had done. They exercised tolerance in particular with respect to the almost independent Bedouin tribes of the desert (Philby 1930, Winder 1965).

It was only under the leadership of ^{C}Abd al-^{C}Azīz II, commonly called Ibn Sa^{C}ūd (1879-1953), that Wahhābī doctrines and practices were revitalized and the Wahhābī state was restored in a new form. As a result the Kingdom of Saudi Arabia was established in 1932.

References

Caskel, W.
    1929   Altes und neues Wahhābitentum, *Ephémérides Orientales* 32 (Leipzig).
Diffelen, R.W. van
    1927   *De leer der Wahhabieten*, Leiden: E.J. Brill.
Hartmann, R.
    1924   Die Wahhābiten, *Zeitschrift der Deutschen Morgen-ländischen Gesellschaft* N.F. 3, pp. 176-213.

Helms, C.M.
1981   *The Cohesion of Saudi Arabia; Evolution of Political Identity,* Baltimore and London: The Johns Hopkins University Press.
Karout, Z.I.
1978   *Anti-Wahhābītische Polemik im iX Jahrhundert,* diss. Bonn.
Laoust, Henri
1939   *Essai sur les doctrines sociales et politiques de Taki-Din Ahmad b. Taimiya: Canoniste hanbalite né à Harran en 661/1362, mort à Damas en 728/1328,* Cairo: Imprimerie de l'Institut Français d'Archéologie Orientale.
1965   *Les schismes dans l'Islam; Introduction à une étude de la religion musulmane,* Paris: Payot.
McMurray, David, A.
1983   The rise of the Wahhābī and Sanusi movements. Unpublished paper, Department of Anthropology, University of Texas at Austin, Spring 1983 (36 + 4 pp.)
Margoliouth, D.S.
1953   Wahhābīya, in: H.A.R. Gibb and J.H. Kramers, ed. *Shorter Encyclopaedia of Islam,* Leiden: E.J. Brill, pp. 618-621.
Musil, A.
1928   *Northern Nejd: A Topographical Itinerary,* New York: The American Society.
Philby, H.St.J.B.
1930   *Arabia.* New York: Charles Scribner's Sons.
Puin, G.R.
1973   Aspekte der Wahhābītischen Reform, auf der Grundlage von Ibn Gennāms 'Raudhat al-afkār', in: *Studien zum Minderheitenproblem im Islam,* Band 1, Bonn, Seminar für Orientalische Sprachen, pp. 45-99.
Rentz, G.S.
1948   Muḥammad ibn ᶜAbd al-Wahhāb (1703/04-1792) and the Beginning of the Unitarian Empire in Arabia. Unpublished Ph.D. dissertation, University of California, Berkeley.
Rida, Muḥammad Rashīd
1344   *Al-Wahhābīya wa'l-Hijāz,* Cairo.
Schacht, J.
1928   Zur Wahhābītischen Literatur, *Zeitschrift für Semitistik und verwandte Gebiete* 6, pp. 200-213.
Winder, R.B.
1965   *Saudi Arabia in the Nineteenth Century,* New York: St. Martin's Press & London, Melbourne and Toronto.

Purity and statecraft:
the Fulani jihād and its empire
Walter E.A. van Beek

THE FULANI EMPIRE OF SOKOTO
AT ITS GREATEST EXTENT

—·—·— border of Empire   0   50   100 miles

AIR

GAO

DAMAGARAM

KANEM

LAKE CHAD

GWANDU
Gwandu
Sokoto
SOKOTO

GURMA

NIGER

Zampara

KATSINA

KANO

BORNU

Kuka

ZARIA

BAUCHI

Mandara

Biu

Kapsiki

NUPE

Unconquered
Plateau
Tribes

BENUE

Yola

YORUBALAND

ADAMAWA

BENIN

IBOLAND

After Johnston 1967

Purity and statecraft. The nineteenth century Fulani jihād of North Nigeria
Walter E.A. van Beek

Introduction

Shading himself from the fire Teri Sunu keeps peering into the dark skies, looking for the trim, bleak sickle of the new moon. His friends around the fire call him back: 'No use looking for the sky, for the new moon. This years' Ramadan will not start until the Sokoto Imam has announced it. Come and listen to the 'poste radio'. Through the cracking and whistling noise a fulfuldé speaking voice is heard, announcing that the moon sickle has been spotted. The 1972 Ramadan has started, in Sokoto, but also in the village of Mogodé, tucked away in the Mandara hills of North Cameroon some 1000 kilometers from Sokoto, as the raven flies.

Such a scene of a pagan community listening to their old Muslim enemy, the Fulani, can be witnessed throughout West-Africa. They may have been scourged by these Fulani in the last two centuries, the fact remains that these isolated communities have been drawn into one of the largest state building movements of Afrika. It was a holy war, a movement to purify Islam, that brought this about, the jihād of Usman dan Fodio.

My aim in this paper is to show why such 'pagan' peoples as the Kapsiki were involved in a puritanic movement, why, in fact, they had to be drawn in through the process of state formation that in itself was a corollary of the Islamic puritan movement. I hope to show that a major impetus of the state building process resides in a complex set of factors, of which the drive for purification is a very important one, but that the outcome of the empire formation for a larger part depends on non-ideological factors. Eventually, the impact of these factors tends to reshape the puritanical movement into an administration, the practical exigencies of which will destroy the original ideals. The quest for purity ends in an imperial organization.

The pre-jihād situation

The history of Northern Nigeria up to the 19th century is dominated by the Hausa city states. Though of one tribal origin, the Hausa never formed a coherent political body. Small states like Kebbi, Zamfara, Gobir and Zazzau tried to gain a lasting ascendancy over one another, and through this internecine warfare, invariably found themselves under the actual or nominal dominion of other powers.

When during the 14th and 15th centuries the Hausa states grew ever more populous and wealthy, they became a potential source of booty and tribute for the eastern Bornu empire that was situated around lake Chad. In the sixteenth century Songhai, operating from Gao, was able to conquer Hausaland, as the different Sarkin (chiefs) of the states failed to unite against the common enemy. The tenuous Songhai hold over the area was interrupted by internal war between the states, and in the 18th century by the short apogee of the Kwararafa Jukun kingdom from the South. From 1734 the area was under Bornu command again (Johnston 1967:14).

The Hausa states, as well as their conquerors, can be best characterised as 'predator states', relying on raids and wars to 'harvest their crop of slaves', the spoils of war feeding the warrior aristocracies (Smaldone 1977:12). Captured slaves were needed for cash crop production and for long distance commerce, in which they were exchanged for horses and - later - guns. Thus, the means of destruction - armies - served as a means of state production (Goody 1968). This dependency on slave raiding is a central issue in the understanding of the results of the jihād, and will be discussed in greater detail later. On this basis the Hausa had built an elaborate state apparatus, with a great number of officials and a strict hierarchical ranking. In the city artesan guilds, often of slave extraction too, were an important part of the society. In the periphery of the city the cultivators raised their crops in a serf-like dependency on the overlords.

Between the largely settled Hausa cultivators, the Fulani lived with their cattle. This tribe, one of the great enigma's of West Africa, is central in the story of nineteenth century puritan Islam. From the tenth century onwards (Hatch 1970) they wandered from their Futa Jalon homeland westwards, gradually drifting into Hausaland at least before the sixteenth century (Johnston 1967:24), arriving in some area's before the Hausa (Webster & Boahen 1967). Eventually they drifted east of lake Chad, even as far as Khartoum. Theirs is the story of the nineteenth century Emirates, theirs is the story of the **jihād**; they purified West-African Islam. Together they number over 6 million, spread out unevenly over the whole of the Sudan belt of West Africa. Their largest concentrations were and are in their Futa homelands, in Mali and in Northern Nigeria. In Hausaland they numbered about 30% of the Hausa population (Hatch 1970, Shaw 1978).

The third party in the political set up were the slaves. Hausa society and to a lesser extent Fulani society fed on captives. Hausa courts were replete with slaves filling in all possible slots in the organization, even occupying important positions like minister of the interior or chief of all slaves (Smith 1978:138, 141). Such slave officials could own slaves themselves. The slaves outside the courts were responsible for most of the staple crop production and made up a considerable part of foot soldiers in the Hausa army (Smith 1960:134).

The fourth party comprised the pagan groups living in the margin of the city state or - later - on the fringes of the empire. The Kapsiki of our introduction are part of this category, as are the numerous tribes of the central Nigerian plateau. These are the people who were habitually raided for slaves; though they never converted to Islam, they do form an important part of the empire, as they form the slave reserve needed for the functioning of the economic and political apparatus.

The Fulani at the end of the eighteenth century by no means presented an undifferentiated unit. Not only were they composed of several large, politically independent clans, many of them did not live as cattle nomads (Monad 1975, Stenning 1959, 1966). In the margin of the cattle raising Fulani and their (ex-)slaves who either raised cattle or cultivated staple crops, the Fulani harboured a large number of scholars, men versed in the Quran and Islamic law, who preached and taught sunnitic Islam of the Maliki school (Lewis 1966:9). In fact, Fulani society was able to sustain an astonishingly large number of Muslim scholars, who wandered with the herdsmen, and - if family circumstances permitted them - took off for their pilgrimage (Last 1967:lxxviii). They had few possessions, being nomads, but nurtured the books they had as priceless treasures. In fact, besides being able to recite the entire Quran in Arabic, they possessed - and knew by heart - whatever book they could get hold of. They travelled extensively to each other, and took years to be taught at the house of another scholar. Islamic teachers of great repute, were sought after throughout the Sudan, and their pupils travelled over thousands of kilometers to them.

This was facilitated by three factors. First, the geographical setting of the Sudan zone makes travel very easy, either on horseback or on foot. Secondly, wherever a scholar went in this zone, he always found fellow Fulani around, to help and house him, and to listen to his teachings and preachings, greatly appreciating his presence. Thirdly, all scholars spoke and wrote in at least three languages, Fulani, Hausa and Arabic. Thus, the whole range of Arabic learning was open to them; in fact they almost routinely travelled to the great Islamic centers of teaching. One example from that period may illustrate this: The famous traveller Barth reports meeting in 1852 in Baghirmi (now in Chad), an elderly and completely blind Fulani called Sambo.

'I could scarcely have expected to find in this out-of-the way place a man not only versed in all branches of Arabic literature, but who had even read (nay, possessed a manuscript of) those portions of Aristotle and Plato which had been translated into .... Arabic, and who possessed the most intimate knowledge of the countries which he had visited.'

This man had studied many years in El Azhar in Egypt, in Zebid in Yemen, famous for the science of logarithms, from Bagdad to Andalos (Barth 1857, III:373). So the intellectual scene of the era was remarkably open, people travelling extensively, writing books in the classical Arabic tradition with the full support of their cattle herding tribesmen (Last 1967: lxxvi).

This is mainly a Fulani picture, though Touareg scholars (Norris 1975:146 ff) and some Hausa scholars (Smith 1978:28ff) fit in too. Despite wars that raged between the Touareg and Fulani at several times, the scholars did keep their contact. The majority of Hausa scholars however, Muslim too, were officials in the court of the Sarkin (kings) of the various states. Their allegiance to Islam (as was to be stated with great vigour by the reformers) was compromised by this dependency. The Sarkin overlords had multiple religious loyalties, being at the same time Muslim Sultan and cult official for the numerous pagan cults. Thus, in the eyes of the Fulani **mallam** (scholar) at least, the Hausa scholars were tainted, an issue on which we will return later.

The Shehu

Despite the range of learning and travelling, most of the religious training was done by kinsmen, uncles or cousins; if possible the father or an an elder brother. The Fulani, however cosmopolitans as they were, remained and still are very clan conscious. Thus, the Toronkawa clan, one large Fulani clan which is closest to the Tucolor of Futa Toro, as a whole has had a tremendous impact on West African history. They are the theologians of this **jihād**, but also of other holy wars: they are the prime movers of at least four empires (Webster & Boahen 1967, Adeleye 1974, Clarke 1982).

The **jihād** that resulted in the Sokoto empire is dominated by one Toronkawa family, that of Usman dan Fodio, a towering figure who is practically a national hero-saint in Nigeria (Shagari & Boyd 1977). Born on 15 December 1754 in the realm of Gobir, the most powerful Hausa state at that time, he lived most of his life as a nomadic scholar, wandering with his kinsmen and their herds. Degel, close to the Gobir centre, was the area of his early years. In his youth he was taught by his father Muhammed Fodio, by an uncle and a distant relative. The latter's teaching took Usman to Agadesh, a renowned center of learning in that era. There he met the most influential Muslim scholar of the late 18th century, el hadj Jibril b. Umar, not a Fulani but of Berber origin (Last 1967:5). Jibril preached a revived, vigorous and uncompromising Islam; his message echoed the Wahhābite teachings, that were gaining acceptance in the Arab peninsula those very years (see Waardenburg, this volume). He had become acquainted with those ideas during his first pilgrimage. When Jibril left for his second journey to Mekka, Usman was called back by his father, so the young man could not perform a pilgrimage. In later years family responsibilities again prohibited Usman from his hadj; this 'failure' was a lifelong regret to him. In many poems he expressed his deep desire to visit the holy places, to walk in the traces of the prophet and to worship Allah as a pilgrim (Last 1967:212). His multiplying commitments kept him from this journey, which would have lasted between eight and ten years.

Through these teachers Usman was introduced to the Quran, to the sunnitic tradition and to the finely tuned jurisprudence and judicial reasoning of the Shari'a in the Maliki school. In addition to this orthodox schooling, he was initiated into Sufism, to one of the many strains of Islamic mysticism i.e. the teachings of al-Qadiri, the great Baghdad mystic Si Mohammed Abdel Qader al Djilani (Triaud 1969:155; Hiskett 1973:60). Among the many 'mystic ways' this Qadiriya order was one the dominant ones of in West Africa. Its spread and influence date from the times of al Maghili in the late fifteenth century (Hiskett 1973:5); from that time the spread and consolidation of Islam went hand in hand with the spread of Sufism (Abun-Nasr 1965:6-7). Qadiriya Sufism, with its strong combination of scholarship, ascetism and mysticism, was to mold the teaching of the Fodio family for generations. After the establishment of the Caliphate (the later phase of the Sokoto empire) the Tijaniya order would encroach upon Qadiriya holdings (Triaud 1969:167; Abdun-Nasr 1965:138 ff.), by means of the empire el Hadj Umar was to carve out from Segu, as well as from within (Triaud 1969:168). Still, Qadiriya remained dominant in Sokoto (Martin 1976).

About the same time the Shehu (which is the usual indication of Usman dan Fodio in the literature, meaning Shaikh in Hausa) was conferred his **ijaza** (licence to preach), a new ruler, Bawa, attained the Hausa throne of Gobir (Johnston 1967:28). As a strong-willed Sarkin, he was hated by the Fulani because of the severity with which he ordered the cattle tax (**jangali**) to be assessed and collected. Many Fulani, refusing to pay this tax, had their cattle seized (Hopen 1958:10). The animosity and friction which this caused, was by no means the first problem between the Gobirawa (Hausa of Gobir) and the Fulani, but proved to be one of the major factors shaping Shehu's course (Johnston 1957: 29). Like many frictions to come, this one was immediately translated into a religious issue, i.e. the absence of Shari'a legitimacy to levy such a cattle tax (Hiskett 1973: 143-4). Shehu Usman pointed out that this tax was not one of the seven forms of taxations authorized by Islamic law; it could be legal if and only if it was a kind of **jiziya**, a tax levied on non-Muslims, as the majority of the Fulani were non-Muslims. However, in that case it should have been a poll-tax and not a cattle tax (Johnston 1967:31).

The Shehu, who was just twenty when he started on his preaching and teaching tours throughout the region, quickly became an established authority on theology and law. Roaming widely from his little township of Degel, which was only a hundred kilometers from the Gobir capital Alkalawa, the Shehu made preaching tours in Zamfara and Kebbi, going as far south as Illo and north till Daura (Smith 1968:143; Hiskett 1973:44). In these other Hausa states, the power of Bawa was much smaller; some of them were vassals of

Gobir, while the eastern ones paid tribute to Bornu. In these tours the Shehu preached the fundamentals of sunnitic Islam: the unity of God, the foundation and pillars of the faith, righteousness and reward in paradise, sin and punishment. As each Islamic theologian he gave minute instructions in ritual and judicial matters. The proper ways of ablutions, prayer and fasting, tithes and alms, oaths and marriage contracts were stressed (Hiskett 1973:49ff). When the Shehu's large successes in Kebbi and Zamfara became known in Al-kalawa, he was invited to the Gobir court. In this as well as later audiences the Shehu took the Sarkin to the task of being a true Muslim prince, to abstain from oppression of fellow-Muslims, and to shun any comprise in religion. Rejecting large alms the ruler offered, the Shehu managed to wrangle some liberties and indulgencies from the Gobir court e.g. liberty to preach freely to all people, Fulani and Hausa, and the alleviation of taxes. The fact that the 75 year old Bawa granted these demands, showed his eagerness to incorporate the new upstart preacher into his dominion, in order to leave a stable state for the next Sultan (Last 1967:7). From this time any person wearing a turban (the token of a Muslim identity) would be respected and no one would be kept from praying or preaching, a major result for the Shehu.

In the next six years Bawa's sons Ya'kub reigned and died in battle, and the might of Gobir waned because of a succession by weak rulers. In the mean time, the Shehu became the nexus of a slowly growing Community, numbering several hundreds of people, who formed the hard core of fervent believers in the later jihād, and whose influence through contact with visiting mallams and through teaching tours far exceeded their numerical importance. In a later stage the Sarkin is reported to have commented on the Shehu's waxing power: 'My father has allowed a seedling to wax, and now it has grown to large to uproot' (Smaldone 1977: 34).

The start of the jihād

Triggered by increasing friction between Hausa rulers and Fulani Muslims, and fired by a strong conviction and a clear sense of vocation, the Shehu set out to attack religious laxity in the Gobir court. In one of his most famous books, he accused the Sarkin court of a great number of serious transgressions, which no Muslim prince should indulge in. These were: officiating in idolatrous rites, non-observance of proper marriage rules, indulgence in heathen divination practices, enslavement of Muslims, alliance with pagan groups, non-observance of modesty, drinking alcoholic beverages, prostitution, and - of course - illegitimate taxes (Johnston 1967:31 ff). The rulers also forced people to serve in the army even though they were Muslims (Clarke 1982:115). The gist of his accusations, in this as well as in later cases, was that the Shari'a was not the basis of official law. A proper **Dar-al-Islam** should follow the Shari'a. To establish this was the single most important purpose of the Shehu's life. He followed three strategies consecutively: reform his fellow Fulani, reform the Hausa court and when the first was completed and the last one failed, to wage the holy war.

So an important 'weapon' in the impending **jihād**, was the Shehus pen. The Shehu, his brother Abdulla, his son Mohammed Bello, his first wife and several of his daughters were accomplished writers and poets in the classical Arabic tradition. The Shehu through his poems recorded his objections to the Hausa rulers, his experiences and his eventual call to the **jihād**. Apart from that, he wrote over fifty scholarly works, discussing doctrinal and judicial matters with local scholars, outlining the proper way for everyday life, explaining the principles of Sufism. The great majority of these works, ranging in size from five folios to substantive thick volumes, was aimed at the Fulani, at raising the standard of Islam (Last 1967: 9). Most books are written in Arabic, and most poems in Fulfulde. From his Hausa writings, little has survived (Hiskett 1973:37).

In accordance with the prophecies of Al-Maghili, people at that time expected the Mahdi, as several local prophets had indicated the years 1200-1204 (1786-1790) for the Mahdi to arrive. Throughout his later life, the Shehu was habitually considered as the Mahdi, though he took great pains to deny it. He did believe the Mahdi traditions, which are perfectly in harmony with sunnitic teaching, but he considered himself one of the forerunners of the Mahdi (Hiskett 1973:122). However, as long as the actual fighting took place the Shehu did not deny his Mahdi-ship too vigorously, as it provided an additional motivation for his people. After the decisive victory, Usman made it clear that neither the advent of the Mahdi nor the End of time were close at hand (Clarke 1982: 120).

While living his austere life in the open countryside of Degel, trying to exhort his fellow Fulani and reform his ever more hostile Hausa ruler, the Shehu in about 1794 had some mystic experiences which helped him shape his further course in life. He reports having seen the saints, and being invested with 'the sword of truth' to use against the enemies of Allah, while his son Mohammed Bello was specially singled out to fight the **jihād** (Last 1967: 10). Though the **jihād** would not start for another decennium, this message undoubtedly assisted in persuading the Shehu's Community that Hausa rule would not be changed by preaching alone.

After a rapid succession of some Gobir Sultans after the death of Bawa in 1795, Yunfa, a former pupil of the Shehu (Last 1967:43), was elected to the throne. Despite their good personal relationship, Yunfa tried to get rid of the Shehu, first by an assassination attempt, then by mounting persecution against the Fulani. His policy wavered with the varying pressures at court. Though at one time he retracted a predecessor's proclamation that forbade preaching Islam, conversion and the wearing of the turban (Last 1967:12), the prevailing mood of his court and the exigencies of his war with Zamfara increasingly turned him against the scholars of the Community. He even sold Muslims into slavery, a capital offense in the eyes of the Shehu (Last 1967:14). After an unfortunate accident between Fulani and the Gobirawa of Yunfa the Shehu's Community fled from Degel to the western border of Gobir, in Gundu. Here they could count on their support from Kebbi and could build their first stronghold, rallying their forces for the cause of the 'Community'. In doing this the Shehu followed the classical pattern of Mohammeds **hijra** i.e. the move to Medina. As Mohammed's exile starts the Muslim calendar, the exile of the Shehu was considered as the start of the **jihād**, and as such of the Sokoto empire.

The sources indicate that the Shehu was at best a reluctant **mujahedin**, who did not seek the holy war (Hiskett 1977:73). On the other hand he did not eschew it. When circumstances temporarily turned against the Community, he proved to be the staunchest supporter of the chosen way. In this he may have been bolstered by the success two Muslim reformers had had a few years earlier in the Fulani/Torankawa homelands Futa Jalon and Futa Toro (Trimingham 1968:161-162). Anyway, people came flocking to the Shehu in his bush outpost of Gudu, and the Community soon grew to ominous proportions, as the Gobir Sultan saw it. After some dalliances Yunfa declared war on the Community; in response the Community in a historic meeting choose the Shehu as its formal leader, as Commander of the Faithful, **Amir al-Mumīnin**, and raised the standard of the **jihād** (Johnston 1967:42). The first battle, at Tabkin Kwatto - since then a pilgrimage center for the Fulani - settled the course of the **jihād**. Against all odds the Fulani resisted the shock of the Hausa cavalry, and rooted the much stronger Gobirawa army. In Bello's own succinct words:

'The Lord broke the army of the godless, so that they fell back, and in their flight they were scattered.... We followed at their heels and slew them that they perished.... All day we pursued them and only at dusk we did return to say the evening prayer and to give thanks to God, the Lord of Creation.' (Bello, cited in Johnston 1967:46.)

The slightly apologetic note that they omitted some prayers, is typical for the strict observance of the rites in the Community.

From this victory omwards the course of the **jihād** was by no means easy. A kind of guerilla warfare developed in which the **mujahedeen** suffered some severe setbacks (Smaldone 1977:38) but in the end they succeeded in defeating Gobir. They took its capital Alkalawa, and killed Yunfa. From there, they started to build their own empire. The crucial issue was the overthrow of Hausa Gobir, called 'the long Campaign', which took from 1804 till 1808; during those years the fate of the **jihād** hung in balance at least three times (Johnston 1967:56).

The reasons for the military success of the Fulani are varied. First the political situation of Gobir never had been strong in itself, as it heavily relied upon slaves and allies for warfare. The Shehu's generals, his son Bello and his brother Abdullah, managed to separate Gobir from all its allies before delivering their final blow. Secondly, though both armies largely depended upon cavalry, the decisive factor in many early battles have been the range, precision and cold-bloodedness of the Fulani archers (Smaldone 1977:25-30). Thirdly, the Fulani generals, despite their incidental vacillations and mistakes, were on the whole much more skillful than their Hausa colleagues. Finally, success came from the general prerequisites of a successful guerilla war: insurgence throughout a vast political arena at the same time, reliance on local domestic production for food and arms, weapons captured from the enemy, and above all a sense of mission, of extraordinary commitment. It is this commitment, the deep conviction of carrying on a **jihād** in the name of God, that made success possible in guerilla warfare. Through the simple act of passing on a **jihād** flag the Shehu could sent forth soldier-scholars to remote areas to spread the rebellion. It is through this commitment that the Fulani generals in every possible instance took the initiative, taking the enemy off guard (Smaldone 1977:34-35). This kind of self abnegating abandonment to the cause of Allah in fact was a major factor in later battles. Though they had only a few dozen horses in their first battle, the Fulani rapidly developed a large cavalry force, which proved decisive in their flexible military strategy. Fighting a **jihād** was fighting on horseback, shock-fighting. Such a cavalry charge, as the one depicted below can only be fought well when death in the battlefield has its own immediate and superlative rewards.

The Cavalry Charge (from Hiskett 1973:85)

Pagan groups, which either as slaves or as allies, fought in the Hausa armies, were invariably overwhelmed by this style of fighting. Their own tactics aim at preserving their own life and at limiting losses more than annihilating the enemy (van Beek 1987).

The same conviction did hold for any military engagement: major battles against Hausa Sultans were **jihād,** but also small skirmishes against insurgents once the empire was established. Even slave raiding among pagans was considered a **jihād.** So each and every campaign was legitimated by the full force of doctrine resulting in a maximum motivation of the soldiers (Smaldone 1977:35).

Building an empire

After the fall of Alkalawa, the **jihād** entered its second stage. Scholar-soldiers carried the banners of the **jihād,** blessed by the Shehu, to the far reaches of Hausaland and beyond. In the period between 1808 and 1812 the theater of war shifted towards the west, east and south, establishing the **Dar-al-Islam** in Bauchi, Gurma, Daura, Kebbi, Zamfara, and Adamawa (see map). Sokoto was built by

Bello as a capital in 1809, as the twin capital of Gwandu (Johnston 1977:56ff).

Building the Caliphate of Sokoto was building the **Dar-al-Islam** and the early Caliphate of Mohammed's successors was the major inspiration of the leaders. The Shehu, bearing the title of **Khalifa**, was not only the undisputed leader of Northern Nigeria, but as **Amir al-Mumīnin** was considered the supreme leader of all Muslims. Though some Islamic doctrines only allow for one supreme Imam (Gibb 1957: 55) there is ample jurisprudence for tolerating two Caliphs as long as they are sufficiently separated in time and space (Last 1967:46-47). In the middle of the nineteenth century, West Africa knew six supreme Imams: Ahmad of Masina, el hadj Umar at Segu, the Askia of Songhai, the Mai of Bornu, the Shehu of Sokoto and the Sultan of Ahir at Agadesh. This proliferation of supreme commanders not' only reflects the loose organization of Islamic institutions in general, but the political situations in the nineteenth century Sahel-Sudan zone too.

Within the empires the same organizational characteristics prevailed. The Emirates carved out by the local **jihād** delegated from Sokoto were under nominal control from the capital only. The Emirs fought their own wars without initial help from the central government, rallied their own following of faithful Fulani, negotiated for allies and ransacked the pagan strongholds in search of slaves. Being scholars of some renown each of them, they formed their own schools, wrote their own books and established their own **Dar-al-Islam**. They invariably and by all means most sincerely ascribed to the religious supremacy of the Shehu - and his successors - and thus to the rightful ascendancy of the central Sokoto government. However, factual rapports between Sokoto and the Emirates were few. The most important ones were the regular levies in wealth and slaves that had to go to Sokoto, and the right of Sokoto to choose a successor for a deceased Emir. Both rights were jealously guarded by the central government and were reciprocated with military assistance when needed and with religious support at all times (Last 1967:103 ff).

When consolidating the Fulani reign, the Shehu sought to establish once and for all the Shari'a as the basis of practical law, as in his view this was the one and only means to build a real **Dar-al-Islam**. In fact, the **jihād** had been fought for this very reason. The hated cattle-tax was abolished, and replaced by approved Muslim taxes, of which the **zakat** was the most important. The Shehu kept his state officials to a minimum: a Vizier, a judge, a chief of police and a land-tax official (Last 1967:57). Though some other officials were appointed later, the number remained a fraction of the population of the Hausa courts (Smith 1978:105-106; 1960:42 ff). The Shehu went to great lengths to have his administration and its courts uphold the values of soberness and scholarship, and to preach these values to his followers (Shagari & Boyd 1977:29). Though his son built the city of Sokoto as the new capital, the Shehu himself lived outside its walls most of his remaining years, preferring a modest house in a nearby village. Here he dwelt with his wives and smaller children, assisted by his trusted and all-important Vizier. Regular conferences were held by the generals who came to consult the Shehu in his village. The Commander of the faithful left wordly affairs to his son and brother, and spent his last five years teaching and writing. Eleven books date from this period (Last 1967:57). They deal with the work of the Community; Mahdism; the charges of Bornu (see below). On Thursday evenings he preached against oppression of the poor, against robbery in the markets and the condoning of crimes, as well as on the more esoteric subjets of Qadiriya Sufism and genealogies (Hiskett 1977:118 ff). He kept reminding his people Mohammed's adhortations about the great **jihād** of the spirit that was to follow their small **jihād** of the war (Shagari & Boyd 1977:28 ff). For him as well as for his son Bello, both types of **jihād** were permanent. Bello's scathing remarks about the spiritual status of the new Community members are revealing; of the ten types of **jihād** participants he describes, only one is a real member: someone who shuns tribalism, has no fear for wordly authority, is a scholar as well as a soldier, has no regard for his own fame or well being, does not value wordly possessions, is not fascinated by horses, does not love fighting, but is motivated only by the love of Allah giving up all possessions and relations, even his life, for the world to come (Last 1967:59). The Shehu and Bello succeeded in some measure in having these values of soberness, austerity and scholarship recognized as the major attitude rulers should have. Throughout the nineteenth century, Sokoto remained both a centre for scholarship and pilgrimage as well as the capital of the largest state in West Africa (Last 1967:113).

Pagans as a resource

No state, however pious, can exist without revenues. The Shari'a-based **zakat** was collected in Sokoto province, but for the outer provinces this was insufficient. The major state income in addition to the **zakat** were the revenues from the political hierarchy: presents from newly appointed officials or aspirant civil servants' donations and levies from the Emirs. Though Emirs were compelled to send only their tax surpluses to the capital, the size of their contributions reflected their own status (Last 1967:105). A fixed portion of any dead Emir's inheritance fell to Sokoto. At least as important (Smith 1978:304) as all these revenues was the share of the booty taken by the Emirs on their own jihād-expeditions. As a devout leader had to go on expedition with great regularity, booty was sent annually to Sokoto, usually in the form of captives. Though instead of slaves the jizya (poll-tax or protection money) could be sent, slaves made up the greater bulk of the spoils of war (Fage 1969, Last 1967:102-107).

Two factors contributed to the success of the empire, increasing the number of slaves. Firstly, the 19th century is one of the few centuries in West African history without a large scale drought (Bryson & Murrey 1977:95 ff). So, the pagan groups (as well as the rest of the empire population) were numerous, as no hunger decimated them. Secondly, in roughly the same period as the jihād the African system of slavery was in a process of transformation (Lovejoy 1983). The abolitionist drive gradually eliminated the transatlantic slave export from the West African coast. Though far removed from the Sokoto center, this had its reverberations for the Caliphate. As Lovejoy convincingly argues, the net result for West Africa was not the demise of slave raiding, nor of slave commerce, let alone of indigenous slavery. The most important immediate result was an abundance of slaves for the internal market, stimulated also by the fact that the traditional 'markets' for slaves - North Africa and the Middle East - were shrinking (Fyle 1974). Thus developed a full-grown 'slave mode of production' (Lovejoy 1983:269 ff), transforming the quest for purity into a state which 'fed on slaves'. Throughout, the various holy wars that swept through sudan Africa (the Sokoto case is one among several) 'created a new slaving frontier on the basis of rejuvenated Islam' (Lovejoy 1983:154). Raiding slaves was a continuous enterprise, with the Caliphate even raiding as far south as the northern limits of the Zaire river, through Ilorin, a dependent emirate (Lovejoy 1981b).

Without this continuous supply of slaves it is difficult to see how the Caliphate could have expanded and consolidated as it has done. Slaves were needed for cultivation of the domestic crops. In order to feed the towns, officials, herdsmen, armies and caravans, plantation villages were set up around the cities, where slaves produced the diverse staple foods (Lovejoy 1978, 1979). They also supplied the great majority of the arts and craftsmen - making weapons - , spun and wove to make clothes and made up a considerable part of the army as foot-soldiers and archers (Fisher 1971a). As indicated above, even government positions were often filled by slaves. The great advantage for the rulers was that they had few allegiances other than towards their master who put them into such a comfortable position, while they could never take his place. As barter value they were of crucial importance for the army too. Warhorses could not be bred on the Sokoto-occupied plains in suffiently large numbers. The large horses used for cavalry came from the North and from the Western Sudan (Johnson 1976), and in both cases had to be bartered for captives (Fage 1969; Flint 1974). So the quest for purity indirectly stimulated the slave trade throught the Sahara and even opened the way for the 'northern' slaves to be sold all the way South, where they were found in Asante (modern Ghana) (Torre 1978:418). The exchange towards the South was especially important in obtaining guns.

The slaves made up a sizeable portion of the total population. For the Sokoto area Barth estimated them at 50% of all inhabitants of the greater Kano-Sokoto region (Barth 1857 I:523). So a steady supply of captives was absolutely essential for the Caliphate. These captives could not be obtained in the vicinity of Sokoto, as few pagan groups lived there. The Caliphate for this purpose followed two courses. First, treaties with enemies were established in order to exchange prisoners of war (Lovejoy 1983:155). More important still, was the continuous raiding of the frontier pagans. The Emirates of the southern and eastern fringes, where large pockets of pagan groups resided, were crucial for this.

As an example the Emirate of Adamawa will serve. In the 1850's it sent 1000 slaves a year to Sokoto as tribute, receiving about 5000 cpatives a year from its dependencies (Lovejoy 1983:157). This emirate formed the easternmost expanse of the empire: its territory now is part of North-Eastern Nigeria and North Cameroon. Tensions between the local Bata and the numerous Fulani of the area had been flaring up into fighting even before the start of the Sokoto-jihād. In 1806 Modibo Adama, a young Fulani scholar, was received with great honors at Sokoto, and was presented a **jihād** flag by the Shehu. With this supreme backing, Adama managed to rally his Fulani tribal kin as well as some local pagan chiefs behind him, and waged a long and arduous series of wars against the many pagans living in the area (Kirk-Greene 1969:129 ff). Some of those resisted themselves very successfully, relying on the natural terrain or on tactical defense. The Mandara mountains, the area where our opening example was situated, are a good example of the kind of refuge the local cultivators sought (van Beek 1978, 1987). So throughout the large Emirate of Adamawa, large pockets of pagan cultivators defended themselves against the more sophisticated war parties of the Fulani **mujahedeen** (Hogben & Kirk-Greene 1966:267). In the hillsides and in the inundated zones of the Logone-Chari confluence, the pagans could effectively keep the Fulani at bay, while the latter dominated the open plains. Though Adama and his successor Lawale regarded the tenacious resistance and continuous presence of large pagan groups as a slur on the Emirate (Kirk-Greene 1969:431-432). After all, converting pagans to Islam is a pious act; enslaving them may be a means to that end, but that was not the goal of the Caliphate slave system. From an analytical point of view, it was essential. Those pagan groups supplied the much needed slaves, and as such the major wealth of the empire, its market commodity, its productive labour. Without the large fringe of slave-raiding Emirates, the Sokoto Caliphate would lack its main revenues: without slaves its domestic production as well as its war system would crumble.

The pagans themselves hardly appreciated their crucial role in preserving the Caliphate. They fought hard and well, and in some cases built up an efficient organisation in resisting **jihād** (Morrison 1982:146); though even their mountain refuges could not prevent them from losing people to the **jihād**ists nor from migrating in large numbers. The results described by an English resident in 1920:

'These are the most lawless, ill-governed places I have seen in Nigeria.... Slave dealing and slave raiding are rampant.... Chiefs of minor importance were given rifles with which they were encouraged to attack the wretched pagans (who are) hiding like frightened monkeys on inaccessible hilltops...of course, everyone goes about fully armed: spears, shields, bows, arrows, clubs etc.' (Kirk-Greene 1958:84)

In some cases the pagans accepted Fulani dominance and paid **jiziya** to escape slavery (Johnston 1967: 84), some chiefs even using the Fulani military might to gain dominion over a reluctant chiefdom (Adler 1984: 356). Many instances refer to the pagans themselves paying tribute in slaves in order to avoid being raided. These slaves, then, were the 'product' of their own internal wars (Vaughan 1977, van Beek 1987).

The Adamawa case was quite typical of the 'outpost' Emirates. Though it lasted about a century and its religious authority and military might never were in doubt, there never was a lasting peace. Adama and his successors continually were fighting uprisings from pagans and incursions from other Emirates on their territory. The Mandara Sultanate was the main adversary for Adamawa, as the Bornu Sultanate was for the whole of the eastern Caliphate. Between their slave raids and external wars, the Emirs had to cope with rebellious kinsmen. From 1878-1898 a great grandson of the Shehu led a group of followers into Mahdism and even established his own community on the west banks of the Mandara mountains (Clarke 1982: 121). From the beginning of the Caliphate (and of the Adamawa Emirate) uprisings were dealt with very severely. Fighting against Sokoto was interpreted as fighting against Islam. In the view of the Shehu and his flagbearers, a clear watershed between Muslim and non-Muslim ran exactly parallel to the distinction for or against Sokoto.

The reason for this is apparent when considering the doctrinal difficulties in waging war against professed Muslims, one of the pivotal problems to which we shall return later. So when the Sultan of Rey Bouba (in North Cameroon) failed to pay tribute, Adama was forced to wage war. The war was not very successful because of lack of proper timing (Mohammadou 1972:178). After the siege of Rey Bouba had ended in a stalemate, the Lamido of Ray, on his own initiative, paid a levy of 1000 hoes, 10 elephants' teeth and 1000 slaves (Mohammadou 1972:182). This element of unclear ascendancy in the Emirate and in the empire was typical. In most areas the Emirs had built their empire in a virtual power vacuum, establishing themselves as rulers where no previous overlords had existed. In a way their **jihād** strategies were aimed at exactly maintaining that kind of vacuum, by eliminating all conflicting claims to power, but without building any administrative organization. The **jihād**-leaders were reluctant organizers, trying to establish a religious/military dominion **per se**. Of the structure of their empire they only built the roof and the foundations, leaving out the living quarters.

Ascetism and war: the two-pronged purity

In the view of the Fulani leaders, the political unrest had important theological advantages. The military instability made for a permanent **jihād**, keeping the people on their religious toes as warriors and - just as important - as scholars. **Jihād** was to be a lifelong enterprise, a way of living and a way of dying. As the **jihād** fought corruption and greed among rival Muslim leaders, those very sins, if checked, would cause the break-down of the empire, as it would add fuel for a legitimate counter **jihād**. Al-Kanemi's reform in the Bornu empire made such a threat very plausible (Webster & Boahen 1967:37). The Shehu was keenly aware of this problem, though for him it was, before all, a moral issue. He saw and foresaw greed and wordliness prevail upon the ideals of Islamic justice, preached and wrote against it as early as 1809, even before the termination of the jihād in Gobir. His poems reflect some bitterness as a few critics accused him of selfish motives:

'I swear by God, the authority of the Shari'a alone. Whoever accepts office to exploit the country for wordly ends, I swear by God, he eats carrion..... I swear by God, it is the knife of Satan cuts him down. (Hiskett 1973:107)

Though most sources are written by the jihādists themselves, the ascetism preached as well as practised by the Shehu and his followers, is beyond all doubt. His view of the jihād was that of a moral reform, first among the Fulani themselves, then among others. His private life was austere and ascetic: strict honesty in all dealings, no striving for wordly possessions. Cled in the simplest of the long Fulani garments, he tried to live in simple quarters the quiet life of scholarship. He condemned music, except a very limited number of instruments (no drums except for war or marriage, no guitars, no flutes etc.), disapproved of dancing, possessions cults and prostitution (Last 1967:235). Of course the practice of venerating trees and rocks on which sacrifices were performed, and divination by sand, by stars and by spirits were unlawful (Clarke 1982:115). He castigated his young warriors who did not wait the proper time before taking a captive woman as their concubine, threatening them with hell fire (Hiskett 1973:106). His Emirs emulated him in this, like Adama's soon Lawale who punished wearers of short garments, and censored morals strictly inside Yola town; he even forbade whistling, smoking or snuff taking (Kirk-Greene 1958-139). Up to 1894 the all important Vizier of the Sokoto Sultan surprised his European visitors with his soberness. They found him 'seated on a mat placed on the mud floor of the small house he occupied in Kano, quietly studying...... an Arabic manuscript....... in a darkened house, without the kingly garments or the least sign of state' (Last 1967:224). Still, neither the Shehu, nor any of his Emirs, really succeeded in stamping out the customs they condemned.

An inspiring example of course can stimulate the quest for purity among followers. The Shehu undoubtedly was such an inspiration for those who came in contact with him, but the majority of the Fulani hardly ever saw him. Some mechanism of social control - apart from the constant inducement of war and adhortations to study the sacred texts was necessary. The Fulani notion of purity did help in this. It did not imply an inwards turning into the deep recesses of the soul, searching for the elusive sins. Nor did the Fulani way of life, derived from the independence of cattle nomadism, favour either public confession or a major role of a controlling third party. The sunnitic orthodoxy, in the Fulani version, was a practical, ritualistic religion; purity could be seen. A man (or woman) who meticulously observed the prayers, fasting and other pillars of Islam, was on the road to purity. Scholarship had to show in teaching, piety in preaching, soberness in style of living and the soldier's abandonment to the cause of Islam was to be tested on each battlefield. So purity shone through in one's actions. Even so, the ideals had to be divulged.

One important way of divulging ideals was and is through praise singers (Last 1967:222). As a special category in society, sometimes with caste-like qualities (Smith 1978:39), the bards were the ones who sang on public or semipublic occasion. Extolling the virtues of the rulers (not necessarily those of Islam, as in less orthodox times they did the same with apostate rulers) and deriding the amoral conduct of eventual adversaries, in the Sohoto empire the bards clearly upheld the values with which the Shehu tried to imbue his people. The poems written by the Shehu, by other leaders or by some saintly (**walī**) woman (Last 1967:223) were recited by them. They sang them at weddings, funerals, commemorations of battles and at the feast of the sheep and the end of Ramadan. These praise singers did and do have sense for political reality. As an institution they belonged more to the Hausa courts (Smith 1960) than to the nomadic Fulani tradition. However, after the Fulani take-over, they shifted their allegiance, honed their Islamic standards and sang in praise of soberness. Their tongue could be sharp as well, ridiculing laxness and wordliness. So, as long as the Shehu and his successors clung to the ideals of the **jihād**, they found a powerful backing in these bards.

Thus, by his writing and by having his sober example divulged, the Shehu tried to reform his own society. Throughout the **jihād** and long before it, the main thrust of his message was to his own Fulani tribesmen. In fact the Shehu spent more time trying to overcome their sins and weaknesses, than in any other endeavour.

The vision of man in the Shehu's movement actually is optimistic. The ideal man is that of the scholar-**cum**-soldier; someone versed in the Quran, in Shari'a law, and at the same time skillful in battle; fearless and faithful. Learning meant a great deal: at one desastrous battle, near Alkalawa, the Fulani suffered a severe setback in their jihād. To stress the completeness of the disaster, Bello remarked that 2000 people had died who knew the Quran by heart (Hiskett 1977:90). Some people lived up to this scholar-soldier ideal, but not everyone. Still, there was a considerable pressure. The Caliphate officials had to conform to this model, as respect for the law and Islam was the source of authority for the whole Caliphate, as it had been the prime mover of the jihād (Last 1967: 232). As long as officials upheld the Shari'a, they were unimpeachable, and the full force of orthodoxy was behind them.

Tribalism was one of the vices the Shehu sought to eliminate: as all people are alike for Allah, they should be alike to one another (provided they are Muslims). Even if he rated family ties and obligations as supremely important, those commitments should be secondary to the following of the Shari'a, secondary to the obedience and subjugation to Allah. One of Adamawa's later Emirs carried out this view to some extreme when as an example he executed one of his nephews who had indulged in robbery, and amputated the foot of a grandson for a similar offense (Kirk-Greene 1969: 144). It was one of the deep tragedies of the jihād that it increasingly turned Fulani against Hausa, instead of Muslims against apostates. The reasons for this gradual tribalization of the jihād are complex, residing in diverging subsistence patterns, the logic and dynamics of political alliances and the strategies for recruiting converts for the movement.

The Shehu never saw the jihād as completed. It was but the first stage of a series of major upheavals leading towards the coming of the Mahdi. The Shehu's own contribution, by no means belittled by himself, was that of the Renewer of Faith, one of the many, one of the last. He tried to have the Muslim Community shut off all ties with unbelievers, thus lending authority to the creation of the walled ribat fortifications, a vision which clashed with the political reality of constant warring and slave raiding. He expected and prophesied the coming of Gog and Magog, 'small people with big ears', who would come a century after the hijra. And as people still point out today: 'There they came, the English!' Last, 1967: 212).

As a theologian and dogmatist the Shehu has been compared with a scholastic author such as Thomas Aquinas (Hiskett 1973:117). The explicit world view and ultimate knowledge that constituted his framework were given in the sacred texts and traditions, and like many Muslim scholars before and after him, Usman's main task consisted in reconciling the discrepancies between his society and the texts. The major way of doing so was changing the society, the minor way was solving all kinds of scholastic riddles on how to apply the texts to reality. One of the most tenacious problems was to determine the state of sinners and the nature of unbelief: 'Does sin turn a Muslim into an unbeliever?' It is characteristic for the theological foundation of the whole jihād, that the war hinged upon this sophisticated question. Following his medieval example, Al-Maghili, the Shehu stated, in defiance of his great and respected teacher el hadj Jibril, that

'as for him who mixes the works of Islam with the works of sin and innovation, he is not an infidel, according to the consensus of the orthodox; but only sins against God and His prophet' (Hiskett 1973: 127).

Still, he took his stand against an overly liberal interpretation: some measure of sinning and some degree of disobedience imply disbelief and do make Muslims into infidels. Drawing this line proved exceptionally difficult, especially when the logic of empire clashed with that of dogmatics. The Shehu's fine set of distinctions was tested to the limit when Bornu shook off its Muslim laxity and initiated a vigourous, successful Islamic reform under Al-Kanemi (Webster & Boahen 1967:38 ff). This eliminated almost all arguments for the Fulani jihād against Bornu, as Al-Kanemi aptly pointed out in his letters to the Shehu (Johnston 1967:105-106). To defend the proceedings and save the impetus of the Fulani jihād, the Shehu hardened his earlier standpoints on disobedience and moved closer to Jibril, who condemned all sin as infidelity. Incidentally this moved the Shehu closer to Wahhābism too. Thus, the Shehu was forced to walk the tight rope between dogma and political reality, in order to uphold his own integrity and preserve the legitimacy of the jihād. But the legimation of actual fighting is a tricky problem in sunnitic orthodoxy in any way (Peters 1977).

Purity and power: the tragic of theocracy

The aim of Usman dan Fodio - and to a large degree his success- was a purification of religion. Within Islam this was not a doctrinal thrust, but a practical one: the people in his days were not living a truly Muslim life, but were corrupted by wealth and paganism. His reform was aimed at changing their ways of life, if possible by changing their ways of thinking. This, of course, runs parallel to the practical side of Islam in general, in which 'doing just things' and 'doing things the right way' is more important than 'believing the right things in the right way'. This insistance on the praxeology of religion, especially to its every day implementation, fits in easily with Islam, though it might eventually appear to be one of the important aspects of puritan systems in general. They measure the heart against the yardstick of the person's actions.

Where religion is dominant, no secularized life is tolerated. In fact, any hint at secularization is viewed as a sin, and a large one at that: shutting off God from the life of the faithful, and denying the influence or presence of God in the individuals life. This anti-secularization stance is quite natural for Islam, but so is the jihād-tradition. In Islam doctrine and tradition the occurence of and the need for periodic reform is clearly indicated. Twelve Renewers of the Faith were prophesied, as well as the Mahdi, so the kind of movement as described here is part and parcel of Islamic preaching. Maybe by force of this traditions and its recurrent implementation, Islam as a religion had succeeded in staying close to its original form. Important in this respect is the model function of the prophet and his Community. Not only Mohammed's way of life and leadership is a model to emulate, but so is his political history, his exile the organization of his Community, his manner of fighting the 'idolators', the organization of the first Caliphate and so on. Usman dan Fodio was very explicit in his following of Mohammed's example, pointing out meticulously all parallels between the great example and the Fulani situation: like Mohammed he started a new epoch from the day of his exile; like Mohammed he preached his troops before battle; leading them in prayer as his prophetic example. His aim in this was never to become a second prophet: that was not his intention. Mohammed's dealings simply offered the only proven and legitimate strategy.

In another Fulani jihād in the 19th century, the same patterns emerged. When Sheikh Amadou, the leader of the Fulani jihād in the Masina, Mali, faced an overwhelming enemy, he told his followers:

'Ce jour est pour nous un nouveau Bedr. Souvenez-vous de la victoire que notre prophète remporta sur les idolatres coalisés. N'a-t-il attaqué l'ennemi avec 313 combattants seulement? Ne remporta-t-il pus une éclatante victoire? A son exemple, nous attaquerons...... avec 313 hommes prêts à combattre'.(Ba & Daget 1962:213)

So Amadou organized his fighters in parties of exactly 313 soldiers, leaving a small force to defend his camp (as did Mohammed). These Masina Fulani attacked their enemy (which they estimated - themselves - at 100.000) and gained a miraculous and decisive victory.

Thus, jihādist puritans not only strive to regain the values and laws of the pristine organisation, they also try to relive its history.

In each **jihād** the original foundation of religion is recreated. Thus, in the present historiography of Northern Nigeria, the time of Ahmado Bello, the Shehu's son and successor, is often compared with that of the first four Caliphs after Mohammed. Bello's era is praised as the only one in which the Shari'a was applied to practical law in full, as the golden age of Northern Nigeria. Still today at Sokoto, the years are counted from both the **hijra** of Mohammed and the Shehu; a great number of miracles are attributed to the Shehu, which in time more and more came to resemble those of Mohammed. So, this kind of puritan movement quite literally is a repristiniza- tion, reliving the redeeming history of the central human figure in that religion.

The idea for a pure state, however, bears some deep contradict- ions, which compromised Mohammed's Caliphate as well as the Sokoto one. Soberness and a simple life not accommodate easily with an empire, and in the Sokoto Caliphate a tension grew between the means and goals of scholars and those of soldiers. The realization of **jihād** purity never was obtained by the majority of the people. As long as a fair number of highly placed persons did realize it, the structure remained intact. So this kind of unobtainable ideal creates differences between people and thus strengthens a pyramidal and authoritative political structure. The first cleavage was between the orthodox **mujahedeen** and the imperial officers. The consolidation of the **Dar-al-Islam** called for different measures than fighting the revolution. The guerilla warfare, which was so effective against the Hausa states, had to be transformed into regular, central campaigns, regulated by a central government. Soldiers could no longer be kept on booty and heavenly rewards as payments, but had to be fed and payed. This tension between the ideal of purity and the praxis of power was a persistent theme in the Sokoto history.

Power, in itself, is a problem for a puritan movement. Centraliza- tion of power is a usual trajectory in the process of differentiation and integration that accompanies state formation (Parsons 1969, Luhman 1982). The ideology of purity, with its insistence on equality of men, is in a sense a current of de-differentiation (Rueschemeyer 1977). The revolutionary movement downplayed inter-personal differ- ences, stressed equality and replaceability, and diminished institu- tionalized differentiation; in short, in Durkheim's terms, a puritan movement tries to replace organic solidarity by the former mechanic one. This may be seen on the macro-level as a means to revitalize a society (Tiryakian 1985), to reaffirm its human roots (Wallace 1956) and to reestablish some fundamental goals of governmental systems. However, as Luhman indicates (1982), the outcome inevitably is on the other side: differentiation reaffirms itself and something akin to the former petrified system reappears. This process, on a much smaller level, can be recognized in Turner's treatment of structure versus communitas (Turner 1969). In ritual, equality, togetherness and shared humanness reign supreme, but daily life inevitably catches up with the sobering realization that some people are more equal than others.

Thus, the following contradictions may serve as a case study in a double transformation: first of all that of a political situation by means of an ideologically triggered revolt. Secondly, the transformation of the ideology itself, in order to accomodate its own succes. Religions are very flexible in this latter kind of transformation (Eisenstadt 1973), partly because the gap between what "is" and what "should be" is unbridgeable. In the political reality this tension between what is right and what is feasible generates creative solutions. For the Fulani four areas of contradiction can be distinguished: life style, finance, war and slave raiding.

Organized campaigning was at odds with the traditional nomadic Fulani way of life. So the Sokoto Caliphs tended to settle the nomads in large camps, and to professionalize cattle-herding - by slaves - thus enhancing proto-urbanisation among their often quite unwilling kinsmen. At the same time, however, the nomadic way of life, without possessions or attachments, lies at the roots of the ideal man. Each Muslim should independently, on his own initiative and of his own free will, seek God and submit to Him. The relative absence of organization, as we noted above, fits in well with this model of man; it also correlates very nicely with a nomadic way of life (Stenning 1966). One more factor in this transition was the growing economic interdependence of nomads, agriculturalists and townspeople. For this moment greater riches in goods (pots, knives, swords, clothing etc.) induced a change against the acclaimed soberness (v. Raay 1975:22).

So in settling the nomads - in which they did not wholly succeed - Caliphs organised their armies but uprooted their own value system. Politically this proved the only way of containing the ever emerging power of the Fulani clan-leaders, which - if unchecked- would put in jeopardy the ideals of the jihād. One other measure was to build ribat, walled fortifications on the border of the empire. The doctrine of the Dar-al-Islam is at odds with such a self-containment of Islamic expansion (Peters 1977:71 ff). In the imperial practice however, it proved to be effective not only in keeping out enemies, but also for keeping in nomads. The jihād aimed at purifying nomads first, and reasonably succeeded in this. Still, this 'pure way of life' in many ways turned out to be a large change in life style for the nomads, than the (later) colonizations by the British (Hopen 1958:15). The roaming nomads became the elite of an empire within a few years; before the **jihād** they were not allowed to own horses or slaves, after the purification they became settled landlords with scores of slaves to till and herd for them (Hopen 1958:17).

A similar clash between doctrine and the logic of empire ocurred in taxes. The abolition of cattle-tax levied by the Hausa Sarkin was one of the principal goals for the revolution. The first measure after defeating Gobir was to abolish this tax. Even if in the province of Sokoto only the **zakat** was levied, in the outlining Emirates the Muslim leaders were forced by financial considerations to levy a similar cattle tax, to be followed by other non-Shari'a taxes (Smith 1978:262). Especially in the central region of the Hausa states, where the Fulani overtook an existing political system, in the latter half of the 19th century these political organizations gradually re-emerged, dictated by the exigencies of political reality (Smith 1960:154). At the end of the century, the Fulani Emirates in their political practice closely resembled their Hausa predecessors. In some of the peripheral Emirates no such intermediary structure existed. In Adamawa, for instance, the Fulani rule retained more of the original **jihād** flavour (Kirk-Greene 1958) than in Sokoto. In those eastern expanses, the constant war kept the ideal of the scholar-soldier more alive than in the center (la Croix 1966). Maybe the greatest threat to this ideal was not the independent nomadic clansman, but the well-fed, immobilized burocrat. The latter's main concern was not fighting the **jihād,** but succession to a lucrative office. A similar clash of priorities lies in the transformation of a scholar-**cum**-soldier into the founder of a dynasty. Of course this pattern is classical Muslim, but its reenactment in the 19th century Sudan is almost a by-law.

In anthropological theory on the origin of the state, war plays a predominant role in state formation (Harris 1975). Most of these theories adress themselves to pristine states (Carneiro 1970), but in secondary states war is a major structuring principle as well (Goody 1968). The Fulani empire is a case in point. As soon as war is waged, an empire is founded. A pre-existing state makes war an even more efficient means to promote state formation (Vansina 1968). However, war in itself is at odds with the quest for purity, however militaristic and expansionist the ideology may seem. Firstly, the ideal pure soldier has to be the one who shuns violence-per-se. Secondly, any battle tends to draw the revolutionaries into further engagements. These later battles have less and less to do with the original quest for purity. In the Fulani case this was clear from the start. The most tenacious problem between state and scholars however, remained the akward political fact that most of the fighting took place against Muslims, i.e. against rival Muslim realms such as Bornu, Mandara or Baghirmi. As is indicated above, this triggered off some doctrinal raffinations, but the issue remained doctrinally doubtful. In the Bornu case a rival **jihād** among the Kanuri did claim similar legitimacy for their counter attacks (Cohen & Brenner 1974:10 ff). In the Masina case, the Fulani theocracy was overrun by a Bambara based **jihād** of el hadj Umar from Segu (Webster & Boahen 1967:37). In both instances, the military and imperial reasons for fighting are infinitely more evident than the doctrinal ones. About the only doctrinal accusation el hadj Umar could level against Sheikh Amadou of Masina, was the latter's alliances with pagan groups, which he was forced to in order to defend himself against Umars predatory expansions (Ba & Daget 1962:260). So doctrine became a reluctant helpmeet in empire building.

Finally, the whole structure of state and the ideal of the scholar-soldier (see above) are made possible by a fundamental conflict between doctrine and practice centering around the pagans and slaves, and - more generally - around inequality in society. Without slaves there are neither scholars nor armies. The preaching of the Shehu stressed the equality of all men, but eventually supported a stratified society, in which professed and ackknowledged Muslims were inferior to other Muslims. The Community of Sheikh Amadou of Masina, at one time wanted to do away with all distinctions, especially those pertaining to the artisans guilds. Amadou, himself the most devout and humble of all West African **jihād** leaders, managed to convince his council that the actual removal of inequality would result in an impractical society which was not what Allah wanted (Ba & Daget 1962:185 ff). The more fundamental opposition between Muslims and pagans - and consequently between free men and slaves - remained a problem (cf. Peacock 1978). Slaves were needed, as was argued above, but full domestic and permanent slavery is difficult to harmonize with the mission to spread the **Dar-al-Islam**, and the potential equality of all men before Allah. In order to function properly, the theocracy needed a pool of non-converts, who would never be converted at all. Expansion is one practical solution for this, as during imperial expansion new peoples are being conquered, and thus supply a continuous input of slaves. When the days of expansion are over, doctrine has to accomodate itself to the fact that permanent pagan settlements reside on its borders. In a large empire such as Sokoto this could be excused by logistical problems of domination over a great distance. In the situation of the much smaller Masina theocracy however, logistical problems were no excuse at all. There, Muslim orthodoxy was forced to make a compact with the pagan groups, such as the Dogon, to have both a safe border and a slave raiding reserve near at hand (Ba & Daget 1962:234; Pern, Alexander & van Beek 1982:57 ff). This factor of slaves as a fundamental resource is somewhat neglected in the literature on state formation (Ajayi & Crowder 1974), while in the discussion on African slavery (Markovitz 1977, Tuden & Plotnicov 1970) the state as such is given little weight.

Eventually, because of the need for slaves, the organizational demands of an empire and the inevitable results of success in war, the theocracy of the **Dar-al-Islam** was gradually restructured into something closely resembling the predator states which it had so succesfully destroyed. So, in the oven of **jihād** purity, doctrine built a clay Utopia, but after the fire had died, the baked model emerged in the form of an empire. But such is the tragedy of theocracy.

References

Abun-Nasr, J.M.
  1965   *The Tijaniyya*. Oxford University Press.
Adeleye, R.A.
  1974   The Sokoto Caliphate in the nineteenth century, in Ajayi & Crowder (eds.) *History of West Africa* Vol. 2. p. 57-92. London.
Adler, A.
  1984   *La mort est la masque du roi. La Royauté sacrée des Moundang du Tchad.* Paris, Payot 1984.
Ajayi, J.F.A. & Crowder
  1974   *History of West Africa*, 2 Vols. London.
Ba, A.H. & Daget, J.
  1962   *L'Empire Peul du Macina. Vol. 1. (1818-1853).* The Hague, Mouton.
Barth, H.
  1857-9 *Travels and Discoveries in Northern and Central Africa.*
Beek, W.E.A. van
  1978   *Bierbrouwers in de bergen; de Kapsiki en Higi van Noord Kameroen en Noord-Oost Nigeria.* ICAU 12, Utrecht.

1986   L'état, ce n'est pas nous. Cultural proletarization in North-Cameroon. Reyntjes, F., van Binsbergen, W. & Hesseling, G. (eds) *Local Community and the State in Africa*, pp 61-92, Antwerp: ASDOC.

1987   *The Kapsiki of the Mandara Hills*. Prospect Heights: Waveland Press.

Biobaku, S; M.A. al-Hajj
1966   The Sudanese Mendiyya and the Niger-Chad region, in I.M. Lewis (ed.) *Islam in Tropical Africa*: pp. 425-451. Oxford: Oxford University Press.

Bryson, R.A. & Murrey, T.J.
1977   *Climates of Hunger. Mankind and the world's changing weather*. Univ. of Wisconsin Press.

Carneiro, R.
1970   A Theory on the Origin of the State, *Science* 169:733-738.

Chatelier Le
1899   *L'Islam dans l'Afrique occidentale*, Paris. Bandiagara.

Clarke, P.B.,
1982   *West Africa and Islam*. Arnold, London.

Cohen, R. & Brenner, L.
1974   Bornu in the nineteenth century in Ayayi, J.F.A. & M. Crowder (eds.) *History of West Africa*. Vol.2. pp. 93-128. London.

Croix, P.F. La
1966   L'Islam Peul de l'Adamaoua in: I.M. Lewis (ed.) *Islam in Tropical Africa*, pp. 401-407. Oxford: Oxford University Press.

Delafosse
1907   *Les pays, les peuples, les langues, l'histoire, les civilisations. Haut Senegal-Niger*. vol. ii: 332 (Bandiagara).

Duysens, B.
1984   *De Sanusiya: militantie en mystiek in de Dar-al-Islam*. (unpubl. paper, Nijmegen).

Eisenstadt, S.N.
1973   *Tradition, Change and Modernity*. New York, John Wiley.

Fage, J.D.
1969   Slavery and the slave trade in the context of West African history. *Journal of African History* X. 3. pp. 393-404.

Flint, J.E.
1974   Economic change in West Africa in the nineteenth century. in: Ajayi, J.F.A. & M. Crowder, *History of West Africa* vol. 2, London. pp. 380-401.

Froehlich, J.C.
    1966   Essai sur les Causes et Méthodes de l'Islamisation de l'Afrique de l'ouest de XIe Siècle au XXe Siècle. in: J.M. Lewis (ed.) *Islam in Tropical Africa.* pp. 160-173. Oxford: Oxford University Press.
Fyle, Ch.
    1974   Reform in West Africa: the abolition of the slave trade. in: Ajayi, J.F.A. & M.Crowder (eds.) *History of West Africa.* vol. 2, pp. 30-56. London.
Fischer, A.G.B. & H.J.
    1971a   *Slavery and Muslim Society in Africa.* Garden City, N.Y.
Fischer, H.J.
    1971b   Prayer and military activity in the history of Muslim Africa south of the Sahara. *Journal of African History* XII. 3. pp. 391-406.
Goody. J.
    1968   *Technology, Tradition and the State in Africa.* Methuen.
Gibb, H.A.R.
    1957   *Islamic Society and the West.* Oxford.
Harris, M.
    1975   *Cows, Pigs, Wars and Witches.* New York, Random House.
Hatch, J.
    1970   *Nigeria. A History.* London.
Hill, P.
    1977   *Population, prosperity and poverty. Rural Kano 1900 and 1970.* Cambridge University Press.
Hiskett, M.
    1973   *The sword of truth. The life and times of the shehu Usuman Dan Fodio.* Oxford: Oxford University Press.
    1979   The nineteenth century jihāds in West-Africa. in: J.E. Flint (ed.). *The Cambridge History of Africa.* vol. 5 pt. 4.
Hogben, S.J. & A.H.M. Kirk Green
    1966   *The Emirates of Northern Nigeria.* London. Oxford Univ. Press.
Hopen, C.E.
    1958   *The Pastoral Fulbe Family in Gwandu.* London.
Hunwick, J.O.
    1966   Religion and the state in the Songhai Empire 1464-1591. in: I.M. Lewis (ed.) *Islam in Tropical Africa.* Oxford U.P. pp. 296-317.
Johnson, M.
    1976   The economic foundations of an Islamic theocracy - the

case of Masina. *Journal of African History* XVII. 4. pp. 481-495.

Johnston, H.A.J.
1967   *The Fulani empire of Sokoto.* Oxford U.P.
Kirk Greene, A.H.M.
1969   *Adamawa; Past and present.* Int. Afr. Inst. London.
Last, M.
1974   Reform in West Africa: the jihād movements of the nineteenth century, in Ajayi, J.F.A. & M. Crowder (eds.) *History of West Africa.* vol. 2, pp. 1-29. London.
1967   *The Sokoto Caliphate.* London.
Lewis, I.M. (ed.)
1966   *Islam in Tropical Africa.* London.
Lovejoy, P.E.
1978   Plantations in the economy of the Sokoto Caliphate, *Journal of African History,* 19, 3:341-368.
1979   The characteristics of plantations in the nineteenth-century Sokoto Caliphate (Islamic West Africa), *American Historical Review,* 84, 4:1267-1292.
1981a   (ed) *The Ideology of Slavery in Africa.* Beverly Hills.
1981b   Slavery in the Sokoto Caliphate, in Lovejoy 1981a.
1983   *Transformations in Slavery. A History of Slavery in Africa.* Cambridge U.P.
Luhman, N.
1982   *The Differentiation of Society.* New York, Columbia U.P.
Markovitz, I.L.
1977   *Power and Class in Africa. An introduction to change and conflict in African politics.* New Jersey, Prentice Hall.
Martin, B.G.
1976   *Muslim Brotherhoods in Nineteenth Century Africa.* Cambridge: Cambridge University Press.
Mohammadou, E.
1978   *Fulbe Hooseere; les royaumes Foulbé du Plateau d'Adamawa au 19e siècle.* ILCAA Afr. Lang. & Ethnogr. VIII.
Mohammadou, E. & A. Hamadjoda
1972   *Les yillaga de la Benoué, Ray ou Rey-Bouba.* Yaoundé.
Mohammadou, E.
1980   *Les Feroobé du Diamaré: Maroua et Petté.* Yaoundé. CFLC.
Monod, T.
1975   *Pastoralism in Tropical Africa.* Oxford: University Press.
Morrison, J.H.
1982   Plateau societies resistance to jihādist penetration. in:

Studies in the history of Plateau State. Nigeria. Ischei (ed.) pp.136-150. Lagos. Nigeria.
Norris, H.T.
1975   *The Tuareqs. Their Islamic Legacy and its diffusion in the Sahel.* Warminster, Arin & Phillips.
Parsons, T.
1969   *Politics and Social Structure,* New York. Free Press.
Peacock, J.L.
1978   *Muslim Puritans.* Univ. of California Press. Berkeley.
Pern, S., B. Alexander & W.E.A. van Beek
1982   *Masked Dancers of West Africa: the Dogon.* Time-Life.
Peters, R.
1977   *Jihâd in Medieval and modern Islam, from Averroes legal handbook 'Bidàyat Al-mudjt A'hid'.* Brill. Leiden.
Raay, H.G.T. van
1975   *Rural planning in a savanne region.* Rotterdam University Press.
Rueschemeyer, D.
1977   Structural Differentiation, Efficiency and Labour. *American Journal of Sociology,* 83: 1-25.
Shagari, A. & Elhaij Shehu & J. Boyd
1977   *Uthman dan Fodio. The theory and practice of his leadership.* Isl. Publ. Bureau. Lagos.
Shaw, T.
1978   *Nigeria. Its archeology and early history.* Thames & Hudson.
Smaldone, J.P.
1977   *Warfare in the Sokoto Caliphate, Historical and sociological perspectives.* Cambridge Univ. Press.
Smith, M.G.
1960   *Government in Zazzau.* Intern. Afr. Inst. Oxford U.P.
1967   A Hausa kingdom: Maradi under Dan Baskore, 1854-75. in: D. Forde and P.M. Kaberry (eds.), *West African Kingdoms in the Nineteenth Century.* pp. 210-244. London.
1964   Historical and cultural conditions of political corruption among the Hausa. *Comparative Studies in Society and History* VI. 2. pp. 164:194.
1966   The jihād of Shehu Dan Fodio: some problems. in: Lewis, I.M. (ed.) *Islam in Tropical Africa.* pp. 408-24. London.
1978   *The affairs of Daura, History and change in a Hausa State (1800-1958).* Univ. of California Press.
Stenning, D.J.
1959   *Savannah Nomads.* Oxford.

1966   Cattle Values and Islamic values in a pastoral population.
in: I.M. Lewis (ed.) Islam in *Tropical Africa.* Oxford U.P.
Triaud, J.L.
1969   La lutte entre la Tidjaniya et la Qadriya dans le Macina
au dix-neuvième siècle. *Annales Univ. Abidjan.* serie F. T1,
fasc. 1, pp. 149-171.
Trimmingham, J.S.
1962   *A history of Islam in West Africa.* Oxford.
1966   The phases of Islamic Expansion and Islamic Culture Zones
in Africa. in: I.M. Lewis (ed.) *Islam in Tropical Africa.*
pp. 127-143. International African Institute. Oxford: Oxford University Press.
1971   *The Sufi orders in Islam.* Clarendon Press. Oxford.
Tuden, A. & L. Plotnicov (eds.)
1970   *Social Stratification in Africa.*   New York, the Free
Press.
Turner, B.S.
1974   *Weber and Islam.* London: Routledge & Kegan Paul.
Turner, V.
1969   *The Ritual Process; Structure and Anti-structure.* Penguin
Vansina, J.
1968   *Kingdoms of the Savannah.* Madison: University of Wisconsin Press.
Vaughan, J.H. jr
1977   Mafakur, a limbic institution of the Margi (Nigeria), in
Miers, S. & I. Kopitoff (eds.) *Slavery in Africa: Historical
and Anthropological Perspectives*, Madison, pp 85-102.
Wallace, A.F.C.
1956   Revitalization Movements: some Theoretical Considerations
for their Comparative Study, *American Anthropologist*
58:264-281.
Webster, J.B. & A.A. Boahen
1967   *The growth of African civilisation. The revolutionary
years: West Africa since 1800.* London.
Willis, J.R.
1967   Jihād Fi Sabil Allàh - its doctrinal basis in Islam and
some aspects of its evolution in nineteenth century West
Africa, *Journal of African History* VIII, 3. pp. 395-415.

Shiᶜite purity: some aspects of the Islamic revolution in Iran
Philip G. Kreyenbroek

Shiᶜite purity: some aspects of the Islamic revolution in Iran
Philip G. Kreyenbroek

Introduction

The Islamic revolutionary movement of Iran is unique among similar movements in the Middle East in that it is, at the time of writing, the only such movement to have played a crucial role in the overthrow of a powerful, Western-backed government, and to assume the leadership of a newly created Islamic Republic. Its characteristic Shiᶜite inspiration and symbolism are shared by the Lebanese Shiᶜite movement, which has been deeply influenced by the Iranian example. There can be no doubt that the Iranian revolution, in every stage of its development, has shown traits which can be termed 'puritan' (1), such as the desire to return to a pristine Islamic ideal, and the development of a new religious ethos calling for the islamisation of society and the purification of the individual.

It is proposed here to give a brief description of the social and political conditions which provoked an Islamic reaction, to examine the thoughts of the two foremost ideologists of the movement, Ayatollah Khomeini and Dr. ᶜAli Shariᶜati, and to discuss the novel understanding of Islamic norms and values which their works inspired (and which was strengthened by the political struggle leading up to the revolution). Finally, some trends that are becoming apparent now that the ideal of an Islamic state has been realised will be tentatively described (2).

The socio-political background

About the conditions which provoked an Islamic reaction (as well as other forms of opposition which we are not immediately concerned with here), there can be little doubt; the rapid programme of secularization and 'westernization' of Iranian society enforced, at times brutally, by the regime of Mohammad Reza Pahlavi, alienated large sections of the community. On the one hand, there were the 'traditional' classes, such as the peasants, the clergy and the traditional merchants (bāzārīs), for whom the old Islamic ways were still functional, and who stood to gain little or nothing from the cultural and economic measures of the regime. On the other side of the social spectrum there were the students and intellectuals who, often brought up in traditional religious homes, were then educated to believe in Western-inspired ideals and values (such as social justice, individual liberties and freedom of expression) which the state failed to realise in practice. Many members of this group were disillusioned, felt themselves trapped in the cultural dichotomy which was so tangible a reality in the Iranian society of the later Pahlavi period, and resented the loss of a clearly definable Iranian cultural identity. Lastly, there were the huge masses of poor urban migrants who had been driven to the city in search of work as a result of the economic measures of the regime (particularly after the short-lived oil-boom of 1974). This urban proletariat was entirely unable to identify with government policies, and increasingly looked to the local clergy for guidance and leadership.

One factor which may help to explain the predominant role of religion in the ensuing political struggle is the fact that secular opposition (whose ideology would, in any case, be harder to understand for the masses than ideas expressed in terms of religion), was severely and effectively repressed by the regime, through its dreaded and hated intelligence organisation (the SAVAK). The clerical classes were also faced with government repression. The regime sought to strip the clergy of all political influence and arrested, tortured and killed some of its more outspoken leaders, thus provoking a sense of outrage among the clergy and the religious laity, as well as some feelings of solidarity among other oppositional groups. Yet at the same time, the Shi^cite 'Church' (i.e. the organizational structure made up of a clerical hierarchy, a network of mosques, charitable institutions etc., with an excellent system of internal communications) was uniquely able to convey to the masses an ideology of political protest couched in traditional religious symbols, which was not only immediately understandable to them, but had the additional advantage of being immune from attacks by the regime.

The traditional Shi^ca

In order to illustrate the profound changes in the interpretation and understanding of religious symbols and values which took place, partly as a result of the teachings of such writers as Shari^cati and Khomeini, it may be useful to give a brief description here of the traditional Shi^cite ethos.

The Shi^cites have always held that, as long as the last legitimate successor of the Prophet Mohammad as leader of the community (i.e. the twelfth or 'hidden' Imam, who disappeared in 873/4 A.C. and whose return is eagerly awaited) remains in occultation, there is no legitimate basis for power on earth. Especially since the Shi^ca became the state religion of Iran under the Safavids after 1500 A.C., the clergy have generally adopted a quietist attitude, tolerating the rule of the secular government of the day as long as it did not too blatantly infringe the rights of 'Church' and faithful. This had also been the attitude of the nine last Imams during their lifetime; it was based on the accepted Shi^ci principle of **taqiya** ('dissimulation', i.e. of one's true beliefs when the expression of these could endanger one's life). The clergy therefore tended to concern itself with matters of devotion and ritual purity, and became actively involved in politics only on a few occasions.

The traditional Shi^ca thus denies implicitly that man could bring about an ideal or even acceptable state of affairs through his own efforts before the coming of the hidden Imam. This helpnessness was symbolized in the minds of 'traditional' Shi^cites by the martyrdom of Imam Hosein (the third Imam, a grandson of the Prophet, who died fighting for his cause at Kerbela in 680 A.C.), which was regarded as a supreme example of man's impotence in the face of the manifestations of evil which are inherent in the world of our times. Thus, the Shi^ca had become a religion of mourning, with institutionalised manifestations of grief, e.g. during ta^cziyas ('passion plays'), **rauza-khvānīs** (gatherings where the story of Hosein's martyrdom is told), and during the processions of the 9th and 10th of the religious month of Moharram, also held to commemorate the events of Kerbela. Apart from being a symbol of martyred innocence, Hosein (like other Shi^cite Imams) was popularly venerated in Iran in his role of a **hājat-deh** ('need-giver'), who grants prayers and brings succour when addressed with proper demonstrations of self-abasement and helpnessness (3).

^CAli Shari^Cati

It was against this 'Safavid' Shi^Cite ethos that the work of Dr. Ali Shari^Cati was chiefly directed. Shari^Cati (1933-1977), the son of an influential reformist religious leader, studied in Paris, where he became well acquainted with Western ideologies (notably Marxism which he rejected, however, on a number of points); on his return to Iran, he began to expound his views on Islam, and soon became the formemost ideologist of 'radical' (as opposed to 'traditional') Shi^Cite Islam. After a term of imprisonment in Iran he fled to England, where he died in 1977. Shari^Cati expressed his views in a steady stream of lectures, books and articles, which met with instant popularity, especially among the young.

Shari^Cati points out that the Persian word for 'religion', **mazhab**, basically means 'road, path': it is intended to lead to a goal, not to be venerated for its own sake. When it becomes an end rather than a means, as has happened in the case of (Shi^Cite) Islam, the traveller gets lost (Algar 1979:93). For this corruption of the true Islamic ethos, Shari^Cati blames the passivity of the masses and the oppressive rule of kings but also, emphatically, the collaboration of Shi^Cite clerics with secular rulers (4).

True Islam, Shari^Cati argues, is a dynamic, vital faith, demanding that its followers emulate, rather than mourn, Hosein's heroic stance at Kerbela: they must fight repression and tyranny in their turn, so as to establish a truly Islamic community (**umma**). This **umma** (5) is to be classless, based on collective ownership and justice, and will be led by a group of 'enlightened thinkers' (**raushan-fekr**, a term normally used in Persian for 'intellectual') who are to be 'recognised' (**tashkhīs**, a Shi^Cite concept) as the most able, by the people. Thus as long as the divinely appointed leader of the community, the Imam, is absent, it is with the people themselves that the ultimate responsibility and sovereignty must rest.

In order to fulfil these obligations, the people must use **ijtihād**, i.e. the right to exercise their own judgement, which in the traditional Shi^Ca is the prerogative of a few high-ranking clerics (mojtahed), whose authority in religious matters must be followed (**taqlīd**) by the community. In Shari^Cati's view, the **ijtihād** of the people is one of the factors which will guard the Islamic community against the decline which he regards as inevitable in other societies. Thus Shari^Cati rejects the concept of clerical authority as such: the official clergy is too much preoccupied with the rules of 'menstruation and parturition' - i.e. with matters of ritualistic purity as opposed to larger moral and ethical issues - and has insufficient knowledge of the real problems facing the Islamic community today. One of the tasks of the 'enlightened thinkers', therefore, will be to strip the official clergy of most of its powers.

By his rejection of the accepted interpretation of **ijtihād** and **taqlīd**, and by his lack of appreciation for the clergy, Shari^cati attacked the very foundations of the Shi^cite 'Church'. Yet it was precisely these elements of the traditional Shi^ca that were widely blamed for causing its backwardness and lack of social engagement. Shari^cati therefore presented an image of Islam which proved to be acceptable and inspiring to large groups of progressive Muslims. His great charisma and unquestionable deep piety, moreover, prevented some of the more orthodox from rejecting his ideas out of hand.

Ayatollah Khomeini

The ideas of Ayatollah Khomeini on the subject of Islamic government, as laid down in a collection of his lectures entitled **Velāyat-e Faqīh**, 'Guardianship of the Jurist' (Khomeini 1978), differ radically from Shari^cati's on most issues, yet they are strikingly similar to these on a number of vital points.

Like Shari^cati, Khomeini claims that Islam is 'a religion of militant individuals, who seek Truth and Justice; it is the faith of people who desire freedom and independence, a religious school of fighters and anti-imperialists' (ibid, 7-8). For the current lapse from this militant ideal, Khomeini blames the imperialist powers (and their lackeys, the Orientalists), who have willfully misrepresented the faith in order to strengthen their hold over the world of Islam: 'for instance they claim that.... Islam consists of nothing but a set of ordinances about menstruation and parturition, that it has a few moral rules, too, but that, for the administration of society, it offers nothing at all' (ibid, 8). This erroneous image of an 'inadequate' Islam has, according to Khomeini, influenced a majority of Muslims, even those who have studied in universities or religious colleges. However, Khomeini points out that if one studies the true Islam, as laid down in the Qoran and the books of Traditions (**hadīth**), one will find that the texts concerned with social, political and administrative issues vastly outnumber those which deal with purely devotional matters. It is in the later religious writings that this trend is reversed.

Divine law, then, is not merely sufficient to serve as the basis of Islamic government, it was revealed for that very purpose. Besides divine law, however, an Islamic community needs a leader to implement and execute that law, as the Prophet Mohammad did in Medina and

Mecca. It was for this purpose, too, that the Caliphate was instituted. Stressing the example of Hosein, who gave his life seeking to depose the usurper Yazid, Khomeini urges Muslims to overthrow the Pahlavi dynasty, and to establish a state based on the principles of Islamic government. The leadership of such a state should be in the hands of the 'religious jurists' (faqīh), who are trained to interpret the divine law, and in particular in the hands of one supreme Faqīh, whose responsibilities - if not his ontological status - would be approximately similar to those of the Prophet and the Imams.

Khomeini rejects the notion that priests must lead a retired life and merely study the ordinances about 'menstruation and parturition', as well as the idea that a distinction should be made between religion and politics. He launches a violent attack on the wide adoption of the principle of taqiya ('dissimulation', see above), which, he says, is not valid at a time when the very essence of Islam is in danger (ibid, 200). The Islamic state envisaged by Khomeini, then, is a militant radical theocracy, led by a strong authoritative clergy, and headed by a supreme Faqīh who has to concern himself with all aspects of government (6).

The new Shiᶜite ethos

Shariᶜati and Khomeini thus differ radically in their interpretation of ijtihād. Shariᶜati transforms the concept into a powerful instrument for change in the hands of the people, intended to form the basis of a political system that could be called democratic, whereas Khomeini does not extend the right of ijtihād beyond a clerical elite with drastically increased powers. Shariᶜati's idea of history, moreover, appears to be that of an ongoing process of change in which Islam, through the ijtihād of the people and the 'enlightened thinkers', will adapt itself and prove its continuing relevance and ultimate truth. Khomeini's Islamic state, on the other hand, is essentially static: it is to be based on laws and ordinances laid down in Scripture and there is no indication that, once an Islamic government has been set up, further fundamental changes are foreseen, or regarded in any way as historically inevitable until the return of the hidden Imam.

Both ideologists agree, however, in rejecting the traditional image of the Shiᶜa as a passivist, dolorous faith chiefly concerned with mourning the tragedy of human powerlessness, and in stressing the relevance of Hosein's stance against tyranny as an example to be followed. Both call for the overthrow of secular despotism, and for the establishment of an Islamic state. A further point of similarity is that the aspirations of both thinkers appear to transcend the boundaries of Shi^cite Iran: Shari^cati, though recognizing that the example of Hosein is relevant primarily to Shi^cites, yet believes that it must ultimately inspire all oppressed nations. Khomeini generally speaks of 'Islam', rather than 'Shi^ca' (which, for him, is the only true version of Islam), and stresses the need for Islamic unity.

In the years preceding the overthrow of the Pahlavi regime in 1979, and particularly in the last, crucial year, this new 'radical' Shi^cite ethos, with its stress on self-reliance and the need for opposition against tyranny, was preached throughout Iran, and was enthusiastically received, it seems, by a majority of believers. At religious gatherings, it was no longer the tragic defeat of ^cAli or the martyrdom of Hosein that were emphasized, nor their role as bringers of succour and comfort, but rather their self-reliance and active struggle against oppression. Solidarity with the poor and the downtrodden (mostaz^cafin) was preached, and the events of 1978 strengthened the popular identification of the revolutionary movement with Hosein, and of the Pahlavi regime with his opponent, the tyrant Yazid. This new self-reliant and activist ethos, engendering a sense of religious (and therefore cultural) identity, thus played a crucial role in the events leading up to the Islamic revolution and was, in turn, strengthened by these.

Another aspect of the new Shi^cite ethos, a strong desire for individual purification, can be explained at least partly as a reaction against the atmosphere of corruption, cynicism and moral laxity which was prevalent among large sections of the upper classes in Pahlavi Iran (cf. Zonis 1971). Thus it was probably disapproval of current, Western-inspired morals that led many women to start wearing the veil (7) as a sign of opposition against the Shah. In order to achieve a state of moral purity (**tazkiya**), the believer must combat and transcend impulses deriving from the 'lower mind' (**nafs-e monfa^cel**), such as greed and lust (Taleqani: 112ff). Although **tazkiya** is thus essentially a personal matter, its outward manifestations, such as wearing the veil, came to be regarded after the revolution as criteria of Islamic behaviour, and what began as a desire for self-purification eventually turned into a legitimisation of social control and repression.

The year of the revolution

Although the history of religious opposition against Mohammad Reza Shah Pahlavi (with Ayatollah Khomeini as its principal leader) goes much further back, the chain of events which led directly to the overthrow of the regime was sparked off on 7 January 1978, by an ill-advised newspaper article by a cabinet minister, attacking Khomeini. As a result, demonstrations of protest and solidarity were held at Qom, which were broken up forcefully by army and police. At least a hundred people were killed, and many more were wounded. In accordance with the Islamic custom of holding commemorative observances forty days after a death, religious leaders now called for renewed demonstrations to be held throughout Iran forty days later. As these, in turn, resulted in further deaths, a chain of demonstrations came to take place every forty days in the following months. The government's severe repression of these and other forms of protest only served to deepen popular feeling against the Shah, while public American support for the regime further inflamed anti-imperialist and anti-western sentiments.

In the period that followed, religious feasts or holidays at times led to huge manifestations of protest against the Shah, culminating in the huge demonstrations of 9 and 10 Moharram (Tāsū^ca and ^cāshūrā, the traditional days of mourning for the martyrdom of Hosein, 10 and 11 December 1978), which showed the massive popular support for a revolution to be led by Khomeini. It was in these days that the change in the Shi^cite ethos manifested itself most clearly: instead of chanting dirges, wailing and beating their chests, people shook their fists and shouted 'Death to the Shah'. By this time, it had become apparent that revolution was inevitable.

It would be a misrepresentation to suggest that the Iranian revolution was brought about on the strength of religious sentiment alone. Clearly, economic issues played an important role, and the participation of such secular political groups as the left-wing activist Fedā'iyān-e Khalq, as well as non-Shi^cite movements such as that of the Kurds, shows that the revolution was supported by a broad spectrum of ideologically divergent groups. In demonstrations, moreover, portraits of Khomeini and Shari^cati were often carried side by side, suggesting a limited awareness on the part of the participants of the deeper implications of the ideas of either thinker. (A note of warning about the implications of Khomeini's 'Guardianship of the Jurist' was in fact sounded by such progressive high-ranking clerics as Ayatollah Shari^catmadari and Ayatollah Taleqani). In the period before the revolution the common aim was, plainly, to overthrow the regime of the Shah and to rid the country of foreign intervention; the emphasis lay on ideals which were shared by all participants, such as political independence from the U.S.A., a sober, earnest life-style, solidarity with the poor, and the abolishment of the hated secret service SAVAK.

One may safely claim, however, that although the Iranian revolution was not exclusively 'Islamic' either in aims or inspiration, it seems doubtful if the downfall of the Shah could have been brought about with such spectacular swiftness either without the charismatic leadership of Ayatollah Khomeini, or without the emergence of the new '-revolutionary' Shi^ca. Combining religious and revolutionary images and values into an apparently coherent system, the new Shi^ca was acceptable as a partner to all participating groups and, even more importantly, proved able to mobilise the masses.

After the revolution

On 16 January 1979, about a year after the first incidents in Qom, the Shah was forced to leave the country. Two weeks later (1 February), Khomeini returned to Iran from exile; on ll February he took over the government of the country, together with the lay Muslim Nationalist Mehdi Bazargan.

The religious leadership now saw itself faced with the daunting task of realizing its ideal of a theocratic Islamic republic which could look for precedents only to the time of Mohammed's leadership in Medina and Mecca, and perhaps to the brief Caliphate of ^cAli. In such fields as economics, the lack of an established Islamic economic theory that went beyond general guidelines and could be applied to specific problems, must have made itself felt almost immediately. Thus, the 1979 Constitution mentions such fundamental principles as 'the provision of basic necessities to all citizens', and forbids 'the infliction of harm upon others, monopoly, hoarding, usury and other evil and forbidden practices', but for specifics it refers to 'the drawing up of the economic plan for the country....' (Algar 1980:43-4), as to a future event.

The newly established 'Khomeinist' Islamic Republican Party (IRP) had a decisive advantage over other political groups, however, in that it could generally count on the allegiance of the established 'Church', and could make use of its extensive and efficient organizational network from the start. Moreover, by assuming the leadership of such local organisations as the **Komītehs** and the Corps of Revolutionary Guards (**Pāsdārān**), and through its influence over the common people generally, the clergy provided the IRP with a strong power-base at the grass-root level. The creation of institutions such as the office of '-Leader' and the Council of Guardians, together with the parliamentary majority of the IRP, placed the legislative and executive powers firmly in the hands of the Khomeinist religious leadership also.

Of the institutions mentioned above, the office of 'Leader' (**Rahbar**) was presumably created for Ayatollah Khomeini, who is mentioned by name in the relevant article of the Constitution (Algar 1980:66). The office bears some resemblance to that of the (supreme) **Faqīh** as envisaged by Khomeini.

According to the Constitution, the Leader must be a **faqīh** who is either recognised and accepted by a decisive majority of the people (as in the case of Khomeini), or designated by a group of experts appointed by the people. He has far-reaching powers, such as appointing the six 'religious jurists' (**foqahā**) on the Council of Guardians, appointing the supreme judicial authority, supreme command over the armed forces, the right to declare war and peace, and the right to dismiss the President following a judgement of the Supreme Court or a vote of the National Consultative Assembly.

The Council of Guardians consists of six 'religious jurists' nominated by the Leader, and six secular jurists elected by the Consultative Assembly. The task of the Council is 'to protect the ordinances of Islam and of the Constitution by assuring that legislation passed by the National Consultative Assembly does not conflict with them' (Algar 1980:60). Thus it has the right to veto any legislation passed by Parliament which it regards as unislamic.

Of the grass-root forces, the **Komītehs** were set up before the revolution, to help and direct local resistance. The activities of these **Komītehs**, whose members tend to be recruited from the lower classes, usually centre around the village or neighbourhood mosque. Although the **Komītehs** were initially politically independent, as a result of their links with the mosques, they soon came to be entirely dominated by the clergy. Generally speaking, they have a reputation for bigotry and brutally repressive behaviour, and their presence makes itself strongly felt locally, especially since, after the revolution, they have become armed. Members of **Komītehs** and other ultra-religious followers of the Khomeinist line are sometimes referred to as **hezbo'llāhī** ('members of the Party of God').

The **Sepāh-e Pāsdārān** ('Corps of Revolutionary Guards') has a similar reputation for religious zeal and intolerance. The Corps was set up shortly after the revolution, apparently in response to leftwing demands for a people's Militia. The **Pāsdārān**, however, are wholly Khomeinist in orientation; their leadership is usually in the hands of high-ranking local cleric (some of these thus command a considerable local force consisting of **Komīteh-members** and **Pāsdārān**). The function of the **Pāsdārān** is, officially, 'to guard the revolution and its achievements' (Algar 1980:60); in practice they combine the tasks of a policeforce with military duties.

The 'Islamic Societies' **Anjoman-e Eslāmī**) were set up to establish or safeguard Islamic standards of behaviour in government offices, banks, schools, universities and other public institutions. Their members are usually strict Muslims. (On the results of such a process of islamization see below). If the **Komītehs**, the **Pāsdārān** and the Islamic Societies thus act as official instruments of social control and repression of 'unislamic' behaviour, the general atmosphere of insecurity and distrust is intensified by the fact that, on the basis of the Islamic principle that a believer must admonish his fellow-men to do what is commendable and prevent them from doing evil, Khomeini has encouraged private individuals to play a similar role. Social spying among neighbours is now a common phenomenon.

As far as political power and control over public life is concerned, then, Khomeini's Islamic revolution has so far been eminently successfull: virtually all key positions of power are in the hands of IRP supporters, and there is hardly any sector of public life that escapes the pervading social control of the **hezbo'llāhīs**. The monolithic power-structure of the Islamic Republic has enabled the IRP to eliminate the entire range of its political opponents, from the communist Tudeh-party to the ultra-orthodox Hojjatiya. Ayatollah Shari^catmadari, once an outspoken critic of the regime, was later virtually excommunicated, and Shari^cati's ideas are ignored by the government. The authoritarian theocratic ideology of the IRP, moreover, appears to deny by its very nature that any legitimate grounds for opposition or protest against the government could exist.

In the more fundamental task of translating Islamic ideals into practical social and economic policies, however, the regime has not met with such conspicuous success. As mentioned earlier, no identifiably Islamic economic system has existed since the days of the Prophet, and the difficulties of evolving such a system would plainly be daunting (8). In practice, there appear to be deep rifts within the IRP on most major socio-economic issues.

As regards justice, in his **Velāyat-e Faqīh** Ayatollah Khomeini (1978: 15-6) criticised and ridiculed the slow, laborious Western-type processes of justice of Pahlavi Iran, and advocated a procedure that would be 'as swift and simple as possible'; he further defended the traditional Islamic custom of public corporal punishment, pointing out that the Prophet himself had carried out the execution of such punishments (ibid, 22). Swift trials and 'Islamic' punishments are now the order of the day, as part of a new judicial system drawn up by Shi^cite jurists. To more liberal Iranians, however, such punishments seem wholly alien (9).

The islamization of the universities (to which end these were closed from 1980 until 1982, and a Council of Cultural Revolution was set up), appears to have consisted in the purging of a number of students and teachers who were considered insufficiently Islamic in outlook (most of the staff, it seems, were later re-instated when no suitable replacements could be found), and in the admission of a disproportionate number of **Kommiteh**-members, **Pāsdārān**, and volunteers for the warfront (**basiji**); furthermore, textbooks were revised in accordance with Islamic principles and beliefs, and compulsory courses in Arabic and religious education were included in the curriculum.

In public life generally, there has been an increasing emphasis on outward conformation to Islamic rules of personal conduct: participation in the communal Friday prayer is regarded as all but compulsory in many places, women are now obliged by law to wear the veil (reports abound of the harassment of women by **hezbo'llāhīs** on account of minor flaws this respect); men and women can appear in public together only if they carry documents to prove that their relationship is a licit one; alcoholic drinks, drugs and pornography are strictly forbidden, and house-searches for such articles by members of the **Komītehs** or **Pāsdārān** have been known to occur. Gh. Sa^{c}edi, a prominent Iranian writer who died in exile in 1985, describes the atmosphere as follows (110):

'... People are afraid to keep any publications or books in their houses, even books which are appreciated by the authorities. Pictures you must hide in a cellar, or tear up and throw away. Instead, you must hang a portrait of the Leader. If you hang it on the wall facing the front door, perhaps it will soften the hearts of the government spies. Music? Forget about music! Music is opium for the soul, and incompatible with Islamic zeal. Not just popular tunes from the bazar, but good, serious music, too, must go...... To go to the beach, to bathe in the waves, is forbidden. From then on, for fear of being shot, people gradually begin to give way. The depravation of the time of the Shah has been replaced by a deeper, a worse depravation. Every hour, a man may contract a temporary marriage (11); every minute, a woman may be forced to accept one......... All forms of amusement are forbidden, and fear makes people deny themselves anything. The only thing left would be eating, but there isn't any food.'

Another dissident author, Hushang Golshiri (1984:53), makes his hero ask if the revolution was fought solely in order to prohibit alcohol. He speaks, no doubt, for many Iranians. The curtailment of individual liberties and the narrow, legalistic interpretation of Islam - so similar, in practice, to the preoccupation with rules of 'menstruation and childbirth' denounced by Shari^{c}ati and Khomeini alike - has disillusioned and alienated many of those who actively supported the Islamic revolution in its earlier stages, particularly those whose inspiration was drawn from the thoughts of Shari^{c}ati.

The political left, the intellectuals and the liberals can thus be described as the great losers of the Iranian revolution. The winners, evidently, are the clergy, whose influence and prestige have soared. Nevertheless, a section of the priesthood has always been sceptical about clerical participation in politics and their uneasiness, it seems, has remained. Another group to have benefited, so far, from the revolution are the traditional merchants (bāzārīs). Their conservative religious outlook generally leads them to accept the current type of islamization of society, and they have gained considerable advantages since the fall of the Shah. Large sections of the mostaz^Cafīn, the 'downtrodden masses' on whose behalf the regime often claims to act, also continue to support the present government. As in the case of the bāzārīs, their strict religious upbringing has generally predisposed these groups to approve of, or at least to tolerate the severe, 'puritan' aspects of the Islamic revolution. Also, many of these people derive a sense of self--esteem, and of participation in the revolution, from their membership of a Komīteh or of the Pāsdārān, or from other activities in support of the Islamic establishment. Economically, the poorer classes have hardly benefited from the revolution, however, and rumours about popular discontent suggest that support for the government among them is neither unanimous nor unconditional.

The war against Iraq has so far inspired a sense of loyalty to the government in many people, and has helped to silence criticism. It does much, moreover, to perpetuate the self-image of the Iranian Shi^Ca as a righteous, militant faith fighting against a godless tyrant. From such things as religious programmes and slogans broadcast by Radio Tehran, it is clear that a stern, activist religious ethos is still officially propagated. It has proved impossible and ultimately undesirable, however, to eradicate the deep-rooted elements of mourning from religious observances and popular sentiment (cf. Hegland 1983:230ff): in a society where martydom for the faith (i.e. death on the front) is a daily reality, admiration for the heroism of martyrs is bound to be combined with grief for their deaths. Such symbols as the fountain spouting red water at the cemetery of Behesht-e Zahra in Tehran indicate how much mourning and martyrdom are again part of the Shi^Cite ethos.

When the country will once more be at peace, however, it seems doubtful if a militant Islamic ethos alone will suffice to ensure the regime of continued popular support. Whether the government, if still in office, will then rely increasingly on the repressive powers of its grass-roots cadres of Islamic activists, cast another external or internal foe in the role of Yazid, or seek to curb some of the present 'puritan' trends, such as the excessive zeal and liberty of Muslim activists in

enforcing 'Islamic' behaviour, thus paving the way for a gradual libe-
ralisation of society, cannot now be foreseen.

Notes

1. For a discussion and definition of the concept of puritanism, see
    Waardenburg (1983).
2. For much of the information presented here about recent develop-
    ments in Iran, the author is indebted Iranian informants whose
    names, for political reasons, cannot be revealed.
3. For a description of this, and a discussion of the changes in
    Shi^Cite ethos generally, see Hegland (1983).
4. For a broader analysis of Shari^Cati's thought see Akhavi (1983).
5. Some discrepancies will be found in the transcription of Persian
    and Arabic terms. Words generally known in their 'Arabic' forms,
    such as **umma** and **ijtihād**, are transcribed in those forms. For other
    terms, a 'Persian' type of transcription is preferred (e.g. **mojtah-
    ed, velāyat**).
6. For a further analysis of Khomeini's thought see Kelidar (1981)
    and Rose (1983). For a translation of his works see Algar (1981).
7. I.e. the **hejab**, which covers the hair and most of the body, but
    not the face.
8. For a discussion of the problems involved in creating an Islamic
    economic system see Katouzian (1983).
9. A poignant description of an 'Islamic' trial is given in a short story
    by Hesam (1983).
10. From Sa^Cedi (1983). Translation by the author.
11. I.e. a Shi^Cite custom by which a man can marry a woman for a
    limited period of time. Often a form of legalised prostitution.

References

Akhavi, S
    1983   'Shariati's Social Thought', in: Keddie 1983: 135-144.
Algar, H.
    1979   (transl.) *On the Sociology of Islam: Lectures by Ali Shari'ati*,
            Berkeley: Mizan Press 1980 (transl.) *Constitution of the
            Islamic Republic of Iran*, Berkeley: Mizan Press
    1981   (trans.) *Islam and Revolution: Writings and Declarations of
            Imam Khomeini*, Berkeley: Mizan Press
Cudsi, A.S. & A.E. Hilal (eds)
    1981   *Islam and Power*, London: Croom Helm.

Golshīrī, H.
1984 *'Fath-nāma-ye Moghān', Zamān-e Nau* 3, 1362: 51-61.
Hegland, M.
1983 'Two Images of Husain: Accomodation and Revolution in an Iranian Village', in: Keddie 1983: 218-235.
Hesām, H.
1983 'Bārān Mībārad', Alefbā, daura-ye dovvom 2, 1362: 139-155.
Katouzian,H.
1983 'Shi^Cism and Islamic Economics', in: Keddie 1983: 154-165.
Keddie, N.R. (ed.)
1983 *Religion and Politics in Iran*, New Haven and London: Yale University Press.
Kelidar, A.
1981 'Ayatollah Khomeini's Concept of Islamic Government', in: Hudsi & Hilal 1981: 75-92.
Khomeinī, mām (Rūho'llāh al-Mūsawī al-Khomeinī)
1978 *Velāyat-e Faqīh: Hokūmat-e Eslāmī*, repr. Tehran (?)
Rose, G.
1983 'The Thought of Khomeini', in: Keddie 1983: 166-188.
Sā^Cedī, Gh.
1983 'Rū-dar-rū'ī bā Khodkoshī-ye Farhangī', *Alefbā*, daura-ye dovvom 3, 1362:1-7.
Tāleqanī, Sayyed Mahmūd
undated Sherkat-e Sahāmī-ye Enteshār *Partaui az Qor'ān, qesmat-e dovvom, joz'-e siyom*, Tehran:
Waardenburg, J.
1983 The puritan Pattern in Islamic Revival Movements', *Schweizerische Zeitschrift für Soziologie / Revue suisse de sociologie* 3: 687-702
Zonis,M.
1971 *The Political Elite of Iran*, Princeton University Press

Purity in the Taiping rebellion
Erik Zürcher

Purity in the Taiping rebellion
Erik Zürcher

The Taiping rebellion: the three main stages of the movement

In the spring of the year 1837, the young school teacher Hong Xiuquan
went to Canton for his third attempt to pass the triennial provincial
examination, and this time again he failed. In Hong the usual feeling
of disappointment and frustration - probably aggravated by the fact
that he came from a poor family belonging to the Hakka minority-
led to a violent crisis. For several days and nights he was delirious:
he shouted incoherent words and had fits of rage. After his recovery
his whole personality appeared to have changed: he was friendly and
composed; he talked with authority; he started writing poems in which
he vaguely referred to his kingship, his divine mission, and his battle
against the demons, and soon became a person of some renown in his
native district.

During his illness Hong had had some strange visions that became
a central theme in Taiping ideology and that have been recorded in
various versions. Angels had carried his soul to heaven, where Hong
had been welcomed by God the Father and his wife, and by God's
eldest son Jesus, who also was married. God revealed to Hong Xiuquan
that he was His second son, the younger brother of Jesus, and
entrusted him with the mission to liberate the world from all 'demons'
and to restore the true faith. Hong received an official seal and a
sword as symbols of his divine mission, and was instructed in the true
doctrine by God himself. Six years later (1843), Hong returned to Canton, where he received a Christian tract from one of the earliest
Chinese protestant evangelists; in that pamphlet he was amazed to find

a confirmation of the teachings he had received during his vision. Deeply impressed, he started to study Christianity, both by oral instruction (a short period of cathechesis under an American Baptist missionary at Canton, 1847) and by unguided reading in the Bible, of which he had found a copy in the so-called 'Gutzlaff version'(1). Inspired by this mixture of ecstatic visions and half-understood Christian ideas, Hong started to preach a new doctrine of salvation, based on devotion, stern morals, and fanatical iconoclasm. Already in 1847 he and his followers (mainly fellow Hakka) were forced to shift their activities to the wild and sparsely inhabited region of 'Thistle Mountain' (Zijing shan), in the southern province of Guangxi, where they established the 'Community of God-worshippers' - the first stage of the movement.

In that remote base area, the brotherhood soon developed into a well-organized, militant sect with branches in many villages where Hakka dominated. Iconoclasm (the destruction of idols and the burning and ransacking of Buddhist and Taoist temples and possibly also Confucian shrines) became politicized and ethnicized: it became a holy war at grass-roots' level. The growing sect of God-worshippers had all the ingredients for such an escalating conflict: ethnic solidarity reinforced by a single and fanatical faith; a holy leader; a constantly increasing membership recruited from small peasants, miners and local bandits; repeated visions and manifestations of God, Jesus and the Holy Spirit speaking through Hong, and, since 1848, also through Yang Xiuqing, a poor charcoal burner and a born military leader and organizer. Yang soon became the factual leader of the whole movement, completely overshadowing Hong, who, however, as God's son remained the highest spiritual authority. Internally, the God-worshippers were organized as a highly disciplined community.

Documents from this first stage show us Hong as the preacher of a simple, very concrete faith. In the beginning, God had revealed the true doctrine - epitomized in the Ten Commandments - to all mankind; in remote Antiquity (the time of the earliest sage-kings of Chinese tradition) the Chinese had lived according to God's commandments, and had led a life of pure morals, frugality and piety. However, since the third century BC Taoist and Buddhist superstitions had got hold of people's minds (2), and China had fallen into the claws of demons, emanations of 'the old snake', the 'red-eyed one', Satan. The believers, led by Hong, had to wage a relentless battle against all forms of superstition in order to bring China back to its pristine purity. True faith is based on a strictly monotheistic belief in one almighty God who is the father of all mankind (and hence on the conviction that 'we all are brothers and sisters'), a very strong awareness of sin (coupled with a very literal interpretation of the Ten Commandments, including the prohibition to represent living beings), and a firm belief in rebirth in Heaven or Hell. Salvation effected through Jesus' self-sacrifice is occasionally mentioned but not elaborated. No role at all is played by the return of the Lord, resurrection and Last Judgement, probably because Hong himself was present as a Messiah.

At first we do not yet find any traces of dynastic aspirations, nor reference to the 'demoniac' nature of the Manchu rulers (who had been ruling China since 1644 as a dynasty of alien conquerors). However, there was much local fighting, and in due course the sect became completely militarized, notably under the practical leadership of Yang Xiuqing. The canon of religious duties became part of a military code of behaviour of extreme severity. The sexes were strictly separated; since women (as 'sisters in God') were considered equal to their 'brothers' (3), Yang organized women batallions led by female officers. Most forms of amusement - notably gambling, smoking tobacco or opium, and alcohol - were outlawed, and there were severe sanctions on sexual licentiousness. The concept of 'brother-and-sisterhood' led to remarkable egalitarian and humanitarian measures such as the prohibition of slavery and of foot-binding, and the abolition of private property: every member had to surrender all his possessions to a 'Holy Store-house' for common use. One is struck by the monolithic structure of power in which civil, military and religious authority coincided: at various levels, officers simultaneously acted as local group-leaders, as military functionaries, and as ministers in worship. Even in the later stages of the movement, of specialized religious functions were ever created.

Around 1850 when the first clashes with government troops took place, the militant sect became politicized: the aims became anti-Manchu and proto-nationalistic, and the war against the powers of evil merged with an anti-dynastic struggle. The rebels let their hair grow (meaning that they openly rejected the humiliating 'pigtail' imposed in 1644 by the Manchu conquerors upon the male population), and for the first time, both in military proclamations and in supernatural revelations, the Manchus were identified with 'the demons' and made responsible for all of China's woes, material (famine, corruption, unbearable taxes) and spiritual (superstition and moral degeneration). The decisive battle took place in december 1850, when the provincial army was completely routed. On January 11, the victory was celebrated with a meeting of prayer and thanksgiving, and at that occasion Hong proclaimed 'The Heavenly Kingdom of Great Peace' (**Taiping tianguo**) (4), to be ruled by himself as the 'Heavenly King'. (The title of 'King' was consciously maintained, because the word **di**, 'Emperor', was only to be used for 'God').

The second stage of the movement (1851-1853) is that of the 'Long March' (to use a modern Chinese simile) - the Taiping on the move. From their remote base-area in Guangxi, the Taiping armies started an amazing series of offensives throughout South China, up to the Yangzi, and from there to Nanking. In March 1853, Nanking was taken, and was re-named 'The Heavenly Capital' (expressly identified with the New Jerusalem). Nanking became the spiritual and administrative centre of the Taiping state, to the dismay of the Qing court in Peking - and to the amazement of the Westerners in Shanghai who, after the first over-optimistic missionary reports about 'a powerful Christian movement in the heart of China', now practically became the neighbours of the Heavenly Court.

In the third phase, till the mid-'fifties, the Taiping effectively ruled a large part of the middle and lower Yangzi basin, since centuries the most important economic area of China - a region roughly as large as France, with about fifty million inhabitants. In many respects, the year 1851 (from the beginning of the Long March) to 1856 (when Yang Xiuqing was killed) constitute the most creative period of the Taiping movement. Already in 1852 a curious military-theocratic power structure crystallized, that at the top consisted of Hong Xiuquan (the Heavenly King) and four other kings associated with the four directions, among whom Yang Xiuqing, the 'Eastern King', was by far the most powerful one. The atmosphere is aptly illustrated by Yang's complete title: 'Yang, the comforter, Gust-of-Wind of the Holy Spirit, **Henai** Teacher, Deliverer from Disease, Assistant to the Left, Commander-in-Chief and Eastern King of the Heaven-ordained Heavenly Kingdom of Great Peace'. After 1852, Hong himself issued few proclamations; most documents came from Yang and from the Western King Xiao Qiaokui, Yang's closest collaborator both in worldly affairs and in the supernatural; if Yang alternately impersonated God the Father and the Holy Spirit, Xiao was supposed to act as a channel for Jesus Christ. Each king had his own **Gefolgschaft** of secundary leaders and thousands of 'clients' - an unstable structure that soon started to disintegrate due to the internal rivalry between the various kings. Only Yang was able to keep them together; after he was murdered by one of his rivals (September 1856), the whole thing collapsed. The remaining years (1857-1868) belong to military history: the successful counter-offensive by the government armies, aided by Charles Gordon's 'Ever Victorious Army' (after some disappointing experiences the Western community in Shanghai had become strongly anti-Taiping); the fall of Nanking (19 July 1864, two weeks after Hung Xiuquan had committed suicide), and the gruesome massacre that followed. Taiping fanaticism lasted till the end: government reports describe how hardly any prisoners could be made, since all Taiping fought themselves to death.

The struggle against 'superstition' went on unabated throughout the Nanking phase; around 1855 virtually every 'idolatrous' temple or shrine in the Taiping territory had been destroyed. Iconoclasm is coupled with virulent anti-Manchu feelings and strong proto-nationalist sentiments: Taiping documents abound with such seemingly modern catch-words and slogans as 'Our people'; 'We the Chinese'; 'Our great heroes of the past'; 'Let the people know that China belongs to the Chinese'; and 'The thousands of years old birth-right of the Chinese people'. But is is also a holy war, for the Manchus are (rather illogically) represented as the 'idolators' par excellence, and the Taiping themselves are the instrument of 'God's fourth outburst of wrath' in human history; the usual scriptural analogies are the Flood and the Exodus from Egypt. Taiping armies are said to have behaved mildly towards cities that were surrendered without fighting, but the slightest resistance was interpreted as 'Satan's work'; and in such cases the whole population was put to the sword (in 1868, when the last resistance was broken, it was estimated that the 'Heavenly Kingdom of Great Peace' had cost China about twenty millions of human lives).

The obsession with egalitarianism and the detailed regulation of life reached its climax in the Nanking phase, notably in the curious 'Agrarian Reform Law' that was promulgated in 1854.(5) It was a (largely theoretical) blue-print for an extreme form of theocratic protocommunism, based on some earlier Taiping institutions like the 'Heavenly Storehouse' (now extended on a national scale, with God the Father as the owner of all property, and the Heavenly King as His caretaker and distributor, and now also applied to land and crops), and the pyramidal structure of the military organization, with at the bottom a 'platoon' of twenty-five men under a 'sergeant', and at the top an 'army' of ca. 13,000 under a 'general'. The same stratification was now applied to the whole population: base groups of twenty-five families under a sergeant, with its own local 'Heavenly Store-house' that absorbed the total agrarian production, up to the highest unit of 156 families under a general. Thus, the agrarian population became a mirror-image of the armed forces, or rather: since every family had to supply one person (man or woman) to the army, the latter was, so to speak, a concentrated form of a piramidally structured population. All land was divided into nine categories of quality, and according to very complicated rules alloted to each single man, woman or child. The groups of twenty-five families were the basic units of education (based on Taiping text-books with highly ideological content); justice; census; taxation, and religious life. On the Sabbath day (Saturday, not Sunday!), the sergeant acted as minister, and it was also he who conducted religious ceremonials at weddings and burials. The sergeant was also charged with education: daily teaching courses in 'canonical literature', viz. the Old and New Testament and a number of Taiping proclamations, songs, and elementary text-books.

In all this the Taiping completely departed from established Chinese tradition - they were, in fact, most drastically (if ineffectively) trying to create a 'new world'. However, the Land Reform Law and other striking innovations launched by the Taiping leaders remained mainly ideological; in actual fact they were only partially implemented, except in the Nanking region.

Needless to say that the traditional basis of literary training and education - the study of the Confucian Classics, and the system of Confucian literary examinations connected with it - was completely abolished. Education wholly served the Taiping ideology. The textbooks used in Taiping elementary education describe, in simple language full of colloquialisms, the main events of 'salvation history': the Creation and a standard selection of events taken from the Bible (with a strong emphasis on God's role as a stern and wrathful patriarch); the story of visions and divine mandate; the struggle against the Manchu-demons, and a number of moralistic precepts. The Taiping even made an attempt to remould the examination system.(6) The themes on which the candidates had to write their papers were based on the Bible and various Taiping 'revelations'; the few essays that have been preserved are of miserable quality, both in style and content. However, here again we find a unique and truly revolutionary experiment, for one of the examinations held in Nanking was reserved for women.

All these measures probably were designed by Yang Xiuqing and his faction. The Heavenly King himself became more and more eclipsed: he lived in the seclusion of his palace, amusing himself with an enormous harem, and gradually becoming insane (specialists have recognized in his later, most incoherent writings the symptoms of a special type of schizophrenia).(7) His role is only mentioned in passages dealing with theology. In the end, he appears to have developed the remarkable idea that Melchisedec (a priest-king from Abraham's time) was no other than Hong himself in an earlier incarnation. (8)

In those years the Nanking court also assumed all the characteristics of a Chinese imperial dynasty with universal pretensions, albeit that the latter were not based on the Confucian dogma of the Mandate of Heaven, but on the universal power and majesty of God (or, by delegation, of his representative on earth). A grandiose court ritual was developed; curious masquerades were organized in which courtiers, disguised in grotesque uniforms, posed as 'barbarian heads of states bringing tribute', and representatives of Western powers were haughtily summoned to pay their respects to the Son of Heaven in Nanking. In Shanghai, the atmosphere became ever more hostile towards the Taiping, and there was increasing willingness to support the Manchu (Qing) regime in its offensive against the rebels.(9) The fall of Nanking was greeted with relief.

Taiping ideology and puritanism: some distinctive features

Obviously, any attempt at cross-cultural comparison implies generalization, and hence loss of specific identity. If we confront sixteenth and seventeenth century Puritanism with its distinctively European background and Protestant features with the Taiping movement in order to find some common ground, we risk to arrive at a somewhat bloodless abstraction. However, overviewing the great number and great variety of sectarian religious movements in Chinese history, one conclusion can be made: if among that plethora of charismatic leaders, millenarian creeds and secret society rebellions there is one movement that could lend itself to a cross-cultural comparison with Puritanism, it is the Taiping revolution. No other movement, not even the ones that are ideologically well-developed, like the series of rebellions organized by the White Lotus Society, exhibit such a range of basic ideas that commonly are associated with the 'Puritan state of mind'.

Provisionally, the following items appear to be significant in the Taiping case:

a) A strong belief in a single, all-powerful God, who has revealed His will and laid down His design for the world in a Scripture of unassailable authority.
b) The conception of a state of 'original purity', an ideal state in the distant past, characterized by faith, piety and morality.
c) The idea of moral degeneration and the loss of the original divine message due to the acceptance of false gods and superstitious rituals.
d) A strong awareness of sin, and of the imminence of God's punishment if mankind does not mend its way.
e) The idea of a Divine Mandate: by a special act of grace, God reveals Himself to the future leader of the movement, and shows him that he is chosen to cleanse the world of sin and superstition.
f) The battle against the world of sin is an all-out offensive against

all 'evil customs' - it requires a total rejection of the traditional way of life.

g) In their personal lives, the believers have to exemplify that rejection: hence stress on an ascetic and disciplined way of life, strict morals, and a drastic prohibition of 'worldly pleasures'.

h) A strongly developed in-group feeling, coupled with the idea that personal gain is a worldly sin, leads to egalitarian experiments and a rejection of private property.

i) The concept of 'being children of God', coupled with a condemnation of Confucian family mores, leads to a certain degree of female emancipation.

j) If the world is ruled by the power of evil, fighting the world also means waging an armed struggle against those who oppose the movement. In the first stage, local fighting leads to a progressive militarization of the movement.

k) Eventually, it also means fighting the ruling dynasty who symbolizes worldly power at its worst. The movement therefore develops into an armed rebellion, without, however, losing its religious orientation.

l) Once the movement has become a regime with a comparatively stable power base and a well-defined territory, a conscious attempt is made to re-create an ideal state of piety and total order, ruled by a military-theocratic elite.

Conclusions

If viewed in the Weberian perspective, the Taiping movement has little to offer. Instead of leading to a more rational conception of the world and of man's place in it, it constituted an unprecedented attempt to destroy Confucianism - a doctrine which, in spite of its religious and cosmological preconceptions, always has represented the more rational trend in pre-modern Chinese thought. Nor can the movement be said to have shown any tendency towards modernization, in spirit of the willingness expressed by one of the Taiping princes (Hong Rengan) to adopt western technology - statements that were made in the last phase of the Heavenly Kingdom, and that well may have been made in order to muster Western support for the tottering Taiping cause.(10) The rise of indigenous Chinese capitalism took place in the milieu of largely westernized entrepreneurs in the large coastal cities in the late nineteenth century, and can by no stretch of imagination be related to the Taiping ideology which, in fact, shows a strong collectivistic - and hence anti-mercantile - bias. And, finally, the roots of the democratic movement in China are to be found in (again, largely westernized) intellectual circles of the early 20th century, and not in the political ideals of the Taiping system with its absolute theocratic authority and its insistence on military 'law and order'.

However, if we widen the concept, and focus on the quest for purity, it is obvious that in many aspects this applies to the Taiping. The Taiping leaders had, in Waardenburg's terms (Waardenburg 1983) indeed, 'recourse to scripture' - both to the Old and New Testament and to their own corpus of revealed 'proclamations' - reliance on the latter of course being justified by the fact that the leader himself was both God's second born son and the recipient of the Father's revelations. In their possession of a special corpus of canonical scriptures of their own the Taiping closely resemble other Chinese sectarian movements; thus, sects of clearly Buddhist inspiration normally base their teachings on the mixture of Buddhist canonical scriptures and their own revealed texts.

'The purification of self and society', the central quest of puritanism, no doubt was one of the main Taiping ideals. In traditional Chinese sectarianism we regularly find the idea - often coupled with eschatological expectations - that mankind has turned away from the virtues of the Golden Age, and that man by the increasing burden of sin and delusion has lost his 'original nature'. However, in no other movement the idea is expressed with such force and insistence as is done in the writings of the Taiping leaders. As is to be expected, the idea is expressed in a mixture of traditional Chinese and Christian images. There is the belief in a Golden Age in the distant past (a Chinese idea found in both the Confucian tradition and in popular religion), but in the Taiping context it is associated with the 'Garden of Eden' complex (hence not interpreted, in the traditional Chinese way, as an obedience to God's commandments). Sin is deeply rooted and all-pervading, society is lost, unless it is 'cleansed' with the most drastic means. Here, again, we find a remarkable case of hybridization. There is a very un-Chinese explanation for the cause of sin and depravity (and one that ever since the 17th century Jesuit mission has been the object of anti-Christian polemics): the force of evil is personified in the figure of Satan, 'the old snake' who has taken possession of the world and who rules it with the help of his 'demons' (identified with the Manchus). However, this personification of evil- no doubt due to Christian influence - is combined with the very old Chinese belief that the saviour, the one who performs the big clean-up, is, and can only be, a saintly ruler. Thus, the purification of society is, **more Sinico,** expressed in political and military terms. Moral purification is a result of dynastic renewal.

Since the Old Snake is crafty and powerful, even the true believers are tempted by him, and have to fight against their bad inclinations, defined as si 'self-centered', 'egocentric', as opposed to qong 'public'- sinfulness persisting even after conversion'. Conversion amounts to a total self-renewal by which the effect of original sin is effaced, just as Hong Xiuquan himself, in one of his early visions, had seen how his breast was opened and his old heart had been replaced by a new one.

Needless to say that the aspects of 'exclusivity' and a particular 'ethos' (Waardenburg 1983) or way of life loom large in both the ideology and the practice of the Taiping movement. If we compare the Taiping ethos with that of other sectarian movements of late imperial times, we find a marked ascetic tendency: prohibition of luxus, drugs, games and other 'frivolous' activities, and a most striking set of taboos in the sexual sphere, even going as far as the physical separation of sexes. This asceticism naturally was combined with rigorous sanctions and punishments. We have statements of foreign observers reporting about the appalling number of persons in Taiping territory executed for even minor offenses, and one Taiping king is even said to have condemned his father and mother to public decapitation because they secretly had had sexual intercourse (11), in spite of the imposed separation of sexes.

The 'exclusivity' of the Taiping is obvious: it is a perfect example of an 'in-group' characterized by shared ideas and ideals as well as by outward forms of behaviour. In Taiping ideology a clear distinction is made between three categories: the true believers who are assured of salvation as long as they strictly follow the rules; the deluded Chinese brethren and sisters whose minds are dominated by the forces of darkness but who still may be won over to the true faith, and the 'demons' - the representatives of the 'barbarian' Manchu government- who are to be destroyed. At another level, exclusivity is expressed in terms of sinocentrism, even if the attitude of the Taiping leaders vis-à-vis the outside world remainded somewhat ambivalent. Their (highly selective) acceptance of Christian lore forced them to recognize the fact that in a distant past God had choosen a region in the far West - Judea - as the scene of his first incarnation, and this awareness of a spiritual centre outside China may have mitigated the sinocentric attitude to some extent, just as it did in the circles of Chinese Christian converts in the 17th century, and, many centuries earlier, **mutatis mutandis** as a consequence of the acceptance of Indian Buddhism. However, in actual practice the age-old pattern of Sinocentrism asserted itself. Already in an early stage of the movement, China is explicitly stated to be a region blessed among the nations: 'the spiritual continent', where the New Jerusalem was to be situated. This attitude became even more marked in the later phases, when Hong Xiuquan assumed all the pretensions of the Chinese universal ruler; it also is apparent, at another level, from the Taiping insistence that they themselves, and not any foreign missionaries, would be responsible for converting the Chinese people to the true faith.

'Eschatology' is no part of the Taiping ideology - for the simple reason that Hong himself occupied the position of the Messiah, charged with the final battle with the forces of evil and with the establishment of the Heavenly Kingdom. Here again we are on the firm ground of Chinese tradition, for quite a number of sectarian leaders in late imperial times pretended to have supernatural status, as manifestations of divine powers such as the future Buddha Maitreya. For the Taiping, the Apocalyps had begun, and was being consummated before their eyes. It is this aspect that makes one hesitate to compare the Taiping with any Western Puritanical movement.

Finally, 'egalitarianism' constitutes one of the most outspoken characteristics of the Taiping ideology - we do not find it to such an extent in any other sectarian group, and it certainly is opposed to Confucian principles. It is most clearly manifested in the famous Taiping land reform program. Land reform - the distribution of agricultural lands among the population imposed by the government - is a familiar phenomenon in Chinese history. However, it had little scriptural support (although some passages from Confucian classics could be adduced to justify the system); in actual practice, it clearly served the double purpose of supplying the state with a regular source of fiscal revenue, and to curb the power of the aristocratic clans with their large private estates. In the Taiping land reform, the ideological legitimation was quite different, as it was explicitly based on the idea of the equality of all human beings before God, and on the necessity to eradicate the sin of selfishness by the abolition of private property. The same basically religious motivation led to what remains one of the most interesting features of the Taiping: the relatively high status accorded to women. Here, again, any comparison with modern emancipatory movements only serves to confuse the issue. The Taiping rejected concubinage and foot-binding (which, it should be remembered, was an erotic device comparable to high heels and mini-skirts in Western society!) because they represented carnal desire, and their other reforms in this field - the incorporation of women in the army, and their access to the Taiping version of the state examinations-were a logical consequence of their religious conviction that all human beings are God's children. That Hong Xiuquan and the other Taiping kings maintained harems of impressive size does not contradict the principle at all: they belonged to the sphere of the divine, just as the Father himself, who in one of Hong's early visions was surrounded by a retinue of beautiful girls.

When placed in its Chinese context, the most striking aspect of the Taiping movement is its total and uncompromising radicalism. No other sect in Chinese history has shown this degree of iconoclasm. The Taiping turned against Chinese tradition at every level. At the local level they destroyed the idols and shrines of popular religion. They also made an attempt to eradicate the institutionalized religions of China - in the Taiping territory no Buddhist or Taoist temple survived. Confucianism was abolished both as a dominating ideology and as a religious system at grass-roots' level (the ancestral cult and the rituals observed in family and clan). At the state level, they attacked the ruling dynasty, not (as other rebel leaders had done in past centuries) because its initial virtue had been dissipated to such an extent that the imperial clan had lost the 'Heavenly Mandate', but because it was an alien and satanic power, the representative of evil in this world. In other sectarian movements some of these elements can be found, but the Taiping were the only ones to combine them into one singularly militant ideology. In the end they failed, partly because of their fanatical zeal and lack of flexibility, and partly because in their militant phase they had created a doctrine that by its exclusive concern with Holy War and charismatic 'personality cult' was unfit to serve as the ideological basis for ruling a country.

Notes

1) For the Christian sources available to the Taiping see Boardman (1952), pp. 41-51.
2) It is interesting to note that Hong's picture of China's ancient spiritual heritage reflects the standpoint of most Christian missionaries in China since the 17th century, particularly in his extreme rejection of Buddhism and Taoism.
3) For the status of women in the Taiping system see Shih (1967), pp. 60-65.
4) The term combines the ancient traditional Chinese ideal of an utopian society of 'Great Peace' (**Taiping**, cf. Shih (1967), pp. 235-239) with the Christian concept of the 'Kingdom of Heaven'.
5) The basic text is the 'Land System of the Heavenly Dynasty', issued early in 1854; English translation in Michael (1971), document 46.

6) Cf. Michael (1966), pp. 75-76 and p. 91. For the revision of the Confucian classics see also Shih (1967), pp. 42-44.
7) Cf. P.M. Yap, 'The Mental Illness of Hong Xiuquan, Leader of the Taiping Rebellion', *Far Eastern Quarterly* 13 (1954), pp. 287-304.
8) Cf. Hebrews 7: 1-2. Hong's conviction that he was a reincarnation of Melchisedec apparently was based on the fact that the latter was called 'King of Salem', or 'King of Peace', which by Hong was interpreted as 'King of Taiping (= Peace)'.
9) For the western increasingly hostile attitude towards the Taiping movement see Gregory (1969), pp. 47 sqq.
10) For Hong Rengan's last-minute program of modernization see Michael (1966), pp. 140-142.
11) Cf. Shih (1967), p. 67.

Bibliography

Boardman, E.P.
  1952 *Christian Influence upon the Ideology of the Taiping Rebellion, 1851-1864*. Madison, Winconsin.
Gregory, J.S.
  1969 *Great Britain and the Taipings*. London.
Meadows, T.T.
  1953 *The Chinese and their Rebellions*. Stanford (original edition London 1856).
Michael, F.
  1966 *The Taiping Rebellion History*. Seattle.
  1971 *The Taiping Rebellion: Documents and Comments*, 2 vols. Seattle.
Overmyer, D.L.
  1976 *Dissenting Sects in Late Traditional China*. Cambridge: Cambridge University Press.
Shih, V.Y.C.
  1967 *The Taiping Ideology its Sources, Interpretation and Influences*. Seattle.
Teng Ssu-yu
  1950 *New Light on the History of the Taiping Rebellion.* Cambridge, Mass.
  1971 *The Taiping Rebellion and Western Powers*. New York.
Wagner, R.G.
  1984 *Reenacting the Heavenly Vision: the Role of Religion in the Taiping Rebellion*. Berkeley, California.

Puritan movements in Suriname and Tanzania
H.U.E."Bonno" Thoden van Velzen

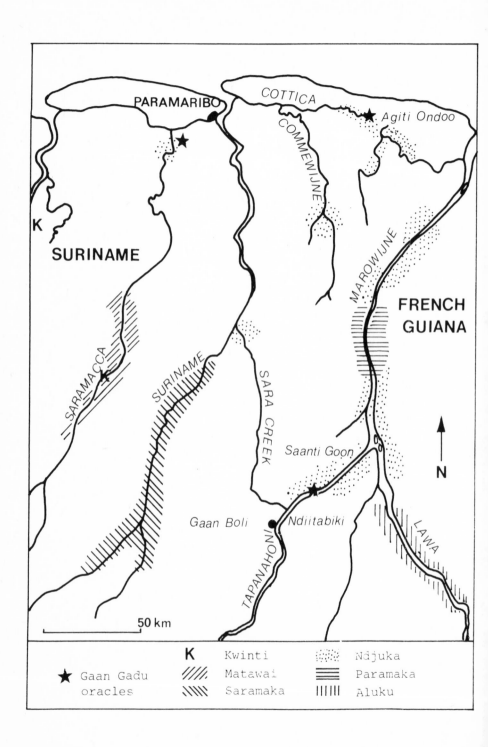

PARAMARIBO

COTTICA

COMMEWIJNE

Agiti Ondoo

K

SURINAME

MAROWIJNE

FRENCH
GUIANA

SARAMACCA

SURINAME

SARA CREEK

Saanti Goon

N

Gaan Boli   *Ndiitabiki*

TAPANAHONI

LAWA

50 km

★ Gaan Gadu
  oracles

K   Kwinti   Ndjuka

/// Matawai   Paramaka

\\\ Saramaka   Aluku

Puritan movements in Suriname and Tanzania
H.U.E."Bonno" Thoden van Velzen

At regular intervals, in many parts of the world, religious communities are shaken by the eruption of puritan movements. Puritans jeopardize the **status quo** by their zeal to cleanse the world. They proceed by disciplining their own unruly selves and by creating strongholds of purity that will serve as bastions for the conversion of the world. Puritans recognize two priorities: to contain the danger from within and to resist temptations originating in the outer world. Puritans sharply dichotomise their moral and social categories. One either belongs to a selected group of warriors in the quest for purity or one represents the forces of darkness. This paper explores the dimensions of two such movements and the 'world' they operate in. At the end, some speculations as to the conditions furthering puritan movements will be suggested (1).

Entrepreneurs as puritans: Ndjuka boatmen

The first example comes from turn-of-the-century Suriname (the former Dutch Guiana). Around 1890, a puritan cult made its first appearance in villages of the Ndjuka Maroons or 'Bush Negroes' of the Tapanahoni river, deep in Suriname's interior. This **Gaan Gadu** ('Great Deity') cult became known throughout the whole of Suriname for its fierce anti- witchcraft campaigns. Humans were seen as sharply divided into three categories: witches, sinners and respectable persons. Witches were considered utterly depraved and irretrie--

vable. For the human community witches were beyond the pale. 'Sinners' could return to the fold after suitable punishment. Responsibility for the world's fate was the burden of all righteous humans, guided by the priests of **Gaan Gadu.**

The quest for purity erupted into iconoclastic purges that swept away most of the traditional spirit-medium cults. In scores of villages, shrines were torn down, spirits exorcized and paraphernalia burnt. Religious practices that failed to bring closer a clean and unsullied world were abandoned. Supernatural beings showing themselves ambivalent towards humanity were no longer recognized as proper agencies for veneration. Determined attempts were undertaken to convert those who lived in ignorance of **Gaan Gadu's** laws. In 1891, the deity's emissaries travelled from the Tapanahoni River to those Ndjukas who had settled in the coastal plain, and to other Maroon groups. **Gaan Gadu's** ambassadors met with considerable success. Within a few years the cult had consolidated its hold over Ndjuka society and won adherents among other Maroon groups as well. The new creed even made inroads into Maroon communities which had embraced Christianity in the past. Covering great distances, Ndjuka and other Maroon converts began to make pilgrimages to the cult's central shrines on the Tapanahoni river (2).

Gold rushes

During the last two decades of the nineteenth century, Suriname and French Guiana became focuses of international economic interest when gold fields were discovered in the interior of both countries. Maroons gained a monopoly over river transport, the only viable link between the ports on the coast and the rich placers deep in the rain forest. The main thrust behind the **Gaan Gadu** cult came from the boat owners (patrons). They seem to have taken the initiative in the witchcraft eradication movement of the early 1890s, and they were known to be the staunchest supporters of the new oracles that functioned as the deity's mouthpieces (Thoden van Velzen 1977).

Boatmen in turn-of-the-century Ndjuka society were affluent. They owned the chief means of production: the boats. They were no longer dependent on the labour of their kinsmen (3). Relationships of dependence between them and their wives' matrilineages could, to considerable extent, be circumvented by buying their food elsewhere. In brief, my argument is that boat owners had a group position to defend, certain economic courses to advocate, and in general were in a position to do so. Wealth assured them of sufficient control of the tribal councils. When such conditions exist, cult teachings will be coloured by the ideological viewpoints of those who control a society's main resources. The new ideology of the 1890s reflected the basic concerns of the boatmen by propagating economic individualism and cultivating suspicion of the poor. The **patron's** distrust of their less successful kinsmen betrayed itself in the specific way witchcraft beliefs were elaborated and defined. Those who met with adversity or debilitating illness were suspect, not the thriving entrepreneurs.

The divine disciplinarian

Gaan Gadu's priests exerted themselves to establish their deity as the supreme divine arbiter. Through their teachings, and through the iconoclastic purges, monolatry was furthered. Throughout the interior of Suriname, a new High God was revered, and the world of the lower supernatural beings ravaged, with only one pantheon of deities left untouched: the all-male **Kumanti** spirit-medium cult. Presumably many boat owners were mediums of such spirits, but perhaps the nature of these spirits, their benevolence, was responsible for the fact that they were spared when the purges demolished traditional religious interests. Whatever the causes of the purges, the result was the creation of a new religious language, a new set of images shared by boatmen of various tribal backgrounds. This standardization of fantasies came at a time when the old boundaries of village and tribal communities had broken down. A bewildering variety of local cults, shrines and spirit mediums had been effectively reduced. With these religious interests, many particularistic religious languages that stood in the way of effective communication among Suriname's Bush Negroes disappeared. The **Gaan Gadu** creed conquered for itself the place as the dominant **lingua franca** of the emotions (4).

Ndjuka boatmen were in need of something akin to science, a corpus of insights into the working of the surrounding world. Such a set of ideas and standardized affects is called here a collective fantasy. This concept of 'fantasy' refers less to 'extravagant ideas that bear no relationship with reality', but rather to 'the imaginative activity which underlies all thought and feeling' (Rycroft 1972: 118). Some of these fantasies strike responsive chords in a great number of people in a certain period. It is then that they may become collective fantasies. A 'collective fantasy' is a symbolic system noted for its visionary images, its philosophy, day dreams and in general for imaginations that are unfamiliar; having no place in ordinary social discourse and often presented implicitly, they strike people as powerful and unusual. A 'collective fantasy' reveals itself through numerous 'symptoms', seemingly isolated pronouncements on the nature of a 'hidden' reality; through strange institutions that play no discernible role in the field of practical action, but above all through images carrying great emotional charges. A collective fantasy may be linked to the world of economic goods and to the entrenched positions of power, but it also enjoys its own sphere of autonomy (Thoden van Velzen 1985).

The collective fantasy espoused by **Gaan Gadu's** priests propagated a view of man's destiny and of the character of the supreme deity that was astoundingly novel and unfamiliar to Ndjukas. The supernatural beings of traditional cosmology were believed to punish departures from prescribed rules of behaviour: infringement of taboos, neglect in the proper execution of ritual, and other fairly well delineated transgressions. **Gaan Gadu** demanded much more of the faithful. This deity scrutinized their acts for traces of moral corruption, and watched their thoughts and feelings as well. **Gaan Gadu** was the deity 'who looks down into our hearts', as it was expressed, 'and from whom we can not hide our evil thoughts'. Such divine monitoring was not limited to the period of contact when the sacred potion was taken: it was a continuing process, a permanent activity. This was a profoundly revolutionary notion, well adapted to the first priority of the ideology: i.e. to smell out witches. However, as I will argue, the collective fantasy was developed well beyond the point of 'instrumentality' or 'ideological needs'.

Barring a few exceptional cases, witches were not believed to be activated by an inherited constitution predisposing them to the crimes concerned (van Wetering 1973: 84). Witchcraft was, rather, a state of mind whereby people were seduced to harm the interests of relatives and neighbours. Each misdeed was believed to pave the way to successively graver ones. The propensity to practise witchcraft grew like a cancer in the body, feeding on it and ultimately destroying it. This process of gradual moral corruption often took years to reach its climax, by which time the depraved person was wholly determined to destroy human life, and was well-equipped to do so. But, along the road to this final station there were stopping-
-places, opportunities where supposedly the individual could resist further temptation and turn back. Hence, a corollary of the theological notion of the omniscient God was the probing of one's conscience by the faithful. They were encouraged to search their heart for feelings of envy, resentment and grudges harboured too long. The notion of guilt was not foreign to traditional Ndjuka religious life, but the way it came to predominate over other feelings

certainly was. The emphasis on the individual, who had to keep to the straight and narrow path under perpetual inner scrutiny and at great pains, was equally novel (5).

Self-examination

Gaan Gadu's priests encouraged self-examination through constant exhortations. They increased distrust of each individual's moral qualifications by demanding a full report on the stature of every deceased. This had to be submitted immediately after the inquest, a traditional institution given added significance. The core of the inquest was the ancient West African tradition of 'carrying the corpse' (Rattray 1927: 167-174), which had been kept alive by Suriname's Maroons. The corpse was tied to a litter and carried through the village on the heads of two bearers. Questions were put to the deceased's spirits by elders following the bier. The spirit replied through the bearers' movements. This was an old form of divination used in the case of every death during earlier times. The new element was that **Gaan Gadu's** priests were not satisfied with an answer to the question as to the cause - which supernaturel agency or what person had killed the deceased - but also insisted on receiving a verdict on his moral character. Each death was then classified as a witch's death (**wisi dede**), a sinner's death (**misi dede**) or a respectable death (**yooka dede**). The first category was the most dishonourable one: it meant either that the deceased had been guilty of witchcraft or that his soul had sunk so low as to be capable of malevolent deeds; had not **Gaan Gadu** intervened the person concerned would certainly have committed such crimes.

Noteworthy too is the unfriendly manner of interrogating the deceased's ghost; the pejorative words used in adressing the spirit, and the ostentatious display of impatience by the interrogating elders. The deceased was considered 'guilty' unless he could prove himself to be innocent. Such 'proof' entailed the successful passing of several tests. The ghost, for instance, must demonstrate its innocence by finding several persons who had concealed themselves in the village: this hide-and-seek was only one of the tests the ghost had to pass. Posthumous punishment was severe, entailing a prohibition to bury the corpse of the witch, and the confiscation of all his property. The mourning ritual was reduced to bare essentials: the bereaved were to show no sign of distress, but were rather supposed to demonstrate their relief by gaiety and laughter.

Apart from the capital sin of witchcraft, the deity would punish suicide attempts, most cases of physical aggression, adultery and homosexuality. The taboos surrounding menstrual seclusion were seen as even more sacred than before: infringements were to be punished as grave misdeeds. In all these cases, the ultimate punishments meted out by **Gaan Gadu** was death, a sinner's death (**misi dede**). The deceased would be left in a hurriedly dug, shallow grave - more than was granted to a witch, but still shameful. In addition, the ordinary elaborate mourning ritual (for decent persons) was reduced to a few libations and prayers in the case of 'witches' and 'sinners'.

The stern disciplinarian character of the new cult was further enhanced by the punishment meted out to those who showed lack of punctually: elders who were late in arriving at **Gaan Gadu's** services were flogged (6), probably as much to their astonishment (no one had ever been punished for such a trivial reason) as to their discomfort (BHW 1892: 142). The priests tried to prevent divorces (MTB 1896: 67), squabbles between spouses (MTB 1895: 49) and wife-beating (BHW 1892: 142). Divine laws seem to have been promulgated on the proper education of children and the inviolability of property, though for these cases I am unable to cite any examples (Burkhart 1898: 27). During the years immediately after the new cult's inception, the priests made sustained efforts to enforce a number of rules affecting many spheres of life (Schneider 1893: 64). They managed to impress the image of a harsh and vindictive deity upon the faithful (BHW 1892: 139-144; MTB 1895: 52).

How alien this type of deity was to ordinary Ndjuka religious conceptions is underlined by the name **Bakaa,** one of the many names borne by the God (MTB 1895: 52). Although the ordinary meaning of **Bakaa** in Ndjuka culture is 'Outsider', someone who is neither a Maroon nor an Amerindian, it refers here to the narrower category of the European. This association between **Gaan Gadu** and the European is still considered important today. People claim, for example, that **Gaan Gadu's** main sanctuary at **Saanti Goon** is guarded by a big white man, who happens to be their deity in visible form. The image of this God, was - to some extent at least - modelled on the European, or, to be more specific, the authoritarian Dutch District Commissioner and his French counterpart, and many other such officials. With these civil servants it was an article of faith that one could not deal successfully with Maroons without firmness: rules had to be spelt out to them and natives would then have to be compelled to keep them with severity (7). Why these Ndjukas would wish to emulate such paternalistic behaviour, or at least identify with it, can only be guessed; perhaps it had something to do with their view of the successful man - a sort of 'superman'. better adapted to the bewildering complexities of a new world than the Maroons themselves? Here one discerns in the stern authoritarian features of the 'new style' deity an attempt to forge links with a wider world.

Clearly, this world required a new type of man. Business transactions and daily social communications were no longer confined to a small circle of relatives and a few white officials. From now on there was to be close contact with other Maroons, with adventurers in search of eldorado, with escapees from Devil's Island and similar penal establishments in French Guiana. The interior had become a much more dangerous and unpredictable place. It was making greater demands too. While there was the challenge of new economic opportunities, of wealth unheard of before, the decisions to be taken could no longer be made jointly with kinsmen. The anxieties thus generated required an outlet. **Gaan Gadu's** priests met this requirement by initiating an anti- witchcraft organization, and by advocating a shift of the psyche's point of gravity towards the superego. The emphasis on the eradication of witchcraft had been the result of considerable popular pressure (8). I do not wish to argue, however, that the priests had no choice but to stress the superego as the psyche's dominant force. Nor would I claim that their attempts met with lasting success. The only thing one can talk about with certainly is the **direction** advocated. To summarize the evidence: the cult attempted to heighten moral sensibility by stressing the scrutiny of conscience, by promulgating a new set of **restrictive** rules, and by conceiving the image of its deity in authoritarian terms.

External Threat

Puritan collective fantasies flourish under threat. Extreme positions, after all, must be justified by a state of emergency. Ndjuka boatmen felt threatened by a host of witches. All of those who could not participate in the lucrative transport industry would come under suspicion. With little or no money, perhaps suffering from poor health, these unfortunate persons had a motive to kill or maim the successful **patrons**. The witch was their arch-enemy. In him, or her in most cases, evil was concentrated. If only those witches could be removed from the face of the earth, how much safer a place it would become! The intensity of anxiety feelings may be gleaned from the posthumous treatment of witches at the **Saanti Goon** sanctuary.

Saanti Goon is **Gaan Gadu's** main sanctuary. It is located in the heart of Ndjuka territory, in the forest opposite the village of Puketi. It consists of two separate locales, two sacred areas. One is on the banks of a creek that flows into the Tapanahoni near the Gaan Olo Falls: this is the witches' 'cemetery'. The area is out of bounds to all Outsiders, and to all others who have no ritual assignment in the area. Only a few handpicked gravediggers (the association responsible for burial and funerary rites), selected and accompanied by **Gaan Gadu's** priests, may enter this area. Along the banks of this creek the corpses of witches were left unburied, pushed into the undergrowth, and covered with a few branches. Gravediggers who penetrated this blighted land prided themselves on their courage. People would call them 'daredevils' (**ogiiman**). This creek was the scene of **Gaan Gadu's** most terrible retribution: for a deceased not to receive a burial, to have one's remains devoured by wild animals and carrion birds, that was the worst fate people imagine. The locale was dominated by the numinous presence of a stern, vindictive deity. Even after the successful revolt of phophet Akalali (9) against the **Gaan Gadu** priesthood (1972), no one, not even the phophet himself, dared to enter this territory.

The second part of the sanctuary, the forest shrine, was the scene of prostration before **Gaan Gadu**. God's Cargoes (**Gadu lai**) were brought to that sacred spot to be divided between the deity and his human servitors, the priests. As I mentioned earlier, after death an inquest was held. The material effects of witches and sinners - those who died a witch's or a sinner's death - were confiscated. The relatives of these witches and sinners were obliged to bring the deceased's effects to **Gaan Gadu's** main oracle at Ndiitabiki were the goods were cleansed and then confiscated in the name of the deity. Part of these were returned to the relatives at the end of the ritual; other goods were placed at **Gaan Gadu's** secret forest shrine at Saanti Goon, and the priests kept some of the more valuable things for themselves.

Judging from the group's reaction to perceived danger, the threat the witches represented must have been frightening. The intensity of feeling can be gauged from the elaborateness of ritual, and its obsessive focussing on the enemy: the witches. I suggest that the puritan creed is a response to these high anxiety levels. If one has to wage war on an enemy, the superego must hold way to prevent the surfacing of dangerous impulses from within, and to avoid the dissipation of energy.

The leadership of these puritan reforms was in the hands of a relatively small group of priests serving the two main oracles of

Gaan Gadu at the Tapanahoni villages of Ndiitabiki and Gaan Boli, and a few dignitaries at their subsidiary oracles in the Cottica region and elsewhere. A group limited in numbers but supported by most of the Ndjuka males in the productive age categories. These boat owners were not under pressure from any external power holder; they moved freely through the Dutch and French colonies, their services as freight carriers much in demand. The puritan response that culminated in the **Gaan Gadu** movement was not a 'religion of the oppressed': neither the variable 'political repression' nor 'economic deprivation' seems to have any explanatory value.

The movement was certainly not nativistic. No effort was undertaken to revitalize ancient institutions, nor did cult adepts exert themselves to effect a repritinization. What is astounding about the heydays of the **Gaan Gadu** movement is the novelty of its major institutions.

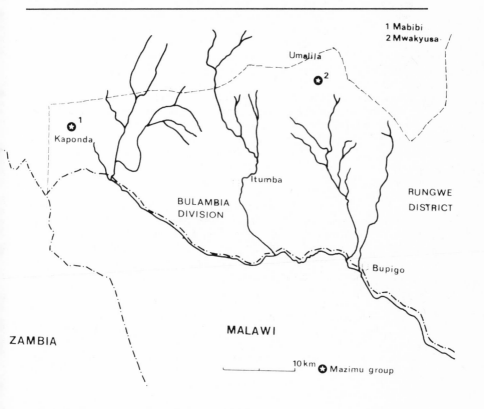

The Mazimu: communities under siege

Total war

In southwestern Tanzania, in the border region of Tanzania, Malawi and Zambia, several groups of **Mazimu** are active. **Mazimu** in the language of one of the ethnic groups living in this area, the Ndali, means ancestor spirits. (**Bazimu** is its equivalent in the language of the Nyiha group; and **Wazimu** in that of the Malila). **Mazimu** is a misnomer (10). The groups that are known under these names are not ancestor cults at all. To be sure, the core of each group consists of a number of mediums who claim to be possessed by ancestor spirits. However, these spirits are never considered to be the ghosts of **specific** ancestors. Moreover, the cult is not associated with ancestor ritual or ancestor shrines. Mediums claim to be possessed by 'the collective of ancestors', or by the spirit of **Mulungu** (God). They might say: 'I am moved by the spirit of God'. Whether the collective of ancestors is meant, or God, mediums feel themselves to be intermediaries of the Divine. In the war being fought between the human community and the forces of darkness, only mediums can link up with the forces of Light, (God, or the collective of ancestors), and tap the power of this supernatural force so that the human community may survive. The mediums are 'the chosen ones', selected by divine wish, to play an important role in the struggle between Good and Evil. Mediums report on what chances to come to their mind: dreams and flashes of insight. These irruptions (11) are believed to have a divine origin. They inform mediums where Evil is hiding; how to destroy it; where to find 'medicines', the counter-weapons in the celestial struggle. Such is the philosophy of the **Mazimu**.

All **Mazimu** are mediums (s. **umushimi**, pl. **inchimi**) or, to put it differently, the test of belonging to the **Mazimu** is mediumship. To be a medium proves that one is chosen by God as his instrument, as a vehicle of the divine that can intervene in human affairs to check the pernicious forces of Evil. But not all mediums are of equal rank or equal calibre. Two categories stand out: 'ordinary' mediums or foot soldiers, and the leaders.

Ecstatic behaviour is the first characteristic of the ordinary medium that strikes the outside observer. In fierce violent spurts, these **inchimi** run zigzagging through the fields, by day or night, in search of the gifts of God or the weapons of Evil. The first category consists solely of medicinal plants. Mediums can be seen uprooting small trees or cacti, feats that they would never be able to perform under ordinary conditions. Usually, they collect leaves, plants or their roots. The second is more heterogeneous. This category encompasses the 'booby traps' (objects of remarkable shape or containing evil medicines) buried in footpaths or hidden under a bridge, at places where people pass by on their daily business, forgetful of the dangers lurking around them. Frequently, mediums try to find the medicines fabricated by traditional medicinemen. These objects are of dubious character to **Mazimu**; some might actually be helpful but they feel ambivalent about them. In their thinking many of these traditional medicines have been tampered with: deliberately by sorcerers, or involuntarily by people who did not intend to harm others, but who were in a sinful state of mind when they set about preparing them. After making their rounds through the area surrounding the congregation of **Mazimu**, they return to the group's leaders to present their booty. The leaders inspect the objects collected, present an estimate of the type and degree of evil hidden in them, and add information about the owner and what he intended to do with it.

Prominent members of the **Mazimu** act quite differently. They do not run through the fields in trance. When they go out to collect medicines, it is usually done in an inconspicuous way. Although they are considered to be the chief instruments of the divine, flashes of inspiration come to them calmly: often it is hard to distinguish between their ordinary behaviour and their mediamistic performance. Much of the divine communication reaches them through their dreams, or through visions that suddenly come to them, without being in trance. When diagnosing patients, or screening witches, while walking absent-mindedly around the persons concerned, sudden hiccups or exclamations (heyooo heyooo) betray seizure by the spirit of God.

Mazimu groups throughout this part of Africa feel entrusted with a divine assignment. They consider it their duty to wage war on the forces of Evil; a perpetual struggle, and a war fought with all means. The witches (**abalozi**) are the enemy to be confronted. The witches are Evil incarnate. The witches contrive that dangers lurk everywhere. This reaches crisis proportions whenever a group of **Mazimu** meet. The witches then rally to surround and engulf the **Mazimu**. Through repeated irruptions, **Mazimu** are aware of these threats. Leaders frequently put their groups on a full alert. They arouse their followers to a sense of imminent danger. The threat could be stemming from the enemy beyond the perimeter of their meeting place or from accomplices of the enemy hiding amongst them. Repeatedly, followers are enjoined to be vigilant. In the middle of the night emergencies are often proclaimed.

Two Mazimu groups

During my field work in Tanzania I spent most of my time with two groups of **Mazimu**. The first worked in Kaponda, not far from the border town of Tunduma (13), and was usually called 'Mabibi's group', or the 'Kaponda group'. Members of this group were recruited from the two main ethnic groups of the area, the Nyiha and Ndali. The leader of this **Mazimu** congregation, Mabibi, was a member of the Ndali ethnic group, most of his assistants were Nyiha. There were hardly any relations of kinship among leaders or followers. The hard core of the Kaponda group consisted of a dozen prominent mediums, and a following of approximately 20 or 30 persons, most of them women. Including patients, at each meeting about 100 persons would show up. Few of the mediums were well-to--do farmers; in fact the whole border region was fairly poor, without cash crops or other sources of financial income.

Although the group's leadership did its utmost to present itself as an embattled minority in a sea of enemies, they could clearly count on the sympathy if not the support of a fairly large group (certainly more than half of the population) of the border area. Patients came from nearby villages and from places across the border in Malawi and Zambia. The Moravians were their staunchest opponents. Well represented among lower-echelon Tanu and government officials, they were feared by **Mazimu** for the sanctions that they could bring to bear on them. On the other hand, they received requests for witch hunts under their (the **Mazimu's)** supervision from villages as far away as twenty or thirty kilometers from their Kaponda base. I was present when Kaponda's **Mazimu** searched the village of Itumba (population 1,000, also a small-scale centre for government services) thirty kilometers from their base, and noticed the widespread support among peasants who were in no way related to the mediums. Many of them had never personally met one of the **Mazimu** from the Kaponda region. Yet, elders with various ethnic backgrounds and from a number of different family groups communally invited them. The large minority of Christians in the village where the **Mazimu** were commissioned to work connived at it; very few spoke out against it.

The second **Mazimu** group operated mainly on the southern fringe of the Umalila plateau among an ethnic group called the Malila. At the end of the 1960s their leader was Mwakyusa. The Malila group was quite differently constituted. Practically all prominent mediums came from a small number of patrilineages. Most female mediums were recruited from these patrilineages as well. The **Mazimu** knew that they represented a faily large section of the population. There was no Christian community in this part of the Umalila plateau. When the mediums moved through the area of scattered farms that formed the community they were never harassed by militant opponents as did occasionally happen with the Kaponda group. Since the introduction of a cash crop, pyrethrum, in the early 1960s, the Malila enjoyed a time of prosperity such as they had never known before.

The enemy within the gates

In Kaponda, Mabibi and a few other mediums directed the group's main activity: the treatment of patients. This is one of the cases I took notes on, a case which is fairly representative of many others regularly brought to the **Mazimu**.

Mabibi summons a patient to come to the unoccupied area in the middle of his house. The women carries her sick baby.
Mabibi: 'Mother, why do you look so sad? Something seems to bother you. Are you angry with yourself? I first summoned you to come here because your child looks so ill. Don't you remember the day when you were soaked with sweat? (Before the answer could be given Mabibi continues his monologue.)
'Now listen carefully. If you feel what I am telling is not the truth, refute it. (A routine suggestion to prevent loss of face. People seldom have recourse to it though.)
'On a certain day when your baby fell ill; did you then consult a medicineman? But all the time you knew it was only yourself who was disposed to do evil. You didn't proper care'.
For half a minute nobody speaks a word. Mabibi, feeling the child's stomach, suddenly starts trembling. (Trembling is considered a sign that the medium is in communication with the supernatural.)
Mabibi: 'If only the government would give me permission to punish evil people, then you would see what we would do with you'. Now Mabibi confronts the patient directly:
'You are an evil woman. When a witch tried to kill you, you decided to offer your child as a sacrifice. Slowly the witch is now eating your baby. But no one gave you permission to sacrifice children. Children are God's property. Please, in the future, watch out what

you are doing'. (Mabibi's assistant turns to me to explain: 'The patient tries to save her own skin by offering her child to the witch) (13).

Mabibi now turns to the people assembled. 'I dreamt that among us here are some people who try to make this meeting as unpleasant as possible. There is one in particular who is very obnoxious. This person does his utmost to disrupt our meeting. I strongly advise this person to quit doing this, otherwise we would feel tempted to make his name public. Please continue with your singing'. (The singing of Moravian hymns is an essential part of the nightly meetings. No official of the Moravian church is present, but people in this area are well-acquainted with their repertoire of church music. The Moravians brought the Gospel to the Nyakyusa in nearby Rungwe District as long as 80 years ago.)

A married couple steps forward. The mother carries her child. Her child is ill. Mabibi walks with great strides around the couple. Now and then he stops pensively. He then turns his face away from his patients. Then he starts questioning them: 'Does your child suffer from diarrhea?' Before they have a chance to reply he puts another question: 'Has someone been selling you bad medicines? 'The man replies to both questions affirmatively. Mabibi: 'You waited for so long, too long. At first you wished to come, particularly when you heard that your child suffers from an intestinal disease. Foolishly you preferred to consult a medineman'.

Mother of patient: 'No, that is not true, we did not consult a medicineman. 'Mabibi repeats his question thrice. Finally the husband concedes: 'Yes, I requested the services of a certain medicineman. My child drank from the medicine that was prepared for him'. Mabibi turned to the child's mother berating her for misleading him. Then he asked her: 'Your child's excrements are black as charcoal'? Before giving her a chance to answer his question he continued: 'Mother, pray to God: your child is very sick'. He touched the stomach of the child thrice and promised to search for medicines at daybreak.

Witches who hide within the **Mazimu** congregation are a paramount danger. They may act as a 'fifth column' for the evil forces on the outside. They have to be detected and neutralized before they can wreck the beneficial work of the mediums. The chief ways in which they operate are to sow discord amongst **Mazimu**, and to hinder the medium's work by enticing them to harbour sinful thoughts. Once the mediums abandon themselves to such desires, their efficacy as tools of God is greatly diminished. Mediums who are afraid to confront the witches, and conceal important insights, form another danger to the congregation. They have been picked by God for this elite unit to perform His work. Any shirking of responsibilities will meet with divine punishment. To be a medium is to have a vocation which imposes heavy burdens. God, who sees everything, scrutinizes all acts and all thinking. Religious notions such as these are taught by all leaders, but in particular by preachers who work by reading a few passages from the Bible, and then extemporize on these subjects. Each **Mazimu** group can boast at least one preacher.

After the leader has diagnosed several patients, and the preacher is given the floor for some minutes, the hour has come for the rank and file of the **Mazimu** to prove their worth. Violent shaking, trembling and running wildly through the barn, precede their public confession. Without such a confession, a medium's work would be seriously hampered. Some confess to sinful thoughts, others to idleness, proneness to drinking, dancing and running after girls. Their public confession is discussed by the leaders. They are reprimanded but subsequently cleansed. Then they can disappear into the night, running through the fields at incredible speed, searching for evil objects and for medicinal plants. When they return after an hour of nocturnal scavenging, their booty is displayed in public, assessed by the leaders, and they receive praise or censure depending on the leaders' estimate of the collection.

After two or three o'clock in the morning, the **Mazimu** congregation enjoys a few hours of sleep. But already before dawn the sleeping mats have been rolled away to make room for a new session. This is invariably opened by the recounting of dreams. Some of these have a nightmarish character: dreamers relate how they were chased by monsters, or by the police. Others revert to a theme that also crops up in ordinary communications: the threat posed by the external world.

Dreams

Here are a few examples of dreams by **Mazimu** from the **Kaponda** region: (a) 'The witches intended to assault our congregation. But something stronger than evil kept them from doing that. That's what I dreamt tonight'.

'I dreamt I encountered a man who challenged me. He said: 'Let's see which one is strongest. I must confess that you are a formidable adversary. You work hard both at home and with the **Mazimu** congregation'.

'I encountered a man who was burying an **amapingo** (bad medicine) in a footpath. When I asked him why he was doing this, he declined to answer. I tried to run away, but he kept up with me and overtook me. I could do nothing else but to sit on the ground and pray for God's protection. It immediately started to rain. The man appeared to be afraid of rain because at once he fled. I went home. When I entered my house I saw my husband with his girl friend. This friend begged me to help; she was sick but had neglected to attend **Mazimu** meetings (Her husband's friend is a member of **Mazimu**; her husband however is not). I refused. I told her I would only give my husband advice'.

Among the **Malila** of the mountains similar 'dream confessions' were publicly delivered, but they were always part of more comprehensive meetings. The **Mazimu** group I knew best met twice a week. When some kind of an emergency occurred, or was felt to occur, extra meetings were convened. One day in the middle of the night strong winds damaged the thatched roofs of houses. On the morrow an extra meeting of **Mazimu** mediums was called. One of the **Mazimu** adepts started by expressing his anxiety that this was the beginning of a counter-offensive by witches. To convince people of the urgency of the situation he disclosed that he had seen the former headman M. move stealthily through the dark to the house of a friend of his, a **Mazimu** as well. Another member of the group then, all of a sudden, had revelations: 'Danger is approaching us'. If we don't move quickly we will suffer again like never before'. Then the leader of this **Mazimu** group spoke: 'I must urge you to be present here next Friday for the singing of hymns. We will also teach people how to live well by cleaning themselves properly, by good cooking, by keeping all domestic utensils is good order'. He read haltingly from the Bible. The **Mazimu** hymns were sung and a few mediums were possessed by 'the spirit of God' (**Imbepe ya Mulungu**). Four ran away to search for medicinal plants. In the meantime the dream confessions started:

Y: 'I dreamt that some people here don't want to tell us what they dream at night. But it is necessary for our survival that we hear all dreams. Don't hide things. I dreamt that a great flood would come, and that we didn't know where to run'.

K: 'I had the same dream. When I returned from Itumba (centre with government officials, local court, primary schools, dispensary) I dreamt that I had met somebody on the way back. He said that we

Mazimu are just a bunch of hooligans. In my dream we caught him, burnt him in a fire, but he escaped. When we chased him he knew to hide himself so well that we couldn't find him anymore. Then I dreamt I was caught by a certain man: he threw me in a deep pond. I started praying. I dreamt an owl was crying on my house roof. I woke up and there was an owl crying on the top of my house. This reminds me that you should never exchange your maize for bananas just because they taste so sweet. It will bring hunger to our families. You will kill your children. Who did this?'

N (female): 'I sent my daughter to do this. After I receive the bananas, I will exchange them for peas'.

Then the discussion focussed for some time on the foolishness of women who give away valuable food for delicacies that had little value as nourishment. It was obvious to me that in this closely-knit group of agnates the attention of men had shifted from impending disaster to the more mundane problems of day-to-day living. The problem of how to control capricious womenhood loomed large in the discussions.

From these homilies the **Mazimu** soon found their way back to the overriding problem of witchcraft. 'When you hear that the witches (**abalozi**) have killed one of our people, come to the meeting place of **Mazimu** forthwith and pray. The witch will be found and then we will beat him till he dies. Certainly we will go to prison, but that won't deter us. To be imprisoned means nothing to us. They won't hold us very long too. When my term is finished, I will be back to beat other witches. Particularly those who move at night will be given no mercy. Even those who just for one occasion buy 'bad medicine' will be thrashed. Let us not forget: this period is the last one; the world is coming to an end'.

Keep your distance

Back to the nocturnal **Mazimu** meeting in Mabibi's group in Kaponda. Among one of the suspicious objects found by the mediums was a small cow horn, often used as a vessel for medicines in this area. Mabibi, while inspecting its contents, drew attention to pubic hair that was put into the horn. In other instances, a strong condemnation would have followed such a discovery. Mabibi mentioned the owner's name and his function in **Tanu** (in those years the name for Tanzania's only political party). He left it at that. Why he chose to remain silent became clear to me when he held his farewell speech to the mediums who were returning to their homes:

'Now you are going home. Some may perhaps feel an inclination to share the experiences of tonight with other people. Don't do that. Keep silent. Those who talk too much spoil our work. Listen but don't say anything. Always remember the witches that are on the loose. The first thing they wish to do is to disrupt our work so that we may no longer find bad medicines'.

And his preacher added:

'Christians accuse us of serving Satan. When you meet with Christians, behave calmly and friendly. Don't argue with them, but listen when they pray. Don't argue with anybody at all, it is bad for our work. Women, when your husbands complain that they were starving while you were here to do the work of **Mazimu**, don't quarrel. Always be kind. Men, you are about to return to your own villages. Don't try to seduce other men's wives; that would make you unfit for serving as God's medium. We have to respect the divine law of fidelity in marriage'.

Attempts at explanation

The **Gaan Gadu** cult that dominated the religious life of the Ndjukas in Suriname's interior at the turn-of-the-century, and the **Mazimu** movements of post-independence Tanzania, shared one characteristic: they erupted in societies that had experienced significant transformations. In Suriname's interior several gold rushes largely destroyed a kin-ordered mode of production. In Tanzania, the combined effects of independence, new economic opportunities, and the introduction of a new medical 'regime' shattered traditional authority structures. The argument presented here is that these religious movements made headway because of the 'thinness' of the new social environment. The old economic and political networks had been weakened considerably, or even, in some areas, had vanished completely. Attempts to understand and experience the world in religious terms could find novel forms under a new leadership.

The transformations of Ndjuka society

Before 1885, Ndjukas were predominantly lumber workers. Each year, for a number of months, they lived in temporary settlements in the coastal plain. Males were accompanied by their women and children. Often a considerable number of matrilineal relatives jointly made the move to the coast. Hence, for most of the nineteenth century, lumbermen and their family lived and worked in the same settlements.

Shared residence, however, can only partially explain the vitality of the quite large corporate kin groups of the time. Their cohesion may be reinforced by economic necessity. Lumbermen needed one another and could not work without the assistance of their family. From time to time tree trunks had to be hauled towards the river. Old and young, male and female, were welcome to contribute their labour. The lumbermen relied on older men and women for a single but essential part of the production process. The few hours (or a few days at most) it took to drag the trunks or logs to the river were decisive for the relations of production: they provided the corporate matrilineal group, with its ideology of mutual sharing and collective responsibility, with a solid economic underpinning.

River transport destroyed the pattern of continuous shared residence. It took boat crews approximately three weeks to complete a trip between the ports on the coast and the placers in the interior. More often than not, they would make several other trips before returning to their villages for a brief visit. The severing of relations of economic dependence was even more significant. Ndjuka males who had set out to work as river carriers were no longer dependent on the assistance of their matrilineal kin: the services of only one or two sons or sister's son were all that was needed. And even this type of minimal dependence could be circumvented by joining forces with an adult kinsman or a friend (a boat crew usually consisted of only two or three men). The relations of production then did **not** oblige the freight carriers to look for support from their kinsmen. Originally an essential support, these relatives had now become a liability.

Ndjuka boatmen working in Suriname and French Guiana lived in a very 'thin' social environment. Not only had corporate kin groups greatly lost their social significance for these boatmen, but no other social figuration of comparable weight had emerged. Through brief visits, Ndjuka boatmen continued to give direction to social affairs in their villages, but their main 'arenas' were the river basins of French Guiana and the border area. There, far from their villages, money was earned, and relations with other men determined. The new social networks that evolved around their work were limited in complexity, usually dyadic relations and often single-stranded. Relations with their colleagues could be very short-lived; for instance, a night in a forest camp, a stopping place on their way to places in the interior; or a few days spent together in a coastal town, waiting for a cargo. In brief, Ndjuka boatmen lived in a 'thin' social environment.

At the end of the century, when a social crust of mutual help and mutual constraint broke away, Ndjukas were thrown back on their own selves and their own resources. The emphasis given by **Gaan Gadu's** priests to self-examination, and to the worship of deities that are strict and vindictive, but moral and predictable, seems to tally well with the requirements of the first generation of boatmen. The same could be argued for that corpus of divine decrees, a set of restrictive rules that served the need for new guidelines in a unfamiliar social environment.

Hence, a relationship can be postulated between the 'thinness' of social networks and efforts to purify the self and society. The relationship, however, is weak. Around 1895, only a few years after its beginning, the iconoclastic purges had spent their force. Turn-of-the-century Ndjuka society also seems to have lost its zeal for disciplining and restricting its members. At least, we have no more indications that any attempts to regulate social life, in excess of what was traditionally prescribed, were ever undertaken. Apparently the 'puritan experiment' was a short-lived one. Around 1900, social conditions in Suriname's interior, in my thinking, favoured puritan regulations but did not demand them. Once Ndjuka boatmen's enthusiasm for the 'puritan experiment' began to cool, the new restrictive regulations were abandoned. However, the emphasis on the purification of self, on self-examination as a necessary condition, did not lapse. I suggest that while they apparently could live without a 'puritan society', to live without safeguards against witchcraft was not a viable option in a society riven by tensions between **patrons** and the 'non productives'. The posthumous punishment of witches did lose nothing of its harshness. Self-examination continued to set the tone in religious debate as a mark of distinction which allowed one to discriminate between the 'good citizen', and the witch or those prone to witchcraft. The **Gaan Gadu** oracles' chief business remained the detection and persecution of witches. In brief, the 'puritan experiment' in Ndjuka society was a discretionary one, to be discontinued without much repercussions. What was essential in 'the experiment' - the anti-witchcraft measures - was to be retained. The anti-witchcraft campaign derived its vitality from ongoing social tensions.

Transformations and the Mazimu

The **Mazimu** groups of southwestern Tanzania lived in a similar 'thin' social environment. This part of Tanzania and adjoining Zambia is usually known as 'the corridor area'. For many generations, peoples had moved through this area in search of a safe place to settle. At least since the beginning of colonial times, Nyakyusa from the crowded Lake Shore area began to expand, pushing many Ndali that inhabited the mountain fringe to the west of them into the 'corridor area'. These Ndali never fully assimilated to the peoples of the 'corridor area'. They had better farming systems which enabled them to occupy the fertile, marshy lands along creeks and rivers. A generation later when the other residents of the area began to understand the fertility of these fields, Ndali occupancy of river gardens became a bone of contention, bringing clear-cut social divisions into areas where people usually were of such diverse origin that antagonistic relations did not crystallize along clear-cut ethnic boundaries. The Ndali also brought another source of division into the 'corridor area': Christianity. Large numbers of them had been converted by Moravian missionaries working in the Ndali mountains or among their neighbours in the east, the Nyakyusa.

During colonial rule, the authority of chiefs, bolstered up by the colonial government, brought some modicum of order into the region. One of the first measures taken by the independent government of Tanzania was to abolish in the rural areas the system of legal and political authority based on chiefs, and to supplant their authority by that of Tanu functionaries. The chiefs were allowed to continue giving direction to traditional rites. But being divested of their worldly power assets, and having to compete for prestigious political offices with relatively young Tanu politicians, many chiefs in the corridor area lost their grip on local affairs. However, Tanu functionaries did not succeed in establishing a respected authority structure either.

The introduction of a 'Western' medical regime in hospitals, clinics dispensaries and primary schools undermined the authority of the medicinemen. This category had been strongly fragmented, without any semblance of hierarchy or fixed relationships. Fierce competition and the absence of authorative centres of divination made the medicinemen an easy target for criticism. Distrust was fanned by the representatives of the alternative 'Western' system. It was in this 'thin' social environment, I suggest, that new religious groupings could emerge which would launch creeds stressing order and discipline while advocating a clear break with the past. Cutting bonds with the two loci of traditional authority, medicinemen and chiefs, they created their own world, communities that failed to establish links with either the political regime or the strong Christian enclaves of the corridor area.

The **Mazimu** groups of Tanzania's border region with their emphasis on the purification of self and society were not short-lived experiments. **Mazimu** adepts could not 'commute' between two social worlds as the Ndjuka boatmen were doing (between their work in French Guiana and their home villages). The **Mazimu** were unable to escape from a world with fragmented authority systems. Their services as 'witch hunters' were much in demand. The traditional religious outlets through ancestor or chiefly cults, were blocked by the destruction of the political base of elders and chiefs. Solutions sponsored by medicinemen were tainted in a comparable way. The purification drive proposed by **Mazimu** did not depend on any obsolete form of authority, nor on newer power structures (government or the associated party system of Tanzania) that lacked a sufficient base in the countryside. The work of Tanzania's puritans probably had the appeal of what the French sociologist Balandier (1955) once called 'a retaking of the initiative' (**une reprise d'initiative**).

Like so many of the early Christians the **Mazimu** of the plain - Mabibi's group of Kaponda - recreated a community cemented by mutual help. During nocturnal meetings a new social ethic was impressed on the believers. They were urged to move gingerly through the land of Satan, neither to seek quarrels nor to let themselves be provoked by people hostile to the movement. Among the **Mazimu** of the plain, who lived among the unconverted, the community could only manifest itself during their weekly meetings, or in the small, almost clandestine gathering of a few adherents.

Among the **Mazimu** of the mountains the community almost coincided with the local group. Most meetings took place during the day and in the middle of Malila villages. The 'search and destroy' actions of mediums, the divination and medical work, all were done in the open and with the cooperation of practically the whole population. But among the Malila too a social ethic was advocated stressing the values of harmonious living and cooperation. Advice on how to prevent matrimonial squabbles was mixed with practical suggestions on hygiene and cooking. Such efforts to recreate the community reveal a longing for a more closely knit society.

No such efforts were apparent among the Ndjukas of 1900. The traditional village community and kin groups were still functioning units. **Gaan Gadu's** followers tried to distance themselves from these communities because they represented a threat to their newly won riches. Religious notions generated among boatmen working in French Guiana were superimposed on their kinsmen living in traditional village communities. This unstable situation could be the chief reason for the early collapse of the puritanical experiments of **Gaan Gadu's** priests.   The movements discussed in this paper have in common that they never came near to winning political hegemony. Rather they represent experiments in puritanism in societies that could still check excesses, and that would not allow those full-fledged tyrannical regimes to mature that have their seeds in puritanism.

Notes

1) I have preferred to use the term 'puritan' as a general name for all those movements which pursue a quest for purity. The disadvantage of doing so is formed by the established connotations of the term 'Puritan' among historians and theologians. For most scholars, 'Puritan' denotes a particular religious movement in Britain and New England and not any other religious phenomenon. Such a restricted use of the term could lead to a confusion of historical specifics with crucial socio-religious characteristics. Essential to the movements I have in mind is the quest for purity and the consequent disciplining of self and reordering of society.

2) The literature on the **Gaan Gadu** movement is extensive. Cf. Thoden van Velzen (1977-1978) and Thoden van Velzen & van Wetering (1983).

3) Cf. de Beet and Thoden van Velzen (1977) for a detailed overview of the transport industry that developed in response to the demands of gold companies and adventurers.

4) These ideas were taken from Horton's influential papers (1970, 1975).

5) Such theological notions smack of Christianity. Although very few Christian missionaries visited the Tapanahoni during the nineteenth century, the Ndjuka were well-acquainted with Christian ideas. But we should be careful about attributing 'conscience probing' and related ideas to the teachings of the missionaries. Acculturation is a much more complex process than the mere exchanging of ideas or the borrowing of cultural traits. I feel equally disinclined to ascribe the notion of **Gaan Gadu** as a divine disciplinarian to the proselytizing of missionaries. In

1890, such concepts were crucial to a new generation of boat owners who longed to gain a better understanding of the world, But even more significant is the fact that the production of this collective fantasy took place under economic and social conditions that had radically changed over the span of only a few years. It seems to me that this must have been greatly disturbing to their peace of mind.

6) Schaerf (1892: 520) published the following rather sensational communication 'Last year some three hundred heathens came together near our new station Wanhatti, to hold a great festival which lasted for several days. They actually threw away their idols and obeahs and took an oath of fidelity to 'Sweli'. (Another of **Gaan Gadu's** names.) By request of the Gr. Ossessi, Captain Brokohamaka conducted this festival, and to show that he was in earnest he publicly put to death man who had beaten his wife'. This last part of the communication seems unreliable. What probably happened was that a man was flogged for breaking the new rule against 'wife beating'. All the same an important sign that the new 'puritan' directions that reached them from chief Oseisie (Osessi) were taken seriously.

7) This point can be substantiated by countless references to official documents and the correspondence between, for example, District Commissioners and the Governor's Office at Paramaribo. Cf. Thoden van Velzen & van Wetering (1983: 135) for more references.

8) The events that precipitated the birth of the **Gaan Gadu** religion bear the mark of a 'grass-roots movement' (Cf. Thoden van Velzen 1978).

9) Most of the material on Akalali, and the psysical appearance of the bush shrine at Saanti Goon, was taken from Thoden van Velzen & van Wetering (1975). After toppling the **Gaan Gadu** priesthood, Akalali opened the sacred dumping place to the public. At first only a few people came, but later hundreds swarmed over the holy refuse-place in search of valuable objects. A year later, when Akalali took me on a tour to Saan Goon, I still saw great quantities of goods in varying stages of decay at the former sanctuary. The weather and luxuriant vegetation had formed green mounds of what must have been some of the earlier dumping sites.

10) **Mazimu** was widely used in what was then called the Bulambia division of then Rungwe district. Although the word is probably of kiNdali origin, many Nyiha, Lambia and Malila used it as well.

At the end of the 1960s, it had gained wide currency as the term for these new religious movements.

11) Although this resembles what psychoanalysts would call 'free association', I have chosen the term 'irruptions', being closer to the German word **Einfall** that Freud used. The concept 'free association' is an incorrect term as Bettelheim (1983: 94-95) has convincingly argued.

12) Mabibi's group is only one of the many **Mazimu** groups active in this part of Tanzania. Others again worked in northern Zambia and Malawi.The orgin of the Tanzanian groups is traced to 'mother movements' in both of those two countries. Much of the history of the **Mazimu** movements is still unclear. Lines of ascendancy between 'mother groups' and their 'offspring' in southern Tanzania were often short-lived. Even the position of influence of leaders south of the border seemed to wane quickly once the new movements had successfully established themselves in Tanzania.

13) The verb is 'ukulejila' meaning 'to offer a child in order to save one's own life'. The word is probably kiNyiha.

References

Abbreviations for missionary journals:
BHW *Berichten uit de Heiden-Wereld*
MTB *Mitteilungen aus der Brüdergemeinde*

Bettelheim, Bruno
    1983   *Freud and Man's Soul.* London: Chatto and Windus; The Hogarth Press.
Balandier, Georges
    1955   *Sociologie Actuelle de l'Afrique Noire.* Paris: Presses Universitaires de France.
Burkhardt, G.
    1898   *Die Mission der Brüdergemeine in Missionsstunden (2);Suriname.* Leipzig: F. Jansa.
de Beet, Chris & H.U.E. Thoden van Velzen
    1977   Bush Negro prophetic movements: religions of despair? *Bijdragen tot de Taal-, Land- en Volkenkunde* 133 (1): 100-35.
Freud, Sigmund (1900)
    1953   *The Interpretation of Dreams. The Standard Edition of the*

Complete Psychological Works of Sigmund Freud, vols. 4,5. London: The Hogarth Press.

Greven, Philip
    1977   *The Protestant Temperament.* New York: Albert Knopf.

Horton, Robin
    1971   African conversion. *Africa* 41 (2): 85-108.
    1975   On the rationality of conversion. *Africa* 41 (2): 219-35; 373-99.

Rattray, R.S.
    1927   *Religion and art in Ashanti.* Oxford: Clarendon.

Rycroft, Charles
    1972   *A Critical Dictionary of Phychoanalysis.* Harmondsworth: Penguin Books.

Schaerf, Br.
    1892   A singular movement among the Bush Negroes. *Periodical accounts relating to the missions of the Church of the United Brethren established among the heathen.* London: The Brethren's Society for the furtherance of the Gospel. pp. 520-21.

Thoden van Velzen, H.U.E.
    1977   Bush Negro regional cults: a materialist explanation, *Regional Cults.* Edited by Richard P. Werbner, pp. 93-118. London: Academic Press.
    1978   The origins of the **Gaan Gadu** movement of the Bush Negroes of Surinam. *Nieuwe West-Indische Gids.* 52: 81-130.

Thoden van Velzen & W. van Wetering
    1975   On the political impact of a prophetic movement in Surinam', *Explorations in the anthropology of religion.* Edited by W.E.A. van Beek and J.H. Scherer, pp.214-233. The Hague: Martinus Nijhoff.
    1983   Affluence, deprivation and the flowering of Bush Negro religious movements. *Bijdragen tot de Taal-, Land- en Volkenkunde* 139 (1): 99-139.

van Wetering, Wilhelmina
    1973   *Hekserij bij de Djuka; een sociologische benadering.* Amsterdam: academic thesis.

The quest for purity in communism
Erik van Ree

The quest for purity in communism
Erik van Ree

Purity and Leninism: the vanguard

In the summer of 1903 the second congress of the Russian Social Democratic Workers Party was convened. It was the setting for violent disagreements between the moderate Mensheviks and the radical Bolsheviks of Vladimir Il'ich Lenin. Lenin was of the opinion that only those who were active in one of the party organizations should be permitted to become members. To his opponent Martov this was unnecessarily restrictive. But Lenin was convinced that an open-door policy would create a situation in which 'every striker' and 'every professor' could call himself a party member. He abhorred that perspective. In a comment on the congress he made the following resumé of his views:

'(It is) my wish, my demand, that the Party, as the vanguard of the class, should be as **organized** as possible, that the Party should admit to its ranks only such elements as allow of at least a minimum of organization. My opponent, on the contrary, **lumps together** in the Party organized and unorganized elements, those who lend themselves to direction and those who do not...This **confusion** is **indead dangerous**' (Lenin 1961b: 258).

Already in 1902 Lenin had created the theoretical foundation of his concept of a vanguard. He developed the separation between party and 'mass' which can be found in Marx' works only in a rudimentary form. In 'What is to be done?' the future leader of the Soviet Union put it thus:

'Since there can be no talk of an independent ideology formulated by the working masses themselves in the process of their movement, the only choice is either bourgeois or socialist ideology. There is no middle course... There is much talk of spontaneity. But the **spontaneous** development of the working-class movement leads to its subordination to bourgeois ideology...' (Lenin 1961a: 384).

The author pleaded for a sharp dividing line between the party and the working class. The party was the repository of socialist consciousness. By themselves the masses could only develop a 'bourgeois' consciousness; they could never submit themselves to the necessary discipline. Lenin's party was a voluntary covenant of 'professional revolutionaries' who would never agree to lose themselves in a broad party of the type Martov envisioned.

Marxist communism in general is known for its labour ethic. That is, except for the inevitable clown in the company, Marx' son-in-law Paul Lafargue, author of *The Right to be Lazy* who depicted communism as the highroad to mankind's glorious idleness. The apostolic principle 'He who does not work shall not eat' was explicitly approved by Marx and Engels. The two prophets of modern communism, taking the working class as their point of reference, disliked the same type of groups as the Puritans did: the **Lumpenproletariat** of beggers, and the group of wealthy parasites into which in their opinion the capitalist class was changing, not to speak of other economically superfluous institutions like monasteries. This labour ethic, too, was to be an instrument for purification. In revolutionary Russia the organization of a disciplined economic process became the focus of Lenin's attention. Labour became a 'matter of honour', if necessary enforced by draconian laws. For Lenin the organization of labour was the central problem after a successful revolution. In his article written in March April 1918 'The Immediate Tasks of the Soviet Government' he expressed this point thus:

'In every socialist revolution, after the proletariat has solved the problem of capturing power, and to the extent that the task of expropriating the expropriators and suppressing their resistance has been carried out in the main, there necessarily comes to the forefront the fundamental task of creating a social system superior to capitalism, namely, raising the productivity of labour, and in this connection (and for this purpose) securing better organization of labour' (Lenin 1965: 257).

In these two respects, the vanguard and the labour ethic, Communism resembles the New England Puritans. Walzer (1982: 317f), in a comparative analysis of Puritanism, Jacobinism and Bolshevism, pointed to the similarity of these radical movements. He sees them as agents of modernization in periods of social transition. They are 'bands of chosen' who act purposefully, élites of 'saints' who cut themselves loose from traditional contexts. They live according to voluntary self-discipline and are involved in a permanent warfare with the existing order in the name of a new one. While the Puritans were the instrument of God, the Bolsheviks had a more impersonal but an equally powerful master: the laws of history, which they wished to serve obediently. The quest for purity was central to all.

For later communist leaders of a more radical kind, such as Joseph Stalin, Mao Zedong, Pol Pot and Kim Il-song, purity became increasingly important. The four leaders liquidated the traditional Leninist party oligarchies and replaced them with their own autocracies, though retaining the façade of party rule. This 'second revolution' was accompanied, and partly motivated, by a continuing process of 'purification'.

Stalinist purity: unity of will

In the transitional period from Lenin to Stalin, a drastic change in the concept of the communist vanguard took place. The Leninist party model set rigid membership criteria, enforced 'iron discipline', but it did not exclude factions, opinion groups within the party. The permanent existence of different 'lines' was recognized and accepted. This Leninist party concept was only a half-way-house between the Menshevik type and a new 'monolithic' kind of party. During the final years of Lenins's life -in 1921 - factions were forbidden in the Russian party. This was probably considered as a temporary measure of expediency. But Stalin turned this measure into his theory of the 'monolithic' party. The essence of this concept was the thesis that the battle of ideas within the party should always lead to 'unity of will' (Stalin 1972: 160) as he formulated it in 1924. All those who did not agree to the new line were 'opportunists'. They had to be expelled.

'Unity of will' put an end to possible differences of opinion as a legitimate phenomenon. Henceforth the party was no longer the party of the communists, but the party of those communists with the 'correct line'. Stalin himself would have turned it around: only the followers of the correct line are communists. The exclusiveness of the vanguard, its sectarian character, became much more pronounced. This revision of Leninist orthodoxy had dramatic implications.

Communist parties consist of opinion groups. Such factions naturally struggle for hegemony. In some communist parties these contests result in more or less lasting coexistence between various factions. The result is a party in which the prominent leaders of the different factions are represented (unofficially) in the Central Committee. The party leader is the **primus inter pares** who quarantees stability. The Communist Party of Vietnam is a good example of this set-up, and so was the Soviet party in Lenin's days, as it is again at present.

The Stalinist theory, however, excluded any compromise. It demanded the definitive victory of one faction (the leader's) and the periodic destruction of all others. This gave the debates in the Soviet party in the 1920s a dramatic undertone. The integrity of the debaters (Stalin, Trotskii, Bukharin et al.) as communists was at stake. This struggle led to the downfall of the 'left and right opportunists' by 1930. That was only the prelude to the apocalyptic storm which raged in the years 1935-1939 when even the moderate Stalinists were exterminated by their more ruthless colleagues. Hundreds of thousands were expelled from the party and the lives of many ended by a shot in the neck. In that way conformity to the will of the leader was established. The vanguard had purified itself.

The 1960s witnessed a similar struggle in China, the Cultural Revolution, where the vanguard started another war against itself. The followers of pure Maoism gained a victory and eliminated the other factions and their leaders, such as president Liu Shaoqi. Since much is widely known about the Stalinist and Maoist purges I shall not discuss them any further. Instead, I will focus on a self-purification that offers clear insights in the devastating power of the quest for purity, that of the party in Pol Pot's Kampuchea and North Korea.

To purify the race and sanitize the country: Kampuchea

The notorious Pol Pot became General Secretary of the communist party of Kampuchea in 1963. At that time he was by no means an autocrat. There were a number of factions which were strongly represented in certain regions, called Zones. The leader himself had his headquarters in the inhospitable Northeast among the mountain tribes. The Eastern Zone was controlled by the moderate 'Internationalists', who were in favour of friendship with the Vietnamese communists. In the Southwest the pro-Chinese 'Maoists' held strong positions. There were several other factions which were less regionally concentrated.

As he told Yougoslavian journalists in 1978 Pol Pot regarded the mountain tribes as belonging to his 'backing base' (Kiernan/Boua 1982: 251). These minorities were, according to his brother-in-law Ieng Sary, faithful to the revolution, non-commercially minded and they possessed 'class hatred' (Kiernan 1985: 274). Pol Pot recruited his followers among the poorest of the peasants and among young people. The Pol Pot faction cherished the thought that the poor are pure and honest and therefore reliable. The young were not yet too much contaminated by the old society, still more pliable.

To the annoyance of their Vietnamese colleagues the Kampuchean communists started a guerilla war in 1967-1968 against Sihanouk. After the **coup d'état** of Lon Nol in 1970 the united resistance, comprising the communists and the prince, was formed. The war was successfully concluded in 1975 by what Pol Pot called a 'total, definitive and **clean** victory' (Kiernan/Boua 1982: 233). But the internal history of the Communist Party of Kampuchea after 1970 was also a war, a long drawn out 'purging war' which ended in 1977-1978 with the liquidation of all the factions by Pol Pot's group.

Craig Etcheson (1984) described the means by which the leader accomplished his 'revolution within the revolution'. The party centre set up camps to give members of the communist youth league and the women's organization a political and administrative training. From there young and fanatical cadres were sent out all over the country to take control of the Zones. In a document of the youth league from 1973 the young are described as 'the central force in the revolutionary movement' (Carney 1977: 33). The youngsters, Pol Pot's right hand, got their own name of honour, 'the dictatorial instrument of the party' (Sihanouk 1980: 28). They spread like waves across the country.

If that was not sufficient to settle the matter, the party centre showed some muscle. It did not shrink back from armed confrontation with the troops of the other factions. For this purpose Pol Pot entered into an alliance with local 'war-lords' such as Ta Mok with whose help he had taken over the Southwest by 1975. Apart from this the General Secretary had a praetorian guard at his disposal, consisting of several divisions which were loyal to him and which were named the 'Unconditionals'. These troops established Pol Pot's hegemony by force of arms. In some areas the leader's soldiers got the nickname 'blackshirts' (Kiernan/Boua 1982: 278) because of their invariably black traditional pyjamas. The last building bricks of their structure of terror was a network of torture camps. In 1975, 'S-21' was founded in Phnom Penh under the command of Brother Deuch, Pol Pot's security chief. Probably some 20,000 party cadres were killed in this temple of horror (Etcheson 1984: 178). By 1977-1978 Pol Pot had succeeded in crushing the factions and established a monolithic party.

Democratic Kampuchea was and remained a rather decentralized, weakly integrated society, held together by the young militants and the army. Regional differences in policy could not be completely eradicated. In 1973 the Democratic Revolution was carried out in the areas under central control. Only by 1977-1978 it could be carried out throughout Kampuchea. The aim was, according to a party document, 'a clean, honest society' (Kiernan 1985: 368). It was a society built upon two basic values: labour and purity.

Pol Pot may have been inspired by the production campaigns in Maoist China. He strived for a 'super great leap forward' (Kiernan/Boua 1982: 228) which had to lead to a very high rate of development in the country. All villages had been divided into **kroms**, groups of 10 to 15 families which worked the land under the command of a chief appointed by the **Angkar** (the Organization, i.e. the Communist Party). The **krom** was a work unit and a social-political entity at the same time. The land and means of production were collectivized. The working days were long and work discipline was very harsh. Many people were 'killed in action' in this labour process, organized on a footing of war. In order to have the women available for production the meals were taken in communal halls. In some villages individual houses were replaced by separate camps for men, women and children. In some cases children were raised apart from their parents by **Angkar** so that the parents could be fully mobilized for work on the fields. Kampuchea became one huge work site. The people built dams and dikes by hand until they literally dropped dead.

According to Etcheson the CPK was inspired by the ideal of a 'pure Khmer society' and the wish 'to purify the race and sanitize the country' (Etcheson 1984: 28-29). Typical reforms were implemented such as the prohibition of wearing colourful **sarongs**. Ith Sarin, a former **Khmer Rouge**, described the mental outlook of the Kampuchean communists in his paper 'Life in the Bureaus of the **Khmer Rouge**'. According to him the party leaders instructed everybody to act as poor peasants. 'Study from the people in order to be like the people' (Sarin 1977: 46) was the slogan. The rule for a proper lifestyle was: work hard and be humble. All party members (with the exception of the most prominent) were expected to perform manual labour. They had to raise pigs, plant rice and dig canals. All human behavior had to be purged from impure elements. One of the rules for a **Khmer Rouge** read: 'Speak, sleep, walk, stand, sit, eat, smoke, play, laugh in a refined unobtrusive manner following the traditions of the people' (idem: 51). Every week so-called 'Lifestyle Meetings' were organized where:

'they criticize each other back and forth on this matter of 'liberalism' in 'drinking, sleeping, walking, talking' which means that some comrades eat differently than they are told, or are sluggardly morning risers or talk too much...Mutual surveillance is the duty of each member...This is a step in 'taming' a man to become a 'machine'...Each member must 'freely' hand himself over to the Organization 'to build'. One must trust completely in the **Angkar** because the Organization has as many eyes as a 'pineapple' and cannot make mistakes (Sarin 1977: 47-48).

Those who did not react positively to criticism had to expect a harsh fate. Michael Vickery, who conscientiously rebutted incorrect horror stories about the **Khmer Rouge** in his book **Cambodja, 1975–1982** (1984) concludes that one could get capital punishment for laziness, verbal resistance, boasting or pretensions, refusal to work, quarreling with your husband or wife, flirting. Executions because of 'illicit flirtations' were quite common. An extremely rigid sexual order was upheld by the laws of the gun and the axe. Children were punished for laughing or joking during work.

To breathe and act in conformity with the will of the leader: Korea

Like the Communist Party of Kampuchea the Korean party consisted of factions. In 1945 the Red Army defeated the Japanese in that country. In its wake two groups of Korean communists who had lived in the USSR for a long time came home. One of these was a group of Koreans, who had obtained Soviet citizenship and were members of the Soviet Communist Party. There was also the 'Kapsan' faction under the leadership of Kim Il-song. During the occupation they had waged a guerilla war against the Japanese in Manchuria, but in the beginning of the 1940s they had fled to Siberia. Kim was Stalin's favourite. He was helped into the saddle by the Red Army. The third faction, the 'local communists', who had organized resistance during colonial occupation in Korea itself, was headed by

Pak Hon-yong. And finally there was the 'Yanan-group' which had fought the Japanese with Mao Zedong in China.

Prior to the armistice in 1953 Kim had already carried through small purges which had resulted in limiting the influence of the three rivalling factions. After the war he destroyed them. Pak Hon-yong was made the scapegoat for the failure of the North Korean troops during the war and executed in December 1955. In 1956-1958 a fierce fight broke out between Kim and the two remaining factions. The Soviet Koreans and the Yanangroup felt stimulated by Khrushchev's destalinization speech and attacked Kim's flirtations with autocracy. Kim arrested them. A massacre was only prevented by strong pressure from Moscow and Beijing.

In 1953, on the eve of the liquidation of the 'local' faction, Thought Examination Meetings were organized in cities and villages (Nam 1974: 114). Party members had to screen their own thoughts, feelings and opinions. In 1958-1959 this was repeated on a larger scale with the Concentrated Guidance Campaign. Every North Korean was obliged to examine in public his or her life history to discover every trace of 'disloyalty' to the leader and root it out. Refugees described this period as one of 'intense and sustained emotional pressure' (Scalapinoel 1972: 833). At the same time the whole country was divided into groups consisting of five families with a party member as chief. The party paper, Kulloja, described the tasks of these small leaders in 1962: 'In this way they can accurately grasp and understand, through their everyday contacts with each family and person, that person's level of knowledge, talents, hopes and ideological trends' (idem: 592). As a result the population was divided into those with 'spotless records' and those with 'complicated backgrounds'.

In 1965 the Resident Perception Project repeated this process once again. This was the stepping stone to a new purge at the top. Ilpyong Kim described this in his **Communist Politics in North Korea** (1975). The first victims were moderate 'Kimilsongists', who were mostly employed in the ideological and economic sphere. They disappeared in 1967. Only two years later it was their opponents' turn to go down - a group of radical military diehards. Both these groups of leaders were convicted to penal servitude or death (An 1983: 16f). Scalapino and Lee (1972: 855) remark that in the course of these campaigns the concept of 'class' in North Korean ideology changed, assuming the added meaning of 'a state of mind, a set of behavior patterns, a life style'. Korean communism set itself to wage a permanent war against 'anti-Party' attitudes in daily life.

As far as we know Kim did not have to resort to such large purges again after 1970. The accent has now shifted to the consolidation of the newly established monolithic regime. The preparation of Kim's eventual succession by his son Kim Chong-il was put on the agenda. In February 1973 the Three Revolution Team Movement emerged (An, 1983; Scalapino Kim, 1983). The movement comprises about forty to fifty thousand youngsters, teaming up in groups of twenty to fifty. They are sent to the major national institutions in order to lead the 'three revolutions': ideological, technical and cultural. These teams of **vigilantes**, who sometimes have the word 'Loyalty' tattooed on their arms (Aims 1983: 15), have their own hierarchy outside the party. In this way they are also able to carry out the 'revolution' within the party. The movement has been under Kim Chong-il's direct control from the very start.

By now this youthful vanguard has been engaged in securing the future succession for their leader for ten years. Cadres who are critical of the idea of a communist dynasty are brushed aside, if the teams have their way. Beside political purges it is a crucial task for the teams to stimulate the masses to perform 'miracles of labour', while being encouraged by slogans like 'speed-war' and '100 day battles', in accordance with the tradition of the Chollima Movement. Chollima was a mythological flying horse which could cover a thousand miles a day. Under this motto the Korean variant of Stakhanovism was organized from the end of the 1950s onwards. Thus, the workers organized themselves in Chollima Teams and tried to break records. Labour was war.

In **Communism in Korea** (1972: 1286f) Scalapino and Lee describe the daily routine of a North Korean worker. The country has an official 48 hour working week, divided over six days. Every morning before work the workers collectively study the writings of Kim Il-song for half an hour. Several times a week they have to take part in military drill for two hours. At least twice or three times a week political meetings have to be attended in the evening, which last two hours each. Then there are monthly get-togethers of Chollima Teams, trade unions, other mass organizations or the party itself. North Korean workers are subjected to a very severe and fatiguing discipline.

Recently Pyongyang published a collection of articles and speeches by Kim junior under the title **On the Juche Idea of our Party** (1985). The concept of **Juche** is difficult to translate, but its meaning comes close to 'selfidentity'. It is a nationalist concept which makes Korean identity the scope of all thinking. The Kim communists feel that Korea should be self-supporting and follow its own model in every respect. The Koreans should shape their own future. According to Kim Chong-il great conflicts were fought out within the party, especially in 1956 and 1967 against the 'factionalists', but finally the leader triumphed. In the 1970s the time had come for the **Juche** program to be fully implemented. Despite Kim Chong-il's preference for the repetition of abstract formulas, a quote may show the North Korean ideological concepts in their mutual relation:

'It is an essential requirement of a working-class party to ensure the unity of ideology and leadership. This is effected by establishing the Party's monolithic ideological system. Only when this is done the whole Party can be armed with the leader's intention and become a living organism, breathing and acting in conformity with his idea and will... Our Party defined new principles of establishing its monolithic ideological system and strengthened this work to meet the needs of the revolution in the 1970s when the proposition was put forward that the whole of society should be modelled on the Juche idea. Today our Party has grown into loyal ranks, and the whole membership thinks and acts according to the will of the Party and the leader...The leader is the centre of the Party's unity and cohesion... The important thing in the Party's unity and cohesion is to achieve the unity of idea and will' (Kim 1985: 96-99).

The psychology of purity

Lenin's concept of the vanguard party was that of an entity which could act **en bloc** in face of the outside world. Discipline was 'externally oriented'. Party members had to support the party program, but otherwise they were only required to be active and carry out decisions. They were not expected to agree with party orders. The Stalinist innovation was to pursue further purification of the already relatively 'pure' Leninist party by excluding anyone who did not show total 'unity of will' with the leader. Bloody purges, culminating in the autocrat's ultimate triumph, resulted. The drive for purity also intensified the labour process, up to and sometimes beyond the limits of human endurance. It also led to excessive control over the individual's lifestyle, which had to be totally cleansed of everything that was frivolous or considered superfluous. On all fronts the Stalinists pushed the quest for purity in Bolshevism much further, a tendency that is part of the explanation for the apocalyptic events in some communist countries.

The communist picture reveals striking similarities with the ethos and the habits in Puritan New England. The rituals for powerful social control, the permanent suffocating mutual surveillance, are examples. In New England sermons were held several times a week. Notes had to be taken down to be discussed in meetings at home. Puritans had to write individual diaries in which their 'progress' in the correct spiritual direction was recorded. In these churches the same typical combination of obedience and a very high level of activism prevailed as in Stalinist parties.

Even more fascinating is the fact that protestant Puritanism also experienced a second, more radical stage: a further purification of the already 'pure' church, It had been a Puritan tenet from the start that 'sinners' should be excluded from the church. But of necessity the church included people who were predestined to go to hell. In the 17th century Calvinist orthodoxy was revised in Massachusetts. Henceforth only 'saints', the future population of heaven, were coopted. Decent, religious people who were not sure of being in God's favour dropped out. Total unity with God (like total unity with the leader three centuries later) now became the hallmark of the community (see Staples, this volume).

These people of New England thought of a way to know who was destined for eternal bliss. The procedure, vividly described by Edmund Morgan (1965), shows a striking similarity with communist 'criticism and self-criticism' sessions. Beside a confession of faith and a promise to live 'without scandals' applicants now had to perform a third act, a 'declaration of their experience of a work of grace' (idem: 62) (see Van der Meijden, this volume). The candidates had to make detailed reports of their lifes' progress and the ways in which they had come to the conviction of being in God's grace. While being cross-examined by the elders and the congregation the candidates had to remain firm and give the 'correct' answers (see Broeyen, this volume). In the end the ability to convey convincingly the personal feeling of being chosen was decisive.

The occurence of similar ultra-puritan phases in protestantism and communism might be partly explained by similar psychological tensions inherent in both the original Leninist and Calvinist systems. For the Calvinist the eradication of sin from one's own life was as essential as the expulsion of sinners out of the church. Being sinful was a sign of being predestined by God to reprobation. On the other hand, being successful and leading a worthy life might be a sign that one was among God's chosen. This in itself leads to a morbid introspection, a permanent urge to root out one's own sins. Protestant sectarians wage two wars, during their whole tiring lives: against Satan's armies and against themselves. But then, one could never be sure of victory. Only God knows one's destiny. However worthily one lived, eternal damnation was always a possibility to be reckoned with.

In orthodox Leninism a similar phenomenon can be observed. Every human thought is class based, and therefore either 'bourgeois' or 'proletarian'. There is no third possibility, Lenin remarked, and he never wavered in this respect. The individual Leninist has constantly to fight against his own 'bourgeois' thoughts, which make him go by the 'wrong line'. This would be like swimming against the current of history, the ultimate crime. On the other hand Lenin never thought the party or himself to be always right. There was no infallible fountain of truth. Party membership was no guarantee of a 'correct line'. However hard one tried to cleanse oneself of bourgeois thought, there was no guarantee against becoming 'objectively a counterrevolutionary'.

Here we find ourselves confronted with a major contradiction. Puritanism and Leninism forced their followers to search obsessively for the pure and righteous path, while God and History were swinging as veritable swords of Damocles over their heads. But then (and this means a horrifying anti-climax) these believers were denied the gratifying feeling of certainty when they made a choice. Thus, individuals and organizations alike may be thrown into a whirlpool of anxiety, fear and feelings of guilt. It is only natural that some parties and churches searched for a way out, in order to destroy the elements of insecurity in their ideologies. They found refuge, an illusionary peace of mind, in a pure and unconditional relation with God or the leader.

Becoming 'ultra-puritan' is a shattering experience, not only for a party or a church but also for individuals. Puritan theologians in America developed a fixed scheme of ten stages through which every person had to pass through reaching the glorious conclusion of being a 'saint'. Morgan (1965: 68f) described these stages. At first the subject becomes acquainted with the church and God's commandments: he is an ordinary believer. But a deeper understanding soon leads to the realization of one's own sinfulness and false pride. It brings him in a state of panic. Eventually one becomes convinced of being doomed ('salvation panic'). But in this deep valley of despair some hope of salvation flickers up. In the end the profound personal conviction of enjoying God's grace triumphs. But the story ends in a paradox, because doubt remains. He who does not doubt is certainly doomed. In this way the Puritan created his own obedient self-confidence, his loneliness, his gloomy happiness. This was the tortuous road of the radical believer.

In 1961 the American psychiatrist Robert Jay Lifton wrote *Thought Reform and the Psychology of Totalism* (1967). He interviewed 40 people who had been in prison in the Chinese People's Republic. In the course of their stay many of them had come to justify their own captivity. The mental changes in the prisoners were brought about by a powerful combination of physical pressure and 'patient re-education'. Lifton also distinguished ten stages of 'being convinced'. To begin with the prisoner is convinced on a political level that the world is not what he thought it was, so the subject accepts the fact that until now he has been a 'tool of imperialism'. He feels guilty. His self-esteem is being undermined, and in long sessions of 'criticism and self-criticism' such overwhelming feelings of guilt are aroused. A 'basic fear' arises, a feeling of being totally and irretrievably lost. Then the helping hand is stretched out. The prisoner gets the chance to make a fresh start on the condition that he is prepared to rewrite his own personal history in communist terms: in other words, to construct a new identity. The victim seizes this way out with both hands, aided by jailers and fellow-prisoners alike, and he experiences a spiritual rebirth.

Lifton remarks correctly that the whole Chinese population went through such a process (in so far as they were in the grip of the authorities), the major difference being that the effects of force is stronger in jail, while outside it is more a question of persuasion. The term 'brainwashing', often used in this context, is misleading because the process has nothing to do with conscious and direct manipulation. The most 'brainwashed' people are the jailers. They make their prisoners by means of shock experience what they themselves have gone through.

The stages mentioned by the Puritan theologians and by Lifton show remarkable similarities. In both cases a new religious or political view of life and the world is the starting point. This is soon mixed with feelings of guilt and fear, leading to a breakdown of identity, a feeling of existential panic. A deep crisis is followed by the creation of a new purified identity, built around a purified notion of the world. A new radical 'saint' is born.

Conclusion

The Leninists (like the Puritans) were inspired by the idea of a disciplined, pure vanguard organization (a church or a party) which excluded either 'sinful' or 'bourgeois'people. This new vanguard was prepared to enforce rigid labour-discipline and an ascetic morality on the population to build up a new, healthy society according to God's commandments or the laws of history.

A process of further 'sectarianization' took place in which the vanguard was still further 'purified'. Only the select intimates of God or the leader were still acceptable. In the case of the movements of Stalin, Mao, Pol Pot and Kim Il-song, this was accompanied by frenzied labour drives and propaganda for an extremely ascetic and totally controlled lifestyle.

Finally we saw that in both original ideological systems (the historical Puritans and Leninism) certain psychological tensions are present which could cause followers to take refuge in this quasi-certainty of unity with the leader or God.

The extreme variants of Puritanism have remained marginal phenomena, mostly concentrated in American church communities. In the international communist movement Stalinist ultra-puritanism was dominant for decades and actively now influences the lives of one third of the world's population.

References

Author unknown
    1983   'Aims and Realities of the Three-Revolution Team Movement', *Vantage Point*. VI, 3: 13-16.
An, Tai Sung
    1983   *North Korea in Transition*. Westport/London: Greenwood Press
Carney, Timothy Michael
    1977   (ed.) *Communist Party Power in Kampuchea (Cambodja): Documents and Discussion*. New York: Cornell University.
Etcheson, Craig
    1984   *The Rise and Demise of Democratic Kampuchea*. Boulder, Colorado/London: Westview Press, Frances Pinter (Publ.).
Hill, Christopher
    1958   *Puritanism and Revolution*. London: Secker and Warburg
    1964   *Society and Puritanism in Pre-Revolutionary England* London: Secker and Warburg
Kiernan, Ben
    1985   *How Pol Pot Came to Power*, London: Verso
Kiernan, Ben & Chanthou Boua (eds.)
    1982   *Peasants and Politics in Kampuchea. 1942-1981.*

London/New York: Zed Press, M.E. Sharpe Inc.

Kim, Ilpyong J.
1975   *Communist Politics in North Korea*. New York: Praeger
        Publishers.
Kim Jong Il
1985   *On the Juche Idea of Our Party*. Pyongyang: Foreign
        Languages Publishing House.
Lenin, V.I.
1961a   'What is to be done?' in: *Collected Works*, vol.5. Moscow:
        Progress Publishers: 347-529
1961b   'One Step Forward, Two Steps Back', in: *Collected Works*,
        vol.7, Moscow: Progress Publishers: 203-425
1965   'The Immediate Tasks of the Soviet Government', in:
        Collected Works, vol.27. Moscow: Progress Publishers
        235-277.
Lifton, Robert Jay
1967   *Thought Reform and the Psychology of Totalism*. Har-
        mondsworth: Pelican Book (1961).
Morgan, Edmund S.
1965   *Visible Saints*. New York: Cornell University Press. (1963).
Nam, Koon Woo
1974   *The North Korean Communist Leadership, 1945-1965*
        Alabama: The University of Alabama Press.
Sarin, Ith
1977   'Life in the Bureaus of the Khmer Rouge', in: Carney,
        1977: 42-55
Scalapino, Robert A., Jun-yop Kim (eds.)
1983   *North Korea Today; Strategic and Domestic Issues*, Berk-
        eley, California: Center for Korean Studies, University of
        California.
Scalapino, Robert A., Chong-Sik Lee
1972   *Communism in Korea*, Berkeley/Los Angeles/London:
        University of California Press.
Sihanouk, Norodom
1980   *War and Hope*. New York: Pantheon Books.
Stalin, J.W.
1972   'Ueber die Grundlagen des Leninismus', in: *Werke Bd.6*,
        Frankfurt: Druck-Verlags-Vertriebs-Kooperative: 62-166.
Vickery, Michael
1984   *Cambodja, 1975-1982*, Boston: South End Press.
Walzer, Michael
1982   *The Revolution of the Saints*. Cambridge, Massachusetts/-
        London: Harvard University Press (1965).

Weber, Max
    1975   *Die protestantische Ethik I*, Hamburg: Siebenstern Tasch-
            enbuch Verlag (1920).

Notes on contributors

Frits G.M. Broeyer is associate professor at the Theological Faculty of the University of Utrecht. He has published widely on the theology of Calvin.

Peter Staples is associate professor of Church History of the Theology Faculty of the University of Utrecht. As a long time editor of *News from the English Churches,* he has published widely on the history of Methodism as well as Anglicanism.

Anne van der Meiden is professor of Mass Communication at the University of Utrecht. He has published on the ultra-orthodox churches in the Netherlands.

Piet Post is teacher at the Teacher Training College in Leeuwarden, specializing in the evangelicals in the Netherlands and has published on religious movements in Holland and on Islam.

Jacques D.J. Waardenburg is professor of Comparative Religion and Phenomenology at the Theological Faculty of the Unversity of Utrecht. He has worked extensively on Islam in the Middle East and in the Netherlands. Among his many publications *Religionen and Religio. Systematische Einführung in die Religionswissenschaft* 1986.

Walter E.A. van Beek is associate professor of Cultural Antropology at the University of Utrecht. He has done fieldwork in North Cameroon and Mali and has published on traditional religion, viz. (with van Baal) *Symbols for Communication; religion in anthropological theory,* 1982.

Philip G. Kreyenbroek is associate professor of Iran Studies at the Faculty of Theology of the University of Amsterdam. He has published on both pre-and post-revolutionary Iran, e.g. *Sraosa in the Zoroastrian Tradition*, 1985.

Erik Zürcher is professor of Sinology at the Institute of Sinology of the University of Leyden. He has published widely on Chinese history.

H.U.E. "Bonno" Thoden van Velzen is professor of Cultural Anthropology at the University of Utrecht. He has done extensive fieldwork in Surinam and Tanzania and is the co-author of *The Great Father and the Danger; Ndjuka collective phantasies*.

Erik van Ree is associate professor of Political Science at the University of Amsterdam, specialized in the politics of communist countries, notably *De Totalitaire Paradox. De terroristische massademocratie van Stalin en Mao*, 1984 (The totalitarian paradox. The terrorist mass democracy of Stalin and Mao).

Index of concepts

Index of personal names